'NONSENSE UPON STILTS'

'NONSENSE UPON STILTS'

Bentham, Burke and Marx on the Rights of Man

Edited
with introductory and
concluding essays by

JEREMY WALDRON

METHUEN
London and New York

First published in 1987 by
Methuen & Co. Ltd
11 New Fetter Lane, London EC4P 4EE

Published in the USA by
Methuen & Co.
in association with Methuen, Inc.
29 West 35th Street, New York, NY 10001

Phototypeset by AKM Associates (UK) Ltd
Ajmal House, Hayes Road, Southall, London
Printed in Great Britain by
St Edmunsbury Press, Bury St Edmunds, Suffolk

British Library Cataloguing in Publication Data
Nonsense upon stilts:
   Bentham, Burke and Marx
   on the rights of man.
   1. Civil rights—History—Sources
   I. Waldron, Jeremy
   323.4'09'03   JC571

ISBN 0-416-91890-5 pbk

Library of Congress Cataloging in Publication Data
'Nonsense upon stilts.'

Bibliography: p.
Includes index.
1. Human rights.
2. Bentham, Jeremy, 1748–1832 ——
Contributions in human rights.
3. Burke, Edmund, 1729–1797 ——
Contributions in human rights.
4. Marx, Karl, 1818–1883 ——
Contributions in human rights.
   I. Title.
   JC571.N655 1987   323.4'01   87–11211

ISBN 0-416-91890-5 (pbk.)

Contents

Acknowledgements

Though this project took more time to put together than it should have, it would have taken even longer had it not been for the encouragement and support of my editor at Methuen, Nancy Marten. I am grateful to her, and also to Robert Goodin, Richard Gunn, Don Herzog, Kristin Luker, Kim Scheppele and Philip Selznick for discussing various parts of it with me. Sections of the concluding essay have been read at seminars as far afield as Berkeley, Chicago, Oxford, London, Edinburgh, Amsterdam, Wellington and Dunedin. I am grateful to the participants for their comments.

Introduction

The idea of human rights is taken more seriously now than it has been for centuries. Not since the heady days of the American and French Revolutions have rights been used so widely as touchstones of political evaluation or as an idiom for the expression of political demands. In the market-place of domestic politics and in international affairs, respect for rights is the new criterion of political legitimacy. A government that respects its citizens' rights is a good government and deserves support; a government that violates human rights should be denied aid and comfort from abroad and shunned in the international community. In moral and political theory, where the idea was for a long time in disrepute, rights are again a serious subject of philosophical enquiry. The literature abounds with discussions of their normative structure, the values like equality and autonomy that are thought to underpin them, the weight that they are supposed to have against other moral considerations, and the relation between moral rights and the rights that are established by positive law. It is common for political philosophers nowadays to claim that the demands of justice are *rights*-based rather than based on considerations of social utility, and many have adopted the Lockean view that the primary function of law and other aspects of social organization is to constitute a framework to uphold and respect the moral rights of individual citizens.[1]

But though these ideas are popular and powerful, they are far from uncontroversial. Recently more and more writers have expressed reservations about the shift away from pragmatic or utilitarian modes of political evaluation, about the fact that we no longer ask what is in the interest of all but, in every case, what individuals are entitled to as a matter of principle. Others are alarmed at what appears to be the ascendancy of an assertive and muscular individualism in this sort of theory at the expense of what they take to be a proper awareness of community, solidarity and civic virtue in human life. Still others are worried by what seems to them to be the abstract and formalistic character of modern claims about universal rights. Modern charters of rights and their philosophical rationalizations are generalizations: they do not seem to pay much attention to the difference that social and historical circumstances may make to the application of anodyne

rights-formulas across a variety of human situations. These misgivings
– which, as I said, are increasingly being voiced – may be regarded as
the shadow that is cast by the ascendancy of rights talk in modern
political discourse.[2]

The utilitarian, collectivist and relativist sentiments that lie behind
these misgivings are uncongenial to many liberals. But whether we
find them initially appealing or not, they deserve the most careful
consideration. Even from a liberal standpoint, the worst that can
happen is that we start taking rights for granted in moral and political
discussion. Few of us want the language of rights to degenerate into a
sort of lingua franca in which moral and political values of all or any
kinds may be expressed. To take rights seriously means to be aware of
what is distinctive and controversial about a claim of right, and that, I
think, is inseparable from an attempt to understand what someone
might be getting at when she repudiates the idea of rights altogether.

What I am trying to do in this book is to put the modern critique of
human rights into some sort of historical perspective. Misgivings
about rights are not a new phenomenon. Just as the theories of
natural rights and of the rights of man that developed in the
seventeenth and eighteenth centuries are the ancestors of the
modern idea of human rights, so the critiques of those theories that
appeared in that period are the starting-point of modern misgivings
about the direction this idea is taking us in our moral and political
thinking.

It would be wrong, of course, to suggest that there is nothing new in
the modern discussion of rights. There are many features that
distinguish it from the debates to which the texts presented here were
contributions. For example modern rights-theorists are more interested than their eighteenth-century ancestors in what are now
known as *welfare* rights and in the idea that rights may express claims
about need and not merely individual freedom. That means modern
theories can take on a more radical aspect than the traditional
theories of classic liberalism. It is no longer widely believed that one
has to step outside the idiom of rights in order to criticize socio-
economic (as opposed to legal and political) arrangements in society.
On the other side of the debate, the explicit development of
sophisticated 'two-level' theories of utilitarianism now lends much
greater credibility to the claim that whatever is of value in the idea of
human rights can be accommodated without abandoning the
tradition of utilitarian argument. And on both sides there is a much
greater willingness to separate the issue of rights from more abstract
'meta-ethical' questions about the reality and objectivity of moral

standards. Talk of rights is no longer seen as posing any greater difficulty in this regard than talk of moral values or moral obligation.

Even so, many of the issues have remained remarkably constant. The abstract universalism of this sort of theory, the individualism of rights, the tension between rights and the demands of community, the use of social contract models in the theory of politics, the absolutism and apparent oversimplification of the claims that rights express, the use and abuse of reason and a priorism in political argument, and the troubled idea of natural law – these issues which lie at the epicentre of the modern controversy have a history as long as the idea of human rights itself. In a recent book Richard Tuck has shown that the modern controversy between the so-called 'Choice' and 'Benefit' theories of rights has its roots in the medieval and early modern emergence of the concept of a right out of the Roman law notions of *ius* and *dominium*.[3] I am hoping to do something similar in this book – though on a much more modest scale – for the modern debate about the abstraction and individualism of this sort of theory. I should add, however, that this is not intended primarily as an exercise in the history of ideas. The aim is to deepen our understanding of the dispute without diminishing the enthusiasm with which we participate in it. I want to do that by focusing on the historical longevity of these misgivings and the perennial character of the controversies they give rise to.

The discussion in this volume centres around three texts: some extracts from Edmund Burke's book *Reflections on the Revolution in France*; a substantial piece from a work by Jeremy Bentham known as *Anarchical Fallacies* (together with a section from one of his papers on fiscal policy entitled 'Supply Without Burthen'); and part of a review essay written by the young Karl Marx entitled 'On the Jewish Question'. Bringing these texts together illustrates strikingly the diversity of viewpoints from which the idea of human rights may be, and has been, attacked. To label them crudely, we have here critiques written from a conservative, a liberal and a socialist point of view. But given that diversity, what is remarkable about these texts is the number of common themes. Bentham, Burke and Marx all attack human rights for what they call their 'abstraction'; they all focus on the theme of individualism versus community, though their respective conceptions of community are of course very different; and they all claim that the rights of man involve a radically impoverished view of the constitution of human society. Looking at these critiques together reveals the richness and complexity of the ideas that lie behind simple terms like 'rights', 'individual' and 'community'. The great ideologies of the west – liberalism, socialism and conservatism – are not utterly alien to one another: they grew up together and have fed on one another's traditions, preoccupations and concerns. The controversies that we will be looking at help to illustrate the point that ideological battle lines are seldom straightforward or binary. They involve the elaboration and repetition of common themes from overlapping points of view.

The texts I have chosen have a further feature that makes them worth bringing together. Each is in some sense a critical response, not only to the idea of human rights, but also to a particular expression of that idea: the 'Declaration of the Rights of Man and the Citizen' proclaimed by the French National Assembly in 1789. Of the three works, Bentham's stands in the most direct relation to that manifesto: *Anarchical Fallacies* is subtitled 'An Examination of the Declarations of Rights Issued During the French Revolution' and, after some introductory remarks, consists of a clause-by-clause analysis of the Declarations in question. (The extract I have reproduced actually addresses the slightly amended Declaration of 1791.) We have reason to believe that it was composed by 1795, but for various reasons it remained unpublished until 1816, and indeed unpublished in English until 1843. Burke's book was written and published in the months immediately following the upheavals of July 1789. Although presented ostensibly as a letter to a citizen of France, and in fact as a response to the propaganda being put about in England by groups like the Constitutional Society and the Revolutionary Society – enthusiasts anxious to transplant the aspirations of 1789 on to English soil – it was quickly recognized as the most eloquent expression of its author's whole outlook on politics and society. Burke's argument about rights, therefore, has to be taken in the context of his wider expression of the conservative outlook, and I have presented it in that context here. The piece by Marx is much later in its composition and addresses the Declaration of Rights as part of a general discussion of emancipation sparked by contemporary Young Hegelian ideas on religious disestablishment and Jewish emancipation in Germany and France. Because all three of these texts address the French Declaration in one form or another, I have included that document as well, with a brief historical introduction.

I have said that one of the aims of bringing together these texts from the late eighteenth and early nineteenth centuries is to enrich and deepen the modern debate between those theorists who remain preoccupied with the individual and her rights and those who are concerned more with the need for community and communal commitments in human life. Some may see this as a misguided and anachronistic exercise – an attempt to sever political writing from its historical context and to dragoon the words of Bentham, Burke and Marx to serve purposes that are quite different in time, shape and character from those that originally provoked them. After all, England in the 1790s and Paris in the 1840s were quite different places from Britain and the USA in the 1980s: those who took part in public debate had different expectations, different fears and different understandings. The things that worry students of political philosophy and contributors, say, to *Political Theory* or *Philosophy and Public Affairs* differ enormously from the things that exercised the readers of the *Deutsche-französische Jahrbücher* or the thousands that made *Reflections on the Revolution in France* a best-seller in 1791. Critics may say instead that we ought to be scrutinizing these texts *historically*, relating them to the pamphlets, speeches, sermons, campaigns, actions and events of which they are a part rather than to the contributions *we* want them to make to issues being debated, mainly in universities, the best part of two centuries later.[4]

It is hard, though, to see why the first of these approaches to a text should necessarily rule the other out. What sort of mistake is it suggested we are making when we adapt a theme or a quotation from Burke, say, or Marx, and use it in a modern debate? Is it that the author would have prohibited such a use of his material had he contemplated it in advance? That sounds crazy: for one thing, all these authors were aware of the transhistorical character of political writing. They drew deeply and sometimes explicitly on traditional texts which, by similar criteria, might have been regarded as anachronistic in *their* time; and they would have been pleased and inspired (maybe flattered) by the prospect of the enduring contribution their writing might make to controversies that would outlive their particular concerns.

Anyway, whatever the authors' expectations, these texts exist in a public realm now with a life and meaning of their own. Is it thought we should impoverish our modern debates by refusing, in a spirit of historically sensitive self-denial, to draw on them for inspiration and argument among ourselves? If we take our own concerns as seriously as it is suggested we should take theirs, this will strike us as a silly form of abstinence. Even the view that we must get hold of an historically accurate interpretation of a text before we have the right to use it in argument is mistaken. Though historically inaccurate, the *received* Plato, the *received* Locke or the *received* Mill may provide (and *have* provided), immensely important and useful arguments for *us* to use in our debates about Utopianism, private property and censorship. Of course, it is also possible for us to impoverish ourselves another way; by failing to relate a text to its historical context, we may make it blander, less interesting, less meaningful, more mysterious, and therefore of less use to us than it would otherwise be. Even if we are deploying a text as a resource in argument and not just as a tool for historical understanding, we might as well make it the best that *it* can be for us, and that will often (though not always) involve some sophisticated awareness of the context from which we are abstracting it.[5] We should remember, however, that historical accuracy and sensitivity are themselves not standards independent of our present projects and preoccupations. The hermeneutical point here is quite complicated, but if we are at all self-conscious about our present concerns, those concerns will include views on why it is important to achieve a sense of the past, and those views will doubtless vary along with some of our other concerns. Our view of what is an accurate and sensitive reading of the text and our view of what is, for present dialectical purposes, an illuminating reading of the text, are not of course identical. But they are not independent of each other either and, in political theory, unless we have some sense of the difference an argument in a text might make, if accepted, to some modern debate, we are unlikely to have a very clear conception of why, as a matter of interpretation, it is important to get it right.

In what follows, each of the extracts will be prefaced by a brief introduction, identifying and commenting on its main themes, and relating them to more general aspects of the author's life, work and influence. But I have also written a general introduction to the volume, which attempts to sketch out the career of natural rights in the seventeenth and eighteenth centuries, and to identify the ways in which the idea had become vulnerable to social and philosophical criticism when it was wheeled out as a revolutionary doctrine in 1789. And then, as it were to close the sandwich, the collection ends with another essay, tracing the career of human rights *since* 1789, and looking to see whether there is anything more to be said in response to the anxieties that continue to exercise socialist, communitarian and utilitarian critics of the idea.

✍ 1 ✍

Natural rights in the seventeenth and eighteenth centuries

I

It is easy for us to take the idea of human rights for granted. But to understand it properly, we need to see it in the context of the ideas to which it has been traditionally opposed. In its classic form the theory of natural rights may be seen as an attack on two quite different approaches to the defence of political absolutism: it is a response to the theory of natural hierarchy, and it is a response to theories of contractual subjection to absolute authority. Both these responses are found in the political philosophy of John Locke, and the argument set out in the *Two Treatises of Government* will serve us, as it served the revolutionaries of the eighteenth century, as the paradigm of a theory of natural rights.[1]

The Lockean philosophy can be viewed, first, as a response to contemporary claims about the divine right of kings and, more generally, to all theories of the natural ordination of political authority. Suppose human beings are taken to be the creatures of a God who has set up a certain order for the world in which they are to live; suppose too that this order can be perceived by them either through the use of reason or through divine revelation or both; and suppose finally that both reason and biblical revelation indicate the indispensability of political authority in human affairs, given the nature of man. Then the question arises: on what basis is this authority to be constituted? Has our Creator Himself instituted the authority needed for human life, designating certain individuals (or certain types of individuals) as natural rulers and placing all others in natural subjection to them? Or is this something He has left for us to work out on our own?

Some of the facts of human life seem to support the first of these hypotheses. Infants are born into a state of helpless dependence upon their parents, and in their childhood are taken to be naturally and properly subject to parental authority. Parents seem to be natural rulers, and the subordination of children to their authority appears to be part of God's plan for mankind. In seventeenth-century society the same was sometimes thought true of the relation between wives and husbands, and also between the members and the head of a household: here too there was a 'natural' order of authority which even consensual relations between adults had to be moulded to fit. This seemed sufficient to establish that the world as God had created it was not naturally devoid of authority relations: in ordering our nature, God had placed us in certain relations of authority. One or two thinkers took the further step of maintaining that God had established an order of specifically *political* authority in the world. Just as Christ was supposed to have established a continuing hierarchy of authority for His church by the appointment of His apostles, establishing a line of rule through apostolic succession, so God was thought to have nominated one or several individuals as kings of the nations of the earth and to have established a procedure for their succession by nomination or inheritance. In England this type of thinking reached its apogee in a book called *Patriarcha* by Sir Robert Filmer, and it was wheeled out with a greater or lesser degree of conviction to bolster some of the claims made by the later Stuart monarchs in seventeenth-century politics.[2]

As I have said, the Lockean theory of natural rights is, in the first instance, a response to this sort of view. In opposition to the divine right of kings, theories of natural rights taught the initial equality of human individuals. John Locke maintained that the natural condition of mankind was one in which

all the Power and Jurisdiction is reciprocal, no one having more than another: there being nothing more evident, than the Creatures of the same species and rank promiscuously born to the same advantages of Nature, and the use of the same faculties, should also be equal one amongst another without Subordination or Subjection, unless the Lord and Master of them all, should by any manifest Declaration of his Will set one above another, and confer on him by an evident and clear appointment an undoubted Right to Dominion and Sovereignty.[3]

Even if one were to take seriously the alleged biblical authority for the divine consecration of kingship (and the biblical texts themselves were contested), the knowledge of who was the rightful heir to that authority had, as Locke argued, been 'so long since utterly lost, that in

all the Races of Mankind and Families of the World, there remains
not to one above another, the least pretence to have the Right of
Inheritance.'[4]

This doctrine of natural equality invited some familiar objections.
After all, it ignored evident differences of age, strength, wisdom and
virtue among human beings. Some philosophers responded to those
objections by flatly denying that the differences were as great as they
were made out. According to Thomas Hobbes, 'when all is reckoned
together, the difference between man, and man, is not so considerable
as that one man can thereupon claim to himselfe any benefit, to
which another may not pretend, as well as he'.[5] There are no
supermen set so strikingly above others as to be able to enforce, by
themselves, a natural right to rule. Locke's strategy, however, was the
more cautious one of pinning down exactly the respects in which
equality was and was not being asserted:

> Though I have said above . . . That all Men by Nature are equal, I
> cannot be supposed to understand all sorts of Equality: Age or
> Virtue may give Men a just Precedency: Excellency of Parts and
> Merit may place others above the Common Level . . . ; and yet all
> this consists with the Equality, which all Men are in, in respect of
> Jurisdiction or Dominion one over another, which was the Equality
> I there spoke of, as proper to the Business in hand, being that equal
> Right that every Man hath, to his Natural Freedom, without being
> subject to the Will or Authority of any other Man.[6]

As this passage also suggests, the doctrine of natural equality was
associated with a claim about freedom: men were born free, not
subject to any political allegiance or obedience. Such a claim could be
attacked in two ways.

The first line of attack was that it appeared to contradict the
natural facts of infancy: as anyone knows who has brought up a baby,
children are born not only in a state of abject dependence but also
into a condition where their liberty (at least in a negative sense) must
be continually infringed if they are to have any hope of surviving and
flourishing. The Lockean position was that this sort of subjection was
different in kind from, and discontinuous with, subjection to political
authority. Parental authority was ordained for a specific purpose: to
protect and nourish children and develop their faculties until they
reached maturity and rationality. It did not give the parents any
legitimate power of life and death over the child nor any right over its
property. Of course, it might be argued that the point of parental
authority was to *prepare* the child for political subjection, to train him

in the discipline, obedience and respect which in adult life he would owe to his political superiors. But Locke maintained that the point of education was the mature and rational exercise of freedom. Though we do not have the full use of our capacities in infancy, it is clear that what we have *in potentia* are capacities for freedom: capacities of understanding, deliberation and will. As Locke put it, 'We are born Free, as we are born Rational; not that we have naturally the Exercise of either: Age that brings one, brings with it the other too.'[7]

The second line of attack on the idea of natural freedom was expressed most forcefully by Jeremy Bentham in *Anarchical Fallacies*: 'All men born free? Absurd and miserable nonsense! When the great complaint – a complaint made perhaps by the very same people at the same time is – that so many men are born slaves.'[8] In reply to this attack, it was important to stress, as Locke did in his more careful formulations, that men were not necessarily born free as a matter of fact, but rather 'born . . . with a *Title* to perfect Freedom'.[9] *Of course* the aim of natural right theories was to criticize those societies in which people were oppressed from birth. The point was to insist that such oppression violated rules of natural law which required (though they did not compel) people to respect one another's freedom. It was not that oppressive human laws did not exist (though some in this tradition had doubts about the point of calling the edicts of a despot *laws*); it was rather that they were taken to have no moral force in the face of our Creator's requirement that each person should be given the opportunity to develop and exercise his capacity to act on his own account as a free and rational agent.

The upshot then was that if government was not naturally ordained though nevertheless indubitably necessary, if authority was not divinely appointed but nevertheless indispensable, it could only be the product of free and equal individuals coming together and choosing to set up political institutions on a basis that reflected their apprehension of the necessity of such institutions in their life in society with others. 'Men being, as has been said, by Nature all free, equal and independent, no one can be put out of this Estate, and subjected to the Political power of another, without his own Consent.'[10] Political society was an artificial institution set up to promote the interests and serve the needs of those who constituted it. It was therefore an institution that must serve the good of all, for it had no other basis of legitimacy than the contribution it made to the lives of those who were from time to time its constituents. If it did not serve the purpose it was instituted for, it could and should be discarded like any other useless artefact and replaced by a new one that did.

I spoke of two lines of absolutist thought to which the theory of natural rights was a response. While the first was a theory about the naturalness of authority, the second was an opposite conviction about the utter conventionality of social and political arrangements. Humans might be equal, free and independent by nature but, in pursuit of stability and the other benefits of secure institutions, there seemed nothing to stop them *giving away* the entirety of their liberty and subjecting themselves voluntarily to the absolute authority of a ruler and the order that he maintained.

> It is lawful for any Man to engage himself as a Slave to whom he pleases; as appears both by Hebrew and Roman laws. Why should it not therefore be as lawful for a People that are at their own Disposal, to deliver themselves to any one or more Persons, and transfer the Right of governing them upon him or them, without recovering any Share of that Right to themselves? . . . A people may choose what Form of Government they please: Neither is the Right which the Sovereign has over his Subjects to be measured by this or that Form . . . but by the Extent of the Will of those who conferred it upon him.[11]

In other words, absolutism did not need problematic doctrines of natural hierarchy. In principle it might claim as much of a basis in the consent of the governed as any other form of government. Every account of the benefits to subjects of absolute rule – benefits like safety, security and stability – could be represented as reasons why consent might be forthcoming. To gain these benefits, people might perfectly well be thought to have sold themselves as slaves to an autocrat.

In *Natural Rights Theories* Richard Tuck has outlined various ways in which such a conventionalist defence of absolutism might be resisted. One strategy – common in sixteenth-century thought – was to concede the possibility that men and women might sell themselves into slavery, but to assume as a matter of factual plausibility that no one would ever bargain away all his rights or every last element of his liberty. If subjection were founded on contract, and if contracts were to be understood in accordance with the intentions of those who entered into them, a principle of 'interpretative charity' might forbid us from imputing to anyone the intention to abandon his rights completely. 'No man can be supposed so void of common sense (unless an absolute Fool, and then he is not capable of making any Bargain) to yield himself so absolutely up to another's disposal, or to renounce all hopes of safety or satisfaction in this life.'[12] A somewhat similar strategy was adopted by Thomas Hobbes (often wrongly regarded as the exponent *par excellence* of this conventionalist theory of absolutism). For Hobbes it was human psychology not charity that precluded the imputation of any intention to abandon all one's rights. Since all actions, including contracts, aimed at some good for the agent, no speech act could ever be taken to aim at the destruction of what was the condition for the individual's good, namely his survival. A contract not to defend oneself against one's sovereign, then, was unintelligible. Indeed, in *De Cive* Hobbes went further and insisted that 'since no man is tyed to impossibilities, they who are threatened either with death (which is the greatest evil to nature) or wounds, or some other bodily hurts, are not stout enough to bear them, are not obliged to endure them'. It was, he said, 'contrary to the very nature of compacts' to bind us to the performance of what was psychologically impossible.[13]

The strategy which became dominant, however, and which nourished the tradition of natural rights, drew not on psychological impossibility nor on interpretative charity, but on the idea of certain *duties* imposed by natural law. Suppose that, as creatures of God, we have a *duty* to sustain our lives, protect ourselves and flourish as best we can. Then not only would it be improbable, but also it would be *wrong* for us to try and alienate the right of self-defence and others like it in a contract of subjection. Such purported contracts would be invalid and ineffectual, from a moral point of view, like one person's attempt to dispose of another's property. This was the approach Locke took. Having insisted that all men were the servants of God, 'sent into the world by his order and about his business', and that they were 'his Property whose Workmanship they are', he inferred that political power could not possibly be 'absolutely Arbitrary over the Lives and Fortunes of the People'. As Locke put it, 'no Body can transfer to another more power than he has in himself; and no Body has an absolute Arbitrary Power over himself, or over any other, to destroy his own Life.'[14]

By taking this perspective on the inalienability of rights, one could see them not merely as inalienable *privileges* (as self-defence was on Hobbes's account) but as inalienable *claim-rights* correlative to the duties of others including those people who aspired to political authority. God has made us, Locke argued, 'to last during his, not one another's pleasure':

> Every one as he is bound to preserve himself, and not to quit his Station wilfully; so by the like reason when his own Preservation

comes not in competition, ought he, as much as he can, to preserve the rest of Mankind, and may not unless it be to do Justice to an Offender take away or impair the life, or what tends to the Preservation of the Life, Liberty, Health, Limb or Goods of another.[15]

It followed that rulers, like all men, had a general background duty not to harm their subjects. Since their subjects could not morally be thought to have freed their rulers from this duty, since it was a duty owed not just to them but to their creator, even conventional political authority must be limited by constraints of natural law. On the basis of considerations like these, theorists in the Lockean tradition were able to assert the inalienability and the imprescriptability of natural rights. Natural rights could not be waived to secure any earthly benefit and, since they were to be understood in the context of the eternal purposes of the divine ruler of mankind, the historical longevity of oppressive and arbitrary politics could not make any difference to the wrongness of absolutism.

To sum up: the relation then between natural rights and the older idea of a divinely ordained law of nature was a complex one. Divine law entered the natural rights theory in at least three ways: first, negatively, in the denial that there was any natural basis for political hierarchy or any natural rulership or subordination among mankind; secondly, in the claim that each person, as God's creature, had a duty to secure her own survival and flourishing in the world; and thirdly, in the view that natural law imposed duties on us all to respect and assist others in this task – duties which no one could say had been waived or set aside in any rationalization of political absolutism.

II

The story of natural rights in the eighteenth century is largely a story about the political deployment of an idea by thinkers who took an increasingly sceptical attitude to its philosophical foundations. The Lockean approach, as we have seen, depended crucially in a number of ways on the notion of divine law. Rights represented the respect owed by ourselves and others to our nature and status as creatures of God. To be sure, one of Locke's theological arguments was purely negative: the argument for juridical equality was based on the *absence* of any indication that God had designated anyone with any special mark of authority rather than on any specific manifestation of divine command. But in a theological vacuum, this would leave us merely with the insight that we have no naturally ordained duty to obey anyone or anything. That sort of Hobbism would provide no basis for natural rights conceived as moral constraints on other people's behaviour. Rights as constraints in Locke's theory were derived from God's commands and God's purposes in creating us. If we were to dispense with God altogether in our metaphysics, we would lose that basis for moral constraint, and the idea that the naked, shivering wretches left over might have sold themselves to a despot in return for security and prosperity would rear its head once again.

Now it is true that the idea of God did not disappear altogether from Enlightenment philosophy. Some of the *philosophes* retained a full-blooded Christian faith, and the developments I am outlining here obviously posed fewer problems for them than for others. In many cases, those who were sceptical about Christianity retained some sort of belief in God (or a god), though it is little more than a deist conclusion for the cosmological argument. But this meagre deism was certainly inadequate for the purposes of a theory of natural rights. In moving from Christian faith to deism, we lose our grip on the ideas of divine purpose, divine intention and divine command. We have to remember that it is the *full theological picture* that is required for the purposes of natural law and natural rights: a mere lingering affection for the infinite, or a hunch that there must be *something* holding up the universe, is not by itself sufficient.

Once divine command was thrown in doubt, was there anything else that could do the job so far as natural law was concerned? There were three options to be explored: one was *nature* or the *natural*, which might function normatively on its own account independently of a creationist teleology; a second was *reason*, which *anyway* was always thought coincident in its conclusions with the revelations of faith in political matters; and the third was *consensus*, that is the convergence of all nations and peoples on certain elementary standards of behaviour. But none of these provided a satisfactory rebuttal to the restless probing of Enlightenment scepticism.

Nature was often appealed to in theories of rights, apart from its status as divine creation. The idea that certain rights might be alienable, for example, was attacked not only as impious but also as unnatural:

Now as no man by nature may abuse, beat, torment, or afflict himself, so by nature no man may give that power to another, seeing he may not doe it to himselfe. . . . They which contract to obey to their own ruine, or having so contracted, they which esteeme such a contract before their owne preservation are felonious to themselves and rebellious to nature.[16]

But if the appeal of 'nature' here is anything more than rhetoric, some account has to be given of how that which simply *is* – a natural fact – can be regarded as normatively loaded. Part of the problem lay in discerning the norms themselves: 'nature red in tooth and claw' was at least as compelling an image as nature conceived of as a harmonious kingdom of ends. David Hume put the point exactly when he wrote that nature considered in itself seemed to have no more regard to good above evil than to heat above cold.[17] In fact Hume's worry about inferring an 'ought' from an 'is' was no mere analytical quibble: it reflected a deep conviction that our impressions of the world revealed an external order that was in itself neutral or indifferent to human purposes or concerns. Even in *human* nature, the most one could find were elementary impulses of self-love and rather narrowly focused sympathy for others. No doubt, a story could be told about the way in which ethical beliefs and principles of justice and right might be constructed on that foundation, but it would not be a story that displayed any particular principles as 'natural'. The most it could show would be that some artificial arrangements were more conducive to utility than others.

The idea of *reason* offered no firmer foundation for principles of right. Although eighteenth-century moral philosophy was largely dominated by ethical rationalism, that remained, as indeed it had for Locke, more a project than an accomplishment.[18] For one thing, reasoning in this sphere required premises. If these were not given by God or by nature, they must have the character of 'intuitions' – axioms of moral thought as inescapably present to our minds as the axioms of arithmetic. (The attempt by Immanuel Kant to infer universal ethical standards from the *form* of reason alone is perhaps a counter-example.[19] But there were many problems with Kant's project, and in any case it had no great influence on Enlightenment or revolutionary political theory. Kant's impact on the rights tradition was to come much later.) The task of finding intuitions which could serve as premises was a difficult one; they had to combine the necessary degree of self-evidence with the substance that would make possible reasoning to interesting conclusions. (We might all agree on the obvious truth of propositions like 'The good should be pursued' and 'That which is wrong should not be done': the problem was to find *synthetic* propositions about the wrongness of particular types of actions or the worth of particular values which were similarly undeniable.)

The most plausible candidates seemed to be the axioms of utility –
the pleasure that everyone sought for themselves (or, through
empathy, for others) and the pain they tried to avoid. If anything like
a rational science of ethics was developed in the Enlightenment
period, it was the theory of utilitarianism. Starting from the
conviction that pleasure or happiness was the only intrinsic value,
and pain or suffering the only evils, it postulated the maximization of
the good of all and the minimization of evil as political aims, and called
on governments to use their best endeavours to discover scientifically
how these goals could best be achieved. Now the idea of utility is not a
new one: expand the definition of happiness widely enough, and relax
one's conception of maximization, and there are few plausible
theories of ethics that cannot be squeezed into this framework. But as
a self-consciously scientific and secular foundation for morality, it was
an eighteenth-century idea, and one that had a very considerable
impact. As we shall see, it provided the basis for a theory of politics
that developed in conscious opposition to the rights tradition. But at
the same time, it influenced all the Enlightenment thinkers, even
those pledged to natural rights. The latter asserted that the
untrammelled pursuit of happiness was one of the rights of man, and
maintained further that people had a right that their governments
should devote themselves in all their actions to the promotion of
general utility.

But conceived apart from utility, the idea of rights remained on
shaky ground. Its proponents could not offer the sort of reasoned
scientific argument from premises to political conclusions that the
utilitarians could. Quite the contrary: their conclusions were
embarrassingly close to (some would say 'identical with') their
premises, and their moral 'reasoning' accordingly very compressed.
Propositions of right were simply announced, not deduced from any
more abstract background principle or value, and the 'theories' in
question had more the character of lists or manifestos than of
articulated structures of logical thought. It was hard for theorists of
rights to find anything to say to Bentham's taunt that their practice
was simply to assert, as a first principle, any political conviction of
theirs that others happened to disagree with.[20]

What about *consensus*? Denis Diderot in his enthusiasm for natural
law claimed that it was to be found not in the reasoning of private
men but in 'the general will of the species': that is 'in the principles
embodied by the written law of every civilized nation; in the social
behaviour of savage and barbarous peoples; in the tacit agreements
obtaining among the enemies of mankind.'[21] For example if all human

societies adhered to some version of the principle that one should abide by one's undertakings – if there was even honour among barbarians and thieves – then keeping faith might be said to belong to all humans as such. The idea was that natural law could be inferred as a sort of lowest common denominator of all the laws and mores of mankind.

But here the moral confidence of the Enlightenment was simply at odds with the evidence provided by its empirical investigations. Diderot's project was, as Peter Gay has pointed out, 'a brave but unsuccessful attempt to rescue what the philosophes should not have tried to rescue'.[22] As early as 1689 John Locke (who was certainly no moral sceptic) had maintained in the course of his argument against innate ideas:

> He that will carefully peruse the history of mankind, and look abroad into the several tribes of men, and with indifferency survey their actions, will be able to satisfy himself that there is scarce that principle of morality to be named . . . which is not, somewhere or other, slighted and condemned by the general fashion of whole societies of men, governed by practical opinions and rules of living quite opposite to others.[23]

Enlightenment anthropology, making the observations that Locke recommended, reached exactly his conclusions. What appeared self-evident in one society seemed absurd and depraved to the members of another. There was no basis in human experience for moral consensus, and certainly not for the sort of universal principles proponents of natural rights were aiming at.

Furthermore, Enlightenment anthropology did not stop at the discovery of moral dissensus. It embarked also on the project, which has dominated all subsequent study of human societies, of trying to understand local moralities as *natural* phenomena and to correlate different mores with the different conditions under which human beings lived. That project, associated in the eighteenth century above all with the work of Montesquieu, threatened natural law both in its mood and in its implications.[24] It treated norms as facts like any others, and looked behind any claim to transcendent authority to the social conditions that were likely to elicit it. Turned on the customs and practices that were at variance with 'natural law', the sociological approach simply confirmed the futility of Diderot's consensus approach: how could there be consensus when the conditions under which humans lived and thought were so various? Turned on the claims of natural law themselves, the approach tended to be a debunking one, exposing them as just one set of conditioned prejudices among others.

I do not want to suggest that the *philosophes* of the Enlightenment were amoralists or thoroughgoing sceptics about social values (though one or two of them were). Most remained firmly wedded to the idea of natural law: Montesquieu, for example, maintained his belief in a transcendent order of justice even when his sociology seemed to leave room for nothing more transcendent than ethical relativism.[25] The point is that by the middle of the eighteenth century, and in the light of their philosophy, the belief in a natural moral order and in universally applicable principles of justice and right could no longer be taken for granted. The ground had been cut from under it, and enlightened reason had not been able to find anything but slogans to take its place. Nevertheless – and it is a sobering thought for a philosopher – the fragility of its foundations did nothing to diminish its political popularity, even among those who professed a concern for truth, knowledge and logic. When in 1787 Alexander Hamilton wrote that 'the sacred rights of Mankind are not to be rummaged for among old parchments or musty records. They are written, as with a sunbeam, in the whole volume of human nature by the hand of Divinity itself, and can never be erased or obscured', there was not a republican in the world with a heart to express his dissent.[26] All the same, these glorious sentiments were terribly vulnerable to polemics and criticism. Their insecure foundations could be exposed at any time, for their conservative, socialist and even utilitarian critics knew full well that behind the fine phrases there was scarcely a philosopher anywhere who would take seriously the epistemological claim that Hamilton was making. When we talk about natural rights in the eighteenth century, we are talking about an idea whose time had come too late in politics to coincide with its philosophical respectability.

III

We have concentrated so far on the classic Lockean doctrine of natural law and natural right, and on the epistemological embarrassment that surrounded it in Enlightenment thought. But there were also other embarrassments for rights theories. In its classic form the idea of natural rights was associated with the theory of the social contract. The claim was not only that humans had certain rights which could not be alienated in society, but also that existing political relationships were in fact founded on an original agreement among the people living in a given territory to establish institutions and procedures for the better protection of these rights. People were supposed to have met together and agreed to pool their resources and entrust their common power to specialized agencies – princes, magistrates and legislators. The authority of those officials was understood entirely in terms of this original agreement; they had no greater authority than that conferred by this trust, and they were answerable for the performance of their functions in the last resort to the people who had vested this authority in them. By the same token, the social contract generated a theory of obligation on the part of the individual citizen. The agencies of government could not do their work of protecting rights and advancing the common good unless everyone stood by his undertaking to support them.

Considered as an historical hypothesis, the social contract was easy to ridicule. Serious historical and anthropological enquiry simply exposed it as a myth. David Hume's attack was typical of the Enlightenment response:

> Almost all the governments which exist at present, or of which there remains any record in story, have been founded originally, either on usurpation or conquest, or both, without any pretence of a fair consent or a voluntary subjection of the people. . . . The face of the earth is continually changing, by the increase of small kingdoms into great empires, by the dissolution of great empires into smaller kingdoms, by the planting of colonies, by the migration of tribes. Is there anything discoverable in these events but force and violence? Where is the mutual agreement or voluntary association so much talked of?[27]

As a moral idea, the social contract seemed equally unconvincing. Are *we* supposed to be bound *now* by the consent of our forefathers at the dawn of time? Or is it our *own* consent that binds us? If it is the latter, what form does that consent take, and when are we supposed to have given it? Since most citizens have no memory of engaging in any such agreement, the social contract theory faces a dilemma. Either consent is inferred too readily from conduct that the agent does not recognize as consenting (Locke's 'tacit consent', for example[28]), in which case the idea of consent adds little to the claim that we are simply obliged to obey the law of the land and that's that. Or the doctrine has the subversive implication that none of us has, and few of us will ever have, any obligation to submit to political authority. Either way it hardly provides an adequate account of politics and law.

But though the fiction of the social contract was vulnerable in these ways, the importance of this attack for the theory of natural rights should not be over-estimated. In principle, natural rights stand independently of the social contract story. If people have certain rights in virtue of their human nature, those rights ought to be respected by the powers that be, no matter how their power was instituted. The fact that power has been based on violence all along and not contract may damage the theory of political obligation, but it does nothing to refute the claim that power should now be exercised in a morally responsible way.

There was also another way in which the social contract could survive as an important political idea. Suppose it were seen not as an historical hypothesis but as a Utopian aspiration: instead of saying that governments have in the past been based on popular consent, we might call instead for a government of the future to *be* instituted on that basis, as a precondition for human freedom and progress. An approach along these lines can be attributed to the greatest political philosopher of the Enlightenment period – Jean-Jacques Rousseau. 'Man was born free,' Rousseau wrote, 'and everywhere he is in chains.'[29] *The Discourse on the Origins of Inequality* purported to tell the story of man's enslavement and of the moral degeneration that accompanied it. On the other hand, Rousseau's most influential work, *The Social Contract*, set out to describe what would be a genuinely free political order 'taking men as they are and laws as they might be'.[30] It does not matter that no such order has ever existed in the world (though, in certain patriotic moods, Rousseau was inclined to identify it with his native Geneva). Rousseau argued instead that the existence of such an order *now and for the future* offered the only hope of reconciling power with liberty, political authority with the moral autonomy of the individual.

This approach was potentially much more radical than the Lockean version of the social contract. Though Locke's theory was revolutionary in its implications, it was committed to the view that most political regimes in the world were in fact legitimate and the only trouble was that sometimes rulers stepped out of line and deviated from the terms of their foundation. Rousseau's theory, by contrast, seemed to suggest that *no* existing regime could be legitimate (again, except maybe Geneva). He laid down as minimum conditions for political respectability conditions that so far no political system had ever satisfied or sought to satisfy, and which he thought might be very difficult to satisfy except under the most favourable conditions. From the Rousseauian point of view, Hume's arguments about the violence on which existing policies were founded were not a refutation of the social contract idea: they were simply further proof that neither morality, nor duty, nor freedom were to be found in political history so far. The Rousseauian conditions were so evidently unsatisfied in the contemporary regimes of western Europe that the presumption would always be in favour of the legitimacy of revolution.

Putting the social contract in the future like this had the further implication that it made popular sovereignty a live issue in political theory. In the classic social contract story, the sovereignty of the people was safely consigned to prehistory. Their one act was to agree at the dawn of time to the institution of political agencies – executive, judicial and legislative. Once that was done, as Locke put it, 'when Society hath placed the Legislative in any Assembly of Men . . . the Legislative can never revert to the people while that Government lasts.'[31] For Rousseau, however, the sovereign acts of the people were something to look forward to and call for, not something to look back on. A free polity would be one in which the people chose the fundamental laws and the people chose the structures of government. True, the people have never embarked on such an enterprise before, but then humanity, throughout its political history, has never been free from oppression or corruption. From this point of view, Rousseau's insistence in *The Social Contract* that the general will of the people could not be represented was crucial. The people must themselves choose their political arrangements if they are to be free: nobody can do that work for them or in their name, and nobody can claim that as a matter of fact it has already been done on their behalf.[32]

There is a long-running controversy about Rousseau's influence on French revolutionary thought, and in particular on the formulation of the Declaration of Rights.[33] It is easy to exaggerate his influence: the Declaration was modelled mainly on the manifestos set out by the Americans some years earlier. But to the extent that it incorporates democratic ideas and ideas about popular sovereignty in law-making and in government, it is certainly Rousseauesque in inspiration or at least inspired by a theoretical milieu in which the influence of Rousseau's ideas and Rousseauesque language was considerable. Certainly there is precious little in the Lockean heritage on which this particular strand of revolutionary thought could be based. And it should be said, finally, that though the doctrine of rights in its classic form was vulnerable in all the ways we have outlined, it was the Rousseauian tinge that made it appear *dangerous* and encouraged ideological opponents to search out and expose its vulnerability.

∾ 2 ∾

The 'Declaration
of the Rights of Man and
the Citizen' 1789

In May 1789, in circumstances of fiscal and constitutional crisis, the Estates General – representatives of the clergy, the nobility and the commoners – were summoned by Louis XVI to Versailles to advise him on the great issues facing the state. In June the Third Estate – the commoners – reconstituted themselves as the National Assembly of France and invited members of the other Estates to join them. The principle on which they did so was that the issues facing the country should be determined on the basis of voting by head, not voting by order or estate with the effective veto that would give to members of the nobility. In the face of aristocratic outrage, the representatives of the commoners met together and committed themselves in the famous 'Tennis Court Oath' not to disband until they had drawn up a new constitution for the realm. Initially it was unclear whether the king would sanction the deliberations of the new body or whether he would join with the conservative majority of nobles and attempt to suppress it. In the event, Louis XVI backed down a little towards the end of June and instructed representatives of the other orders to join the Third Estate in its meetings. This was generally taken to be a defeat for the monarchy, representing an effective – though certainly not an explicit – recognition of the National Assembly as such.

On 9 July the committee of the Assembly entrusted with the preparation of a new constitution submitted a preliminary report in which it recommended that the constitution should be prefaced with a declaration of rights, enumerating the general philosophic principles on which the rest of the document would be based. In fact various versions of such a declaration were already being prepared. Prominent among those who were working on such projects was the Marquis de Lafayette, a young liberal nobleman who had fought in the American War of Independence and was on familiar terms with many of the leaders of the American republic. The story is told that in his home in Paris, Lafayette had a copy of the Declaration of Independence on display in one panel of a double frame. Anyone who asked what the other empty panel was for was told it awaited the publication of a French counterpart of the American Declaration.[1]

Throughout the first half of 1789 Lafayette's Declaration had undergone a number of drafts, the later ones somewhat more radical as events moved quickly in France. We know that he consulted closely with Thomas Jefferson – then American minister in Paris – on the project and that Jefferson made a number of comments and suggestions.[2] But not all Lafayette's American friends shared his enthusiasm. It has to be remembered that at this stage the American attitude towards rights manifestos was ambivalent. The Declaration of Independence had asserted the 'unalienable Rights', with which all men had been endowed, of 'Life, Liberty and the Pursuit of Happiness'. But the contemporary American constitution did not include a Bill of Rights (that was added in 1791), and it was seen by many of its drafters as an attempt to provide stable institutions of government for a people recovering from revolutionary war rather than as an embodiment of radical aspirations. Several Americans expressed their reservations about 'the Grossness of [Lafayette's] Ignorance of Government and History',[3] while others – more confident in radical politics – had reservations about the concessions the young noble still made, at least in his early drafts, to the principles of monarchy, social distinction and political stability.

When a draft was eventually presented to the National Assembly on 11 July 1789, it was in circumstances of grave emergency: the king had ordered foreign mercenaries who were loyal to him to Paris and Versailles 'to preserve order' and Paris itself was facing a degree of social chaos, political crisis and a severe shortage of food. Thomas Paine (Burke's great opponent) later asserted that 'the particular reason for bringing [the Declaration] forward at this moment, (M. de Lafayette has since informed me) was, that if the National Assembly should fall in the threatened destruction that then surrounded it, some trace of its principles might have the chance of surviving the wreck.'[4] Lafayette's biographers have summarized his speech introducing the Declaration in these terms:

> The justly appreciated report of the Committee on the Constitution had proposed that the Assembly give its attention first to a declaration of rights. Whether the Assembly offered the nation such a 'manifesto of indisputable truths' immediately or only as a

preamble to the 'great work' of a completed constitution, it should, he declared, give primary consideration to stating the basic principles of any constitution, of any system of laws, no matter how simple and commonplace such principles might be. Such a statement would have two practical purposes: it would serve as a reminder of 'the sentiments which nature has implanted in the hearts of every man,' and it would 'express those verities from which all institutions should derive,' providing 'an unerring guide' for the nation's representatives, 'constantly sending them back to the source of natural and social right.' The universal recognition of these eternal verities was all the more engaging because 'for a nation to love freedom, it need only know it,' and 'for it to be free, it need only wish to be.'[5]

The speech was applauded and the document submitted to various *bureaux* of the Assembly for further consideration. There were also other more or less well worked out proposals along similar lines to consider, by men like Sieyes, Mounier and Mirabeau. But the immediate impact of Lafayette's presentation was considerable. The Declaration and his speech circulated quickly in Paris and no doubt contributed to the atmosphere in which the Bastille was stormed, and the king apprehended and brought from Versailles to Paris, a few days later.

When Lafayette's document was referred, the assumption was that a declaration of rights should not be promulgated in advance of the new constitution. But on 27 July the Committee on the Constitution recommended that a declaration should be published, on its own if necessary, as soon as possible. Some deputies expressed misgivings about the wisdom of this course, fearing that a declaration of rights without a constitution would simply foment disorder, aggravate the violent expression of grievances and give rise in the medium term to expectations that any later constitution would be bound to disappoint. But other deputies were less cautious about entrusting the people with a knowledge of their rights and, like Lafayette, were anxious to establish the basic principles of a new order immediately in the face of the counter-revolutionary threat. The committee's proposal was accepted, further drafting and discussion were undertaken, and in its final form the 'Declaration of the Rights of Man and the Citizen' was adopted by the National Assembly on 26 August 1789.

That document, in a slightly amended form, was eventually prefixed to the constitution of 1791, and it was updated from time to time in the turbulent years that followed. It is, however, the 1789 version which has had the greatest influence in world politics and political philosophy, and that is still the version to which 'the French people solemnly proclaims its attachment' in the modern constitution of the Fifth Republic.[6]

Declaration of the Rights of Man and the Citizen 1789

The Representatives of the French People constituted in National Assembly,

Considering that ignorance, forgetfulness or contempt of the rights of man are the sole causes of public misfortune and governmental depravity,

Have resolved to expound in a solemn declaration the natural, inalienable and sacred rights of man,

So that this declaration, perpetually present to all members of the body social, shall be a constant reminder to them of their rights and duties;

So that, since it will be possible at any moment to compare the acts of the legislative authority and those of the executive authority with the final end of all political institutions, those acts shall thereby be the more respected;

So that the claims of the citizenry, founded thenceforth on simple and uncontestable principles, shall always tend to the support of the constitution and to the common good.

Consequently the *National Assembly* recognizes and declares in the presence and under the auspices of the Supreme Being the following rights of man and of the citizen:

1 In respect of their rights men are born and remain free and equal. The only permissible basis for social distinctions is public utility.
2 The final end of every political institution is the preservation of the natural and imprescriptible rights of man. These rights are those of liberty, property, security and resistance to oppression.
3 The basis of all sovereignty lies, essentially, in the Nation. No corporation nor individual may exercise any authority that is not expressly derived therefrom.
4 Liberty is the capacity to do anything that does no harm to others. Hence the only limitations on the individual's exercise of his natural rights are those which ensure the enjoyment of these same rights to all other individuals. These limits can be established only by legislation.

5 Legislation is entitled to forbid only those actions which are harmful to society. Nothing not forbidden by legislation may be prohibited nor may any individual be compelled to do anything that legislation has not prescribed.

6 Legislation is the expression of the general will. All citizens have a right to participate in shaping it either in person, or through their representatives. It must be the same for all, whether it punishes or it protects. Since all citizens are equal in its eyes, all are equally eligible for all positions, posts and public employments in accordance with their abilities and with no other distinctions than those provided by their virtues and their talents.

7 No individual may be accused, arrested or detained except in the cases prescribed by legislation and according to the procedures it has laid down. Those who solicit, further, execute or arrange for the execution of arbitrary commands must be punished; but every citizen charged or detained by virtue of legislation must immediately obey; resistance renders him culpable.

8 The only punishments established by legislation must be ones that are strictly and obviously necessary, and no individual may be punished except by virtue of a law passed and promulgated prior to the crime and applied in due legal form.

9 Since every individual is presumed innocent until found guilty, legislation must severely repress all use of force beyond that which is necessary to secure his person in those cases where it is deemed indispensable to arrest him.

10 Nobody must be persecuted on account of his opinions, including religious ones, provided that the manifestation of these does not disturb the public order established by legislation.

11 The free communication of thoughts and opinions is one of the most precious rights of man; hence every citizen may speak, write and publish freely, save that he must answer for any abuse of such freedom according to the cases established by legislation.

12 In order to guarantee the rights of man and the citizen, a police force is necessary: it follows that such a force is established for the public weal and not for the private advantage of those to whom it is entrusted.

13 The upkeep of the police force and the expenses of public administration necessitate public taxation. This must be borne by all citizens equally, according to their means.

14 All citizens, individually or through their representatives, possess the right to assure themselves that a need for taxation exists, to accept it by free consent, to monitor the way it is being used and

to prescribe the base, the allocation, collection and duration of the tax.

15 Society possesses the right to demand from every public servant an account of his administration.

16 A society in which rights are not secured nor the separation of powers established is a society without a constitution.

17 Since property is an inviolable and sacred right, no individual may be deprived of it unless some public necessity, legally certified as such, clearly requires it; and subject always to a just and previously determined compensation.

⽤ 3 ⮑

Jeremy Bentham's
Anarchical Fallacies

I

Jeremy Bentham was born in 1748, the son of a wealthy member of
the legal profession. Educated at Westminster School and Queen's
College, Oxford (where he received his first degree at the age of 16),
and admitted to the Bar in 1769, he soon forswore the practice of law
as it is for the more solitary, less remunerative, but temperamentally
more congenial study of the law as it ought to be.

Of the three great critics of rights we are examining, it was
Bentham who was most evidently a product of the intellectual
optimism that dominated European thought in the eighteenth
century. Under the influence of the Enlightenment thinkers, Cesare
Beccaria and Claude Helvetius, Bentham developed a precisely
formulated version of utilitarianism as a distinctive perspective for
evaluating law, politics and social institutions. That theory was most
clearly set out in his *Introduction to the Principles of Morals and
Legislation* published in 1789, and it remained a centre of gravity for
all his subsequent work.

The utilitarianism of Bentham's *Introduction* is based on the
premise that 'Nature has placed mankind under the governance of
two sovereign masters, *pain* and *pleasure*',[1] and that it is futile to
expect anyone to follow an ethic that does not have these as its
primary points of reference. The principle of utility passes this test,
for, as Bentham put it, it 'approves or disapproves of every action
whatsoever, according to the tendency which it appears to have to
augment or diminish the happiness of the party whose interest is in
question.'[2] It also provides a clear meaning for the otherwise fictitious
idea of *the interest of the community*: that is simply 'the sum of the
interests of the members who compose it'.[3] In other words the public
interest was seen as reducible directly to the interests of individuals,
expressed in terms of those individuals' experiences of pleasure and
pain. In Chapter 4 of the book Bentham went on to propose a method

for determining the amount of pleasure or pain that each individual might suffer in relation to some proposed course of action. The value of a given pleasure or pain consequent on some action was to comprise its subjective intensity, its duration, the probability of its occurrence, its propinquity or remoteness in time (regarded by Bentham as a factor independent of its probability), and its fecundity (that is the other pleasures and pains to which it, in turn, gave rise). Adding and multiplying along these dimensions for numbers of people, one could determine more or less precisely which of a set of alternative actions would have the best effects.[4] This paradigm of moral calculation dominated Bentham's thought all his life. He did not believe it should be applied meticulously 'to every moral judgement, or to every legislative operation'.[5] And he did believe that it should be supplemented by what he called 'axioms of mental pathology', that is empirical generalizations 'expressive of the connexion between such occurrences as are continually taking place, or liable to take place, and the pleasures and pains which are representing the result of them.'[6] (The law of the diminishing marginal utility of money would be a good example.) But the calculus of utility was 'always to be kept in view' and provided the only scientific basis there could be for moral thinking.[7]

In his earliest writings, *A Fragment on Government* and the manuscripts of *A Comment upon the Commentaries* and *Of Laws in General*, Bentham attacked established theories of the common law and the English constitution, ridiculing what he called the 'fictions' of natural law and the social contract and insisting on understanding law in terms of the determinate commands of an identifiable sovereign backed up by the threat of sanctions of one kind or another. Since law sprang from the human will, law-making was to be evaluated in the same way as all other human conduct – by its tendency to promote the happiness of those affected. On this account, the jurist had a two-fold function. It was, first, to find out what the existing state of the law was, and the effects of its operation on society. And second, to work out what utility demanded in the particular circumstances of a given society, to propose rules, schemes and institutions for putting these demands into effect, and to persuade powerful sovereigns to include those proposals in the contents of their sanctioned commands.

Against the background of this jurisprudence, Bentham acquired a penchant for the elaboration of legislative schemes for practical reform and institutional design. He was not content to leave these in his library, but sent a steady stream of them in the direction of any sovereigns he thought might be motivated to carry them into effect. Recipients of these proposals included not only the government of his own country, but also those of Russia, France, Spain and the new regimes in North and South America. Despite these efforts, Bentham's schemes were almost uniformly unsuccessful at the political level. The lasting legacy of his work has been more a certain spirit of reformist thought than any institutional achievement. The most severe disappointment of all was Bentham's long campaign to sell his novel conception of prison and workhouse architecture and management – the scheme he called the *Panopticon* – to the British government.[8] A number of commentators have traced his disillusionment with benevolent (read 'utilitarian') despotism and his growing affinity for democracy to setbacks such as these.[9] Certainly the *Panopticon* project was an obsession for Bentham for much of the 1790s; when he resumed more abstract theoretical work in 1803, he inclined much more towards the idea that the promotion in politics of the greatest happiness of the greatest number could be secured only by giving the greatest number some degree of influence over the personal fortunes of their legislators, and making the latter effectively accountable to them.

In the early nineteenth century he worked on a number of projects of a philosophical kind – such as a study of the nature of thought and language – as well as issues of political economy and legal and constitutional theory. During this period the previously solitary Bentham accumulated a number of acolytes who took on the task of making his often illegible and chaotic manuscripts available in orderly form to the general public. (This process continues, with no obvious end in sight, to this day.)[10] He died, surrounded by these acolytes and by well over 70,000 pages of manuscript material, in 1832.

The material from which the bulk of the following extract is taken is a document which includes four distinct critical reviews of the various declarations of rights made by or proposed to the French National Assembly in the revolutionary period 1789–95. The most important as well as the most extensive of these is the second – the response to the 1791 Declaration. But though this material is directed specifically at the details of those historical manifestos, the critique of natural rights is a theme that runs all through Bentham's writing, from beginning to end. In *A Fragment on Government*, published in 1776, Bentham attacked the invocation by Blackstone of Lockean natural law ideas as a basis for English constitutional theory. In the same year he collaborated with John Lind in the production of a pamphlet called *An Answer to the Declaration of the American*

Congress; there the theory of natural rights was denounced as a series of 'vague and declamatory generalities', which were not only 'repugnant to the British Constitution' but also 'subversive of every actual or imaginable kind of government'.[11] It is, however, worth remembering that, like Burke, Bentham was not an enemy of the American cause. When his attack on American natural rights theory was resumed in 1789, he was careful to add: 'Who can help lamenting that so rational a cause should be rested upon reasons, so much fitter to beget objections than to remove them?'[12]

His reaction to the revolution in France in that year was like that of the majority of his thinking contemporaries: initial enthusiasm, turned to disappointment by the events of the 1790s, and issuing in downright hostility by 1796. The enthusiasm rested in part on the discernment of a new opportunity for the employment of his own talents as legislative adviser to a new regime. He offered a number of schemes and pamphlets to the revolutionary authorities (including floor design and ground-rules for a legislative assembly), and in 1792 was made an Honorary Citizen of the French Republic for his pains.[13] But even while that honour was being formally conferred, Bentham was beginning to write scathingly about events in France, and by 1796 he had repudiated not only the revolutionary ideal, but also republicanism and (for the time being) the cause of parliamentary reform in England.[14] In 1791 his brother wrote to him from abroad and said that in his travels he had come across 'some hundreds of pages of verbiage on *liberté* and *droits d'homme* which a few lines of your principles would show as clear as the sun at noon.'[15] Bentham began working on those lines in 1795 and finished them in 1796. Originally entitled *Pestulance Unmasked*, the manuscript lay 'very quietly upon my shelf' until 1801 when it was offered for publication to an anti-Jacobin magazine under the title

No French Nonsense: or A Cross Buttock for the first Declaration of Rights: together with a kick of the A—— for the Second . . . by a practitioner of the Old English Art of Self Defence.[16]

Unfortunately, however, it was not to be published in English (under this title or any other) until after Bentham's death. An edition appeared in France in 1816, translated by Bentham's editor and popularizer, Etienne Dumont. But it did not see the light of day in England until the appearance of Bentham's *Collected Works* in the edition put together by John Bowring in 1843. There is a substantial extract in Bhiku Parekh's book, *Bentham's Political Thought*, published in 1973.[17] No version of it has yet appeared in the edition of

Bentham's works presently being assembled in London.

As well as the extract from *Anarchical Fallacies*, I have also included here a brief extract from a paper entitled 'Supply Without Burthern; or Escheat *vice* Taxation', which Bentham wrote in 1794. Political economy was one of the areas on which Bentham thought a utilitarian adviser ought to have something to say, and in his *Manual of Political Economy* (1793) Bentham had argued, along familiar lines, that government interference with the economy was detrimental to the happiness and prosperity of the nation. The 'Supply Without Burthern' proposal developed this theme in the area of fiscal economy and property rights. Bentham proposed that government interference by way of taxation could be reduced by allowing much of the fiscal burden of government to fall upon deceased estates rather than on the property or income of the living. He conceded that in cases where the deceased had close relatives or dependants, the estate should pass to them. But in other cases, where the estate would by the existing operation of law pass to some distant relative, no serious harm or disappointment would be caused by diverting it to the Exchequer instead. The point of the proposal was not merely fiscal: inheritance was the one area where a value like social equality (valued instrumentally by Bentham in view of the diminishing marginal utility of resources) could be pursued without threatening the security of proprietors' expectations. Elsewhere in his economic writings, Bentham had argued that equality must always yield to security.[18] But security of expectation was not, he reckoned, an important consideration in the inheritance of an estate by a distant and non-dependent cousin of the deceased.

As in many of his works, Bentham attempted to anticipate objections to his scheme. The extract I have included is his preemptive response to the objection that taxing estates in this way would violate natural law. However, it is clear that in answering this objection, Bentham goes far beyond what is necessary for that purpose: he is clearly expressing a rage and impatience with the whole idea of natural law and natural rights which reflects his general, and nor merely his fiscal concerns. Werner Stark writes that what we have here is 'a passionate denunciation of the theory and practice of the law of nature',[19] and goes on to note that these pages were written at the time of the Terror in France, when it seemed that the mob and the guillotine, rather than the kingdom of ends, were the results of the practical application of theories of natural right.

At any rate, the pamphlet (presented as a sketch for a larger book on the subject, which, as far as we know, Bentham never attempted) was duly sent to the Exchequer for consideration. Like all Bentham's similar proposals, it was ignored.

II

I have taken the title of this collection from a well-known phrase that Bentham used in *Anarchical Fallacies* to attack the view that the object of all government is 'the preservation of the natural and imprescriptible rights of man'. *'Natural rights is simple nonsense'*, retorted Bentham, 'natural and imprescriptible rights, rhetorical nonsense, – nonsense upon stilts' (p. 53).[20] The passage continues with Bentham claiming that 'this rhetorical nonsense ends in the old strain of mischievous nonsense'; and perhaps this term 'mischievous nonsense' sums up better than anything else Bentham's attitude to the idea of natural rights. The way I propose to approach Bentham's critique, then, is to ask, first, why he thought this talk of rights was *nonsensical* and, second, what *mischief* he thought this nonsense made in politics and social life.

The charge of nonsense has two counts to it. On the one hand, Bentham viewed talk of natural rights as literally *non-sense* – that is devoid of meaning (rather in the way members of the Vienna Circle were later to characterize the sentences of theology and metaphysics). On the other hand, he was able to point out contradiction after contradiction in the texts of the Declarations of Rights. That seemed to indicate that he thought the phraseology of the Declarations *did* have a meaning, but one which went all over the place and more or less guaranteed their falsity.

Themes of language, meaning, sense and nonsensicality dominated Bentham's work. Throughout all his work, there is a powerful commitment to the view that clarity will never be achieved in politics and the study of law 'till that universal precept . . . be steadily pursued, "Define your words" '. Like an earlier English philosopher, Thomas Hobbes, Bentham was convinced that one of the main sources of conflict in politics was verbal vagueness, equivocality and confusion.[21] In his early writings on jurisprudence, we find a preoccupation with 'fictions', that is expressions which in themselves refer to nothing but which are nevertheless used as though they were meaningful, and assertions which at face value seem evidently false but which are nevertheless accepted and given legal effect in order to secure some desired outcome. In these early writings definition is understood along familiar empiricist lines: the resolution of complex ideas into the simple elements of sense experience that compose them.[22] But gradually Bentham developed his own distinctive approach to the science of conceptual definition – an approach he called 'paraphrasis' and which is roughly the elucidation of the use of a term not in isolation but by an account of the sentences in which the term is used:

> A word may be said to be expounded by *paraphrasis*, when not that *word* alone is translated into other *words*, but some whole sentence of which it forms a part is translated into another sentence, the words of which latter are expressive of such ideas as are *simple* or are more immediately resolvable into simple ones than those of the former.[23]

So one does not insist as a condition of meaningfulness that every *word* must refer, simply or as a complex, to elements of sense experience; rather one insists that a word is meaningful only if the meaning of every *sentence* in which it occurs can be rendered by another which has that sort of empirical reference. For example the word 'sake' is meaningful not because *it* picks out an empirical idea but because we have a way of understanding sentences like 'He did this for her sake' which make it clear what elements of sense experience are being referred to.

The triumph of Benthamite jurisprudence was the elucidation by paraphrasis of the meaning of terms like 'right' and 'duty' in the context of positive law. As they stood, 'right' and 'duty' were fictitious terms for Bentham, whereas terms like 'law', 'sanction' and 'sovereign' were not. The former did not stand for anything tangible, but the latter picked out identifiable, even if complex, things that we could hear, see and experience – things like commands, commanders and the deliberate infliction of pain. So if propositions about right and duty could somehow be translated into propositions about laws and sanctions, they could be given a sense. To talk of a duty, Bentham suggested, was to talk of an action required by a sovereign on pain of some sanction. Talk of rights could then be reduced to sovereigns and sanctions indirectly via that analysis of duty: to have a right is to be the beneficiary of a duty – that is for it to be the case that one benefits from another's performance of an action required of her by a sovereign on pain of a sanction. The positivist implications of his analysis were clear. If sentences containing 'duty' and 'right' depended for their sense on the sense of other sentences about sovereigns, commands and sanction, talk of natural duties and natural rights would reduce to nonsense unless one were willing to refer to the natural law commands of a divine sovereign. But Bentham noted wryly that the revolutionaries of the Enlightenment were very

reluctant to make that move: 'The natural rights we hear so much of
. . . are of all things the farthest from being divine rights. For in no
mouths are they so frequent nor so much insisted upon as in the
mouths of those by whom the existence of a divine law and of a divine
lawgiver are equally denied' (p. 73). Take away the lawgiver, and you
take away the law; and 'right' and 'duty' are left high and dry, devoid
of any sense. 'Right and law are correlative terms: as much so as son
and father. A natural right is a son that never had a father' (p. 73).

At one point in *Anarchical Fallacies* Bentham suggests that the
crucial linguistic error involved here is the transformation of the
adjective 'right' (as in 'This action is right') into a noun ('I have a right
to perform this action'). He notes that since this transformation is
verbally easier in English than in French, we should not have
expected this brand of nonsense to surface so strikingly in France (p.
68). It should be clear, however, that this is not the real nub of
Bentham's worry. In a legal context an occurrence of the noun 'right'
can be paraphrased as easily as the adjective: it is a useful and
intelligible fiction. On Bentham's considered account, the nonsense
of natural rights has to do, not with the formation of the substantive,
but with the severance of a juridical notion from the context of
positive law.

Like logical positivists in the twentieth century, Bentham of course
accepted that language devoid of meaning might nevertheless have a
use. He was quite clear about the political usefulness of rights-talk.

> When a man has a political caprice to gratify, and is determined to
> gratify it, if possible, at any price, when he feels an ardent desire to
> see it gratified but can give no reason why it should be gratified,
> when he finds it necessary to get the multitude to join with him, but
> either stoops not to enquire whether they would be the better or
> the happier for doing so, or feels himself at a loss to prove it, he sets
> up a cry of rights. (p. 73).

But such a cry is just a form of verbal bludgeoning. Expressions of
natural right, says Bentham, 'owe the influence they unhappily
possess to the confidence they display'. But they also presage a darker
form of political influence: 'When I hear of natural rights . . . I always
see in the background a cluster of daggers or of pikes introduced into
the National Assembly' (p. 74). As we shall see, Bentham has much to
say against the wickedness of the political philosophy associated with
natural rights. But here the point is that claims and counterclaims
whose vehemence is inversely proportional to their meaningfulness
can be resolved only by violence. Making no sense, they can

evoke no reply. They are not true or false, but either prevail or are suppressed.

> Of a positive assertion thus irrational, the natural effect where it fails of producing irrational acquiescence, is to produce equally irrational denial. . . . When we have said this much on either side, it is to no purpose to say more; there we are completely at a stand; argument such as this can go no further on either side, – or neither yields, – or passion triumphs alone – the stronger sweeping the weaker away.[24]

The interesting thing is that, unlike modern positivists, Bentham did not deny all meaning to *ethical* evaluations of the law. On the contrary, drawing his celebrated distinction between 'descriptive' and 'censorial' jurisprudence, he took it as his life's work to show how the law of England and of other countries fell far short of any rational standards of evaluation. It *was* sensible, he claimed, to ask and argue about what the law *ought* to be, or whether a particular law was *good* or *bad*. If I say, 'Such-and-such a law ought not to be made', what is expressed? 'This and this only,' said Bentham, 'that a sentiment of dissatisfaction is excited in my breast by any such law.' Equally if I say no such law *shall* be made, I express the view that 'the sentiment of dissatisfaction in me is so strong as to have given birth to a determined will that no such law shall ever pass.' These are intelligible albeit subjective sentiments. But feelings and resolutions like these can also be defended with *reasons*, and Bentham maintains that 'this reason, if there be any which deserves the name, is always a proposition of fact relative to the question of utility.'[25]

Utilitarian argument, then, can be used to establish the validity of moral propositions about the law and, by the same token, if the law in question confers some benefit on an assignable person, it can be used to establish the validity of moral propositions about legal rights. It certainly makes sense, according to Bentham, to maintain that so-and-so *ought* to have some particular legal right. But sense disappears when that is represented by the claim that so-and-so *already* has some natural right in virtue of which the legal right is called for: 'Reasons for wishing there were such things as rights are not rights; a reason for wishing that a certain right were established, is not that right – want is not supply – hunger is not bread' (p. 53). That something ought to be done makes sense in terms of the basic principle of morality; and even the idea that we have moral duties can be paraphrased in this way, as well as in terms of positive law. But, as far as one can tell, Bentham remained obdurate in his refusal to paraphrase talk of moral *rights* in terms of moral duties and moral 'ought's. Though he took 'moral rightness' to mean conduciveness to the principle of utility, he refused to give the substantive term 'right' a moral sense. I must say that I can see no justification for that refusal.[26]

Apart from the meaninglessness of its main term, talk of natural rights was saturated with other forms of 'nonsense', according to Bentham, in particular equivocations, ambiguity and contradictions.

The equivocation which most enraged him was on the terms 'can' and 'cannot' in assertions like the following in the Declaration of Rights: 'Social distinctions *cannot* be founded, but upon common utility' (Article I); 'Whatever is not forbidden by the law, *cannot* be hindered' (Article V); 'Property being an inviolable and sacred right, no-one *can* be deprived of it . . .' (Article XVII). In these and similar phrases, the ground shifts uneasily between claims about physical, moral and legal impossibility. The ambiguous connotations of the phrase '*natural law*' suggest that something contrary to nature cannot physically take place. But that will hardly do in a political context where, as Bentham noted, the main *complaint* is that the 'impossible' (in whatever sense is meant here) *has* been and *is* being done, and that violations of natural law *are* being committed. What is meant is presumably either that the act in question is morally impossible – that is incapable of being right or justified in any circumstances – or that it is legally impossible – that is null and void and having no binding effect in law. Now, on its own, neither of these is satisfactory: the first falls foul of Bentham's consequentialism; the second is contradicted by his legal positivism. But the combination of these spurious claims is deadly to sound reasoning: 'Shuffled backwards and forwards amidst these three species of impossibility – physical, legal, and moral – the mind can find no resting place: it loses its footing altogether, and becomes an easy prey to the violence that wields these arms.'[27]

Bentham believed that contradictions abounded in the language of rights. They could be found, not only in the formulation of the particular rights – he singled out the right of property for particular attention, noting that 'what is every man's right is no man's right; so that the effect of this part of the oracle, if observed, would be, not to establish property, but to extinguish it' (p. 58) – but also most importantly in the overall spirit of the Declaration. The tenor of the Declaration, in its greater part, is to assert very general claims in apparently absolute form, such as a claim to unbounded liberty, an uncompromising claim to democracy, a claim to absolute property, and so on. But, as Bentham noted, no political regime of any sort can possibly be established in which such things are maintained as absolutes. There have to be *some* constraints on liberty (if only to make meaningful freedom available to anyone), *some* constraints on property (in order to give effective property rights to any or all), and so on. Now the proponents of the Declaration were not completely devoid of common sense and they recognized these points. But the exceptions and limitations they accepted were tucked away in the latter parts of the document where they would not detract too much from the appearance of absolutism so far as the particular rights were concerned. The result, Bentham says, is not what one would have wanted – namely a *clearly qualified* commitment to liberty, property, democracy, and so on – but a tissue of contradictions:

> In vain would it be said, that though no bounds are here assigned to any of these rights, yet it is to be understood as taken for granted and tacitly admitted and assumed that they are to have bounds; viz. such bounds as it is understood will be set them by the laws. Vain, I say, would be this apology; for the supposition would be contra-dictory to the express declaration of the article itself. . . . It would be self-contradictory, because these rights are, in the same breath in which their existence is declared, declared to be imprescriptable; and imprescriptable . . . means nothing unless it excludes the interference of the laws.[28]

When the qualifications *are* revealed, they are inevitably cast in language so vague as to undermine *any* force (let alone any *absolute* force) that the initial claims may have had. In other words, the framers of a Declaration like this face a dilemma.

> In regard to the rights thus declared, mention will either be made of the exceptions and modifications that may be made to them by the laws themselves, or there will not. In the former case, the observance of the declaration will be impracticable; nor can the law in its details stir a step without flying in the face of it. In the other case, it fails thereby altogether of its only object, the setting limits to the exercise of the legislative power.[29]

The only way to avoid the Scylla of absolutism and the Charybdis of legalism is to follow the course that Bentham discerns in the Declaration: to brazen it out with contradictions.

III

We have dwelt long enough on the accusation that the Declaration of Rights is nonsense. In the case of the Declaration of American

Independence and the constitutions of the states, Bentham was prepared to strike a sympathetic note in his linguistic critique: 'Who can help lamenting that so rational a cause should be rested upon reasons, so much fitter to beget objections, than to remove them?'[30] But by the mid-1790s he was convinced that talk of natural rights was not merely nonsense in a good cause, but 'terrorist language', 'mischievous' and 'dangerous nonsense'. Natural rights were described as 'the mortal enemies of law, the subverters of government, and the assassins of security' (p. 73). He now maintained that the morality of the Declaration was on a par with its logic: wild, unjustified, contradictory and potentially anarchic.

We have already seen that Bentham, in common with a number of writers in the eighteenth century, had grave doubts about contractualist theories of the origin of government and about the idea of a state of nature governed by natural law which such speculations presupposed. For Bentham human life without positive law would have a Hobbesian character: it would be savage, miserable and insecure. Now such a situation was by no means unthinkable. The achievements of law were security, society and economy; but these were fragile achievements, and if law were attacked, there was always the danger – as the Terror of the 1790s had shown – of a collapse back into the chaos and insecurity of life without order. Against this background, then, the imperatives of politics were twofold. First, whatever the origin of government in a particular society, nothing should be done to undermine the possibility that that society should continue to be ruled by law. Even if its history was distasteful to the morally fastidious, its future depended on the persistence of law, however violently that had been initially established. Second, 'the happiness of society should be the one object kept in view by the members of the government in all their measures' (p. 55). This was to be the Law and the Prophets of utilitarian political morality. Both imperatives, Bentham argued, were ignored or undermined by those who based their politics on the idea of natural tights.

We have seen that he thought talk of rights abstracted from positive law was nonsensical. But this in itself does not capture the *antipathy* between law and natural rights. Theories of natural rights deny the very existence of laws made contrary to their prescriptions; in so doing, they undermine the clarity and determinacy of the concept of law, derogating from the one great advantage it has as an undisputed co-ordinating focus for expectations in society. In terms of Bentham's jurisprudence the inchoate vagaries of common law were bad enough; the idea of a natural law criterion of validity for codes and statutes would be ruinous. Certainly, he conceded, there were bad laws – laws which should never have been passed. But Bentham maintained that a society in which it is impossible for people to know what is law and what is not (even if the arcane law is perfectly just) is incomparably worse than a society in which the law is well known and some of the known laws are bad. In other words, Bentham's legal positivism was not just an analytical position: it was grounded firmly in a sense of the human advantages of determinate, posited forms of social organization.

A legal positivist need not refrain from moral criticism of the law. Bentham saw an important difference between the anarchist and 'the rational censor of the laws'. The latter can also be a good subject: he calls for the repeal of the law he opposes, but acknowledges its existence in the mean time. Bentham is famous for the suggestion that the jurist's function is to 'censor freely' but 'obey punctually'.[31] But a moral requirement of unthinking compliance with positive law does not seem to have been his considered view. In a later part of *Anarchical Fallacies* he ridiculed a doctrine expressed in the 1795 'Declaration of the Duties of Man and the Citizen' to the effect that 'he who openly violates the law, declares himself in a state of war with society':

> In kindness to one set of button-makers, we have a silly law in England, condemning the whole country to wear now and for everlasting a sort of buttons they do not like. A more silly law can scarcely be imagined. . . . In London you may see every day, in any street, men, women, and children violating these and other such wholesome laws . . . with sufficient openness. Since all these wicked uncivic button-wearers have declared war against society, what say you, Citizen Legal-epigram-maker . . . to a few four-and-twenty pounders filled with grapeshot to clear the streets of them?[32]

Bentham's complaint, then, against the proponents of natural right was not that they were inclined in certain circumstances to disobedience. Rather it was that they responded over-dramatically to the badness or silliness of a law when it was repugnant to one of their rights, calling for resistance to and the overthrow of the entire system of government. The proponents of rights not only denied the *existence* of a silly or repugnant law, but also called upon all mankind to rise and resists its execution. It is not noncompliance but the revolutionary call to arms, with its associated anarchy, terror and insecurity, which is the focus of Bentham's concern. *Disobedience* and *rebellion* are quite different things, and Bentham resisted all attempts by proponents of rights and proponents of the duties of citizenship to identify the two.

Again, part of the problem lies with the apparent absolutism of the Declaration of Rights. It puts forward as the absolute minimum conditions of political legitimacy principles which, if they have any place at all in the theory of politics, are more properly regarded as counsels of Utopian aspiration:

> A government which should fulfil the expectations here held out, would be a government of absolute perfection. The instance of a government fulfilling these expectations never has taken place, nor till men are angels, ever can take place. Against every government which fails in any degree of fulfilling these expectations, then, it is the professed object of this manifesto to excite insurrection: here as elsewhere, it is therefore its direct object to excite insurrection at all times against every government whatsoever.[33]

The offence of incitement to insurrection is compounded in natural rights theories by the wrongheadedness of the political principles on which the Declaration is based. According to Bentham almost every article stands convicted of 'hasty generalization – the great stumbling block of intellectual vanity' (p. 48). Ideals like equality, liberty and democracy are asserted as general principles without any consideration of the particular consequences their operation would have for the well-being of men and women. Equality and democracy are Bentham's favourite targets. The claim, for example, that all are equal in rights rides roughshod over the distinctions society has found it useful to make:

> The apprentice, then, is equal in rights to his master.... The case is the same as between ward and guardian. So again as between wife and husband. The madman has as good a right to confine anybody else, as anybody else has to confine him. The idiot has as much right to govern everybody, as anybody can have to govern him. (p. 51)

Without distinctions like these, a system of legal and political equality is 'democracy run mad – [laws] made by men, women, and children, – convicts, madmen and so on.' But to establish such distinctions, it is not enough to spout slogans or parrot traditional categories; we must, says Bentham, investigate in detail what will serve the requirements of social utility.

The point about consequences pervades the whole of Bentham's critique of rights. He is convinced that by shying away from consequentialist analysis, the framers of the Declaration are guilty of shallow and superficial thought leading to crazy and ill-considered action:

> The dictates of reason and utility are the result of circumstances which require genius to discover, strength of mind to weigh, and patience to investigate: the language of natural rights require[s] nothing but a hard front, a hard heart and an unblushing countenance. It is from beginning to end so much flat assertion: it neither has anything to do with reason nor will endure the mention of it. It lays down as a fundamental and inviolable principle whatever is in dispute. (p. 74)

To know what legal rights people should have, and whether they should be equal or unequal, it is necessary to enquire into the time, place and circumstances in which the right is to operate. Moreover, 'the right itself must be specifically described, not jumbled with an indistinguisable heap of others, under any such vague general terms as property, liberty and the like' (p. 54).

In political thinking we should not descend from general principles to particular applications. Instead our method should be roughly inductive. If it is fundamental laws we are after, then

> the proper order is – first to digest the laws of detail, and when they are settled and found to be fit for use, then, and not till then, to select and frame in *terminis*, by abstraction, such propositions as may be capable of being given without self-contradiction as fundamental laws.[34]

The alternative course – committing oneself to general principles as fundamental laws in *advance* of a detailed investigation – is so contrary to reason, Bentham suggests, as to betray much darker motives than any genuine concern for human welfare. The promulgation of these manifestos as the last word on government is evidence of 'self conceit and tyranny exalted into insanity' (p. 54). A legislator concerned for the general good will recognize that his laws must be changed as circumstances change, and not feel threatened by that. Conversely those who wish to make their legislation immutable must repudiate any concern for changing circumstances. They are saying in effect:

> Our will shall consequently reign without control and forever: reign now we are living, reign after we are dead. . . . Future governments will not have honesty enough to be trusted with the determination of what rights shall be maintained, what abrogated – what laws kept in force, what repealed. (p. 54)

Like his companions in this volume, Burke and Marx, Bentham would have no truck with the philosopher's pretension to lay down abstract principles as timeless rules for all forms of society. Like them he was convinced that the circumstances of human life were too varied and too ephemeral to allow us to pin down the demands of social utility in a few abstract formulations.

The final count in Bentham's indictment of the rights of man was the threat they posed to social solidarity. No one can doubt, he thought, that the motives of those who propounded these manifestos were self-serving. But their tendency was also to heighten and exacerbate selfishness in general in society.

> The great enemies of public peace are the selfish and the dissocial passions – necessary as they are – the one to the very existence of each individual, the other to his security. On the part of these affections, a deficiency in point of strength is never to be apprehended: all that is to be apprehended in respect of them, is to be apprehended on the side of their excess. Society is held together only by the sacrifices that men can be induced to make of the gratifications they demand: to obtain these sacrifices is the great difficulty, the great task of government. What has been the object, the perpetual and palpable object, of this declaration of pretended rights? To add as much force as possible to these passions, but already too strong, – to burst the cords that hold them in, – to say to the selfish passions, there – everywhere – is your prey! – to the angry passions, there – everywhere – is your enemy. Such is the morality of this celebrated manifesto.[35]

Unlike Marx and Burke, Bentham located self-interest at the core of his theory of human nature. But like them, he saw the possibility of human society as depending utterly on the extent to which people could be inclined to pursue interests other than those that were narrowly their own. The great and recurring theme in all three of these attacks is that the rights of man embody as the be-all and end-all of politics a demand for the immediate and unqualified gratification of purely selfish individual desires. While it is true that certain considerations of self-interest have an intrinsic urgency that can be ignored in a society only at its peril, none of these writers was prepared to found political community exclusively on that prerequisite. Each of them offered a wider vision – the altruism of Bentham's principle of utility, the intergenerational wisdom of Burke's traditions, and the co-operative fulfilment of Marxian species-being. For all of them, human life, to be bearable, involved a substantial commitment to living together in community that is belied by the abstract egoism of a theory of human rights.

Anarchical Fallacies;

being an examination of the
Declaration of Rights issued
during the French Revolution

by Jeremy Bentham

Preliminary Observations

THE Declaration of Rights – I mean the paper published under that name by the French National Assembly in 1791 – assumes for its subject-matter a field of disquisition as unbounded in point of extent as it is important in its nature. But the more ample the extent given to any proposition or string of propositions, the more difficult it is to keep the import of it confined without deviation, within the bounds of truth and reason. If in the smallest corners of the field it ranges over, it fail of coinciding with the line of rigid rectitude, no sooner is the aberration pointed out, than (inasmuch as there is no medium between truth and falsehood) its pretensions to the appellation of a truism are gone, and whoever looks upon it must recognise it to be false and erroneous – and if, as here, political conduct be the theme, so far as the error extends and fails of being detected, pernicious.

In a work of such extreme importance with a view to practice, and which throughout keeps practice so closely and immediately and professedly in view, a single error may be attended with the most fatal consequences. The more extensive the propositions, the more consummate will be the knowledge, the more exquisite the skill, indispensably requisite to confine them in all points within the pale of truth. The most consummate ability in the whole nation could not have been too much for the task – one may venture to say, it would not have been equal to it. But that, in the sanctioning of each proposition, the most consummate ability should happen to be vested in the heads of the sorry majority in whose hands the plenitude of power happened on that same occasion to be vested, is an event against which the chances are almost as infinity to one.

Here, then, is a radical and all-pervading error – the attempting to give to a work on such a subject the sanction of government; especially of such a government – a government composed of members so numerous, so unequal in talent, as well as discordant in inclinations and affections. Had it been the work of a single hand, and that a private one, and in that character given to the world, every good effect would have been produced by it that could be produced by it when published as the work of government, without any of the bad effects which in case of the smallest error must result from it when given as the work of government.

The revolution, which threw the government into the hands of the penners and adopters of this declaration, having been the effect of insurrection, the grand object evidently is to justify the cause. But by justifying it, they invite it: in justifying past insurrection, they plant and cultivate a propensity to perpetual insurrection in time future; they sow the seeds of anarchy broad-cast: in justifying the demolition of existing authorities, they undermine all future ones, their own consequently in the number. Shallow and reckless vanity! – They imitate in their conduct the author of that fabled law, according to which the assassination of the prince upon the throne gave to the assassin a title to succeed him. *'People, behold your rights! If a single article of them be violated, insurrection is not your right only, but the most sacred of your duties.'* Such is the constant language, for such is the professed object of this source and model of all laws – this self-consecrated oracle of all nations.

The more *abstract* – that is, the more *extensive* the proposition is, the more liable is it to involve a fallacy. Of fallacies, one of the most natural modifications is that which is called *begging the question* – the abuse of making the abstract proposition resorted to for proof, a lever for introducing, in the company of *other* propositions that are nothing to the purpose, the very proposition which is admitted to stand in need of proof.

Is the provision in question fit in point of expediency to be passed into a law for the government of the French nation? That, *mutatis mutandis*, would have been the question put in England: that was the proper question to have been put in relation to each provision it was proposed should enter into the composition of the body of French laws.

Instead of that, as often as the utility of a provision appeared (by reason of the wideness of its extent, for instance) of a doubtful nature, the way taken to clear the doubt was to assert it to be a provision fit to be made law for all men – for all Frenchmen – and for all Englishmen, for example, into the bargain. This medium of proof was the more alluring, inasmuch as to the advantage of removing opposition, was added the pleasure, the sort of titillation so exquisite to the nerve of vanity in a French heart – the satisfaction, to use a homely, but not the less apposite proverb, of teaching grandmothers to suck eggs. Hark! ye citizens of the other side of the water! Can you tell us what rights you have belonging to you? No, that you can't. It's *we* that understand rights: not our own only, but yours into the bargain; while you poor simple souls! know nothing about the matter.

Hasty generalization, the great stumbling-block of intellectual vanity! – hasty generalization, the rock that even genius itself is so apt to split upon! – hasty generalization, the bane of prudence and of science!

†
. . .

The great enemies of public peace are the selfish and dissocial passions: – necessary as they are – the one to the very existence of each individual, the other to his security. On the part of these affections, a deficiency in point of strength is never to be apprehended: all that is to be apprehended in respect of them, is to be apprehended on the side of their excess. Society is held together only by the sacrifices that men can be induced to make of the gratifications they demand: to obtain these sacrifices is the great difficulty, the great task of government. What has been the object, the perpetual and palpable object, of this declaration of pretended rights? To add as much force as possible to these passions, already but too strong, – to burst the cords that hold them in, – to say to the selfish passions, there – everywhere – is your prey! – to the angry passions, there – everywhere – is your enemy.

Such is the morality of this celebrated manifesto, rendered famous by the same qualities that gave celebrity to the incendiary of the Ephesian temple.

The logic of it is of a piece with its morality: – a perpetual vein of nonsense, flowing from a perpetual abuse of words, – words having a variety of meanings, where words with single meanings were equally at hand – the same words used in a variety of meanings in the same page, – words used in meanings not their own, where proper words were equally at hand, – words and propositions of the most unbounded signification, turned loose without any of those exceptions or modifications which are so necessary on every occasion to reduce their import within the compass, not only of right reason, but even of the design in hand, of whatever nature it may be; – the same

† denotes an omission in the text

inaccuracy, the same inattention in the penning of this cluster of truths on which the fate of nations was to hang, as if it had been an oriental tale, or an allegory for a magazine: – stale epigrams, instead of necessary distinctions, – figurative expressions preferred to simple ones, – sentimental conceit as trite as they are unmeaning, preferred to apt and precise expressions, – frippery ornament preferred to the majestic simplicity of good sound sense, – and the acts of the senate loaded and disfigured by the tinsel of the playhouse.

In a play or a novel, an improper word is but a word: and the impropriety, whether noticed or not, is attended with no consequences. In a body of laws – especially of laws given as constitutional and fundamental ones – an improper word may be a national calamity: – and civil war may be the consequence of it. Out of one foolish word may start a thousand daggers.

Imputations like these may appear general and declamatory – and rightly so, if they stood alone: but they will be justified even to satiety by the details that follow. Scarcely an article, which in rummaging it, will not be found a true Pandora's box.

In running over the several articles, I shall on the occasion of each article point out, in the first place, the errors it contains in theory; and then, in the second place, the mischiefs it is pregnant with in practice.

The criticism is verbal: – true, but what else can it be? Words – words without a meaning, or with a meaning too flatly false to be maintained by anybody, are the stuff it is made of. Look to the letter, you find nonsense – look beyond the letter, you find nothing.

Article I

Men (all men) are born and remain free, and equal in respect of rights. Social distinctions cannot be founded, but upon common utility.

* * *

All men are born free? All men remain free? No, not a single man: not a single man that ever was, or is, or will be. All men, on the contrary, are born in subjection, and the most absolute subjection – the subjection of a helpless child to the parents on whom he depends every moment for his existence. In this subjection every man is born – in this subjection he continues for years – for a great number of years – and the existence of the individual and of the species depends upon his so doing.

What is the state of things to which the supposed existence of these supposed rights is meant to bear reference? – a state of things prior to the existence of government, or a state of things subsequent to the existence of government? If to a state prior to the existence of government, what would the existence of such rights as these be to the purpose, even if it were true, in any country where there is such a thing as government? If to a state of things subsequent to the formation of government – if in a country where there is a government, in what single instance – in the instance of what single government, is it true? Setting aside the case of parent and child, let any man name that single government under which any such equality is recognised.

All men born free? Absurd and miserable nonsense! When the great complaint – a complaint made perhaps by the very same people at the same time, is – that so many men are born slaves. Oh! but when we acknowledge them to be born slaves, we refer to the laws in being; which laws being void, as being contrary to those laws of nature which are the efficient causes of those rights of man that we are declaring, the men in question are free in one sense, though slaves in another; – slaves, and free, at the same time: – free in respect of the laws of nature – slaves in respect of the pretended human laws, which, though called laws, are no laws at all, as being contrary to the laws of nature. For such is the difference – the great and perpetual difference, betwixt the good subject, the rational censor of the laws, and the anarchist – between the moderate man and the man of violence. The rational censor, acknowledging the existence of the law he disapproves, proposes the repeal of it: the anarchist, setting up his will and fancy for a law before which all mankind are called upon to bow down at the first word – the anarchist, trampling on truth and decency, denies the validity of the law in question, – denies the existence of it in the character of a law, and calls upon all mankind to rise up in a mass, and resist the execution of it.

All men are born equal in rights. The rights of the heir of the most indigent family equal to the rights of the heir of the most wealthy? In what case is this true? I say nothing of hereditary *dignities* and *powers*. Inequalities such as these being proscribed under and by the French government in France, are consequently proscribed by that government under every other government, and consequently have no existence anywhere. For the total subjection of every other government to French government, is a fundamental principle in the law of universal independence – the French law. Yet neither was this true at the time of issuing this Declaration of Rights, nor was it meant to be so afterwards. The 13th article, which we shall come to in its place, proceeds on the contrary supposition: for, considering its other attributes, inconsistency could not be wanting to the list. It can scarcely be more hostile to all other laws than it is at variance with itself.

All men (i.e. all human creatures of both sexes) *remain equal in rights.* All men, meaning doubtless all human creatures. The apprentice, then, is equal in rights to his master; he has as much liberty with relation to the master, as the master has with relation to him; he has as much right to command and to punish him; he is as much owner and master of the master's house, as the master himself. The case is the same as between ward and guardian. So again as between wife and husband. The madman has as good a right to confine anybody else, as anybody else has to confine him. The idiot has as much right to govern everybody, as anybody can have to govern him. The physician and the nurse, when called in by the next friend of a sick man seized with a delirium, have no more right to prevent his throwing himself out of the window, than he has to throw them out of it. All this is plainly and incontestably included in this article of the Declaration of Rights: in the very words of it, and in the meaning – if it have any meaning. Was this the meaning of the authors of it? – or did they mean to admit this explanation as to some of the instances, and to explain the article away as to the rest? Not being idiots, nor lunatics, nor under a delirium, they would explain it away with regard to the madman, and the man under a delirium. Considering that a child may become an orphan as soon as it has seen the light, and that in that case, if not subject to government, it must perish, they would explain it away, I think, and contradict themselves, in the case of guardian and ward. In the case of master and apprentice, I would not take upon me to decide; it may have been their meaning to proscribe that relation altogether; – at least, this may have been the case, as soon as the repugnancy between that institution and this oracle was pointed out; for the professed object and destination of it is to be the standard of truth and falsehood, of right and wrong, in everything that relates to government. But to this standard, and to this article of it, the subjection of the apprentice to the master is flatly and diametrically repugnant. If it do not proscribe and exclude this inequality, it proscribes none: if it do not do this mischief, it does nothing.

. . .

Article II

The end in view of every political association is the preservation of the natural and imprescriptible rights of man. These rights are liberty, property, security, and resistance to oppression.

Sentence 1. The end in view of every political association, is the preservation of the natural and imprescriptible rights of man.

More confusion – more nonsense, – and the nonsense, as usual, dangerous nonsense. The words can scarcely be said to have a meaning: but if they have, or rather if they had a meaning, these would be the propositions either asserted or implied:

1 That there are such things as rights anterior to the establishment of governments: for natural, as applied to rights, if it mean anything, is meant to stand in opposition to *legal*, – to such rights as are acknowledged to owe their existence to government, and are consequently posterior in their date to the establishment of government.

2 That these rights *can not* be abrogated by government: for *can not* is implied in the form of the word imprescriptible, and the sense it wears when so applied, is the cut-throat sense above explained.

3 That the governments that exist derive their origin from formal associations, or what are now called *conventions*: associations entered into by a partnership contract, with all the members for partners, – entered into at a day prefixed, for a predetermined purpose, the formation of a new government where there was none before (for as to formal meetings holden under the controul of an existing government, they are evidently out of question here) in which it seems again to be implied in the way of inference, though a necessary and an unavoidable inference, that all governments (that is, self-called governments, knots of persons exercising the powers of government) that have had any other origin than an association of the above description, are illegal, that is, no governments at all; resistance to them, and subversion of them, lawful and commendable; and so on.

Such are the notions implied in this first part of the article. How stands the truth of things? That there are no such things as natural rights – no such things as rights anterior to the establishment of government – no such things as natural rights opposed to, in contradistinction to, legal: that the expression is merely figurative; that when used in the moment you attempt to give it a literal meaning it leads to error, and to that sort of error that leads to mischief – to the extremity of mischief.

We know what it is for men to live without government – and living without government, to live without rights: we know what it is for men to live without government, for we see instances of such a way of life – we see it in many savage nations, or rather races of mankind; for instance, among the savages of New South Wales, whose way of living is so well known to us: no habit of obedience, and thence no government – no government, and thence no laws – no laws, and thence no such things as rights – no security – no property: – liberty, as against regular controul, the controul of laws and government – perfect; but as against all irregular controul, the mandates of stronger individuals, none. In this state, at a time earlier than the commencement of history – in this same state, judging from analogy, we, the inhabitants of the part of the globe we call Europe, were; – no government, consequently no rights: no rights, consequently no property – no legal security – no legal liberty: security not more than belongs to beasts – forecast and sense of insecurity keener – consequently in point of happiness below the level of the brutal race.

In proportion to the want of happiness resulting from the want of rights, a reason exists for wishing that there were such things as rights. But reasons for wishing there were such things as rights, are not rights; – a reason for wishing that a certain right were established, is not that right – want is not supply – hunger is not bread.

That which has no existence cannot be destroyed – that which cannot be destroyed cannot require anything to preserve it from destruction. *Natural rights* is simple nonsense: natural and imprescriptible rights, rhetorical nonsense, – nonsense upon stilts. But this rhetorical nonsense ends in the old strain of mischievous nonsense: for immediately a list of these pretended natural rights is given, and those are so expressed as to present to view legal rights. And of these rights, whatever they are, there is not, it seems, any one of which any government *can*, upon any occasion whatever, abrogate the smallest particle.

So much for terrorist language. What is the language of reason and plain sense upon this same subject? That in proportion as it is *right* or *proper, i.e.* advantageous to the society in question, that this or that right – a right to this or that effect – should be established and maintained, in that same proportion it is *wrong* that it should be abrogated: but that as there is no *right*, which ought not to be maintained so long as it is upon the whole advantageous to the society that it should be maintained, so there is no right which, when the abolition of it is advantageous to society, should not be abolished. To know whether it would be more for the advantage of society that this or that right should be maintained or abolished, the time at which the question about maintaining or abolishing is proposed, must be given, and the circumstances under which it is proposed to maintain or abolish it; the right itself must be specifically described, not jumbled with an undistinguisable heap of others, under any such vague general terms as property, liberty, and the like.

One thing, in the midst of all this confusion, is but too plain. They know not of what they are talking under the name of natural rights and yet they would have them imprescriptible – proof against all the power of the laws – pregnant with occasions summoning the members of the community to rise up in resistance against the laws. What, then, was their object in declaring the existence of imprescriptible rights, and without specifying a single one by any such mark as it could be known by? This and no other – to excite and keep up a spirit of resistance to all laws – a spirit of insurrection against all governments – against the governments of all other nations instantly, – against the government of their own nation – against the government they themselves were pretending to establish – even that, as soon as their own reign should be at an end. In us is the perfection of virtue and wisdom: in all mankind besides, the extremity of wickedness and folly. Our will shall consequently reign without controul, and for ever: reign now we are living – reign after we are dead.

All nations – all future ages – shall be, for they are predestined to be, our slaves.

Future governments will not have honesty enough to be trusted with the determination of what rights shall be maintained, what abrogated – what laws kept in force, what repealed. Future subjects (I should say future citizens, for French government does not admit of subjects) will not have wit enough to be trusted with the choice whether to submit to the determination of the government of their time, or to resist it. Governments, citizens – all to the end of time – all must be kept in chains.

Such are their maxims – such their premises – for it is by such premises only that the doctrine of imprescriptible rights and un-repealable laws can be supported.

What is the real source of these imprescriptible rights – these unrepealable laws? Power turned blind by looking from its own height: self-conceit and tyranny exalted into insanity. No man was to have any other man for a servant, yet all men were forever to be their slaves. Making laws with imposture in their mouths, under pretence of declaring them – giving for laws anything that came uppermost, and these unrepealable ones, on pretence of finding them ready made.

Made by what? Not by a God – they allow of none; but by their goddess, Nature.

The origination of governments from a contract is a pure fiction, or in other words, a falsehood. It never has been known to be true in any instance; the allegation of it does mischief, by involving the subject in error and confusion, and is neither necessary nor useful to any good purpose.

All governments that we have any account of have been gradually established by habit, after having been formed by force; unless in the instance of governments formed by individuals who have been emancipated, or have emancipated themselves, from governments already formed, the governments under which they were born – a rare case, and from which nothing follows with regard to the rest. What signifies it how governments are formed? Is it the less proper – the less conducive to the happiness of society – that the happiness of society should be the one object kept in view by the members of the government in all their measures? Is it the less the interest of men to be happy – less to be wished that they may be so – less the moral duty of their governors to make them so, as far as they can, at Mogadore than at Philadelphia?

Whence is it, but from government, that contracts derive their binding force? Contracts came from government, not government from contracts. It is from the habit of enforcing contracts, and seeing them enforced, that governments are chiefly indebted for whatever disposition they have to observe them.

Sentence 2. These rights (these imprescriptible as well as natural rights,) are liberty, property, security, and resistance to oppression.

Observe the extent of these pretended rights, each of them belonging to every man, and all of them without bounds. Unbounded liberty; that is, amongst other things, the liberty of doing or not doing on every occasion whatever each man pleases: – Unbounded property; that is, the right of doing with everything around him (with every *thing* at least, if not with every person,) whatsoever he pleases; communicating that right to anybody, and withholding it from anybody: – Unbounded security; that is, security for such his liberty, for such his property, and for his person, against every defalcation that can be called for on any account in respect of any of them: – Unbounded resistance to oppression; that is, unbounded exercise of the faculty of guarding himself against whatever unpleasant circumstance may present itself to his imagination or his passions under that name.

· · ·

Unbounded liberty – I must still say unbounded liberty; – for though the next article but one returns to the charge, and gives such a definition of liberty as seems intended to set bounds to it, yet in effect the limitation amounts to nothing; and when, as here, no warning is given of any exception in the texture of the general rule, every exception which turns up is, not a confirmation but a contradiction of the rule: – liberty, without any pre-announced or intelligible bounds; and as to the other rights, they remain unbounded to the end: rights of man composed of a system of contradictions and impossibilities.

In vain would it be said, that though no bounds are here assigned to any of these rights, yet it is to be understood as taken for granted, and tacitly admitted and assumed, that they are to have bounds; viz. such bounds as it is understood will be set them by the laws. Vain, I say, would be this apology; for the supposition would be contradictory to the express declaration of the article itself, and would defeat the very object which the whole declaration has in view. It would be self-contradictory, because these rights are, in the same breath in which their existence is declared, declared to be imprescriptible; and imprescriptible, or, as we in England should say, indefeasible, means nothing unless it exclude the interference of the laws.

It would be not only inconsistent with itself, but inconsistent with the declared and sole object of the declaration, if it did not exclude the interference of the laws. It is against the laws themselves, and the laws only, that this declaration is levelled. It is for the hands of the legislator and all legislators, and none but legislators, that the shackles it provides are intended, – it is against the apprehended encroachments of legislators that the rights in question, the liberty and property, and so forth, are intended to be made secure, – it is to such encroachments, and damages, and dangers, that whatever security it professes to give has respect. Precious security for unbounded rights against legislators, if the extent of those rights in every direction were purposely left to depend upon the will and pleasure of those very legislators!

Nonsensical or nugatory, and in both cases, mischievous: such is the alternative.

So much for all these pretended indefeasible rights in the lump: their inconsistency with each other, as well as the inconsistency of them in the character of indefeasible rights with the existence of government and all peaceable society, will appear still more plainly when we examine them one by one.

1. *Liberty*, then, is imprescriptible – incapable of being taken away – – out of the power of any government ever to take away: liberty, –

that is, every branch of liberty – every individual exercise of liberty; for no line is drawn – no distinction – no exception made. What these instructors as well as governors of mankind appear not to know, is, that all rights are made at the expense of liberty – all laws by which rights are created or confirmed. No right without a correspondent obligation. Liberty, as against the coercion of the law, may, it is true, be given by the simple removal of the obligation by which that coercion was applied – by the simple repeal of the coercing law. But as against the coercion applicable by individual to individual, no liberty can be given to one man but in proportion as it is taken from another. All coercive laws, therefore (that is, all laws but constitutional laws, and laws repealing or modifying coercive laws,) and in particular all laws creative of liberty, are, as far as they go, abrogative of liberty. Not here and there a law only – not this or that possible law, but almost all laws, are therefore repugnant to these natural and imprescriptible rights: consequently null and void, calling for resistance and insurrection, and so on, as before.

Laws creative of rights of property are also struck at by the same anathema. How is property given? By restraining liberty; that is, by taking it away so far as is necessary for the purpose. How is your house made yours? By debarring every one else from the liberty of entering it without your leave. But

2. *Property.* Property stands second on the list, – proprietary rights are in the number of the natural and imprescriptible rights of man – of the rights which a man is not indebted for to the laws, and which cannot be taken from him by the laws. Men – that is, every man (for a general expression given without exception is an universal one) has a right to property, to proprietary rights, *a right which* cannot be taken away from him by the laws. To proprietary rights. Good: but in relation to what subject? for as to proprietary rights – without a subject to which they are referable – without a subject in or in relation to which they can be exercised – they will hardly be of much value, they will hardly be worth taking care of, with so much solemnity. In vain would all the laws in the world have ascertained that I have a right to something. If this be all they have done for me – if there be no specific subject in relation to which my proprietary rights are established, I must either take what I want without right, or starve. As there is no such subject specified with relation to each man, or to any man (indeed how could there be?) the necessary inference (taking the passage literally) is, that every man has all manner of proprietary rights with relation to every subject of property without exception: in a word, that every man has a right to everything. Unfortunately, in

most matters of property, what is every man's right is no man's right; so that the effect of this part of the oracle, if observed, would be, not to establish property, but to extinguish it – to render it impossible ever to be revived: and this is one of the rights declared to be imprescriptible.

It will probably be acknowledged, that according to this construction, the clause in question is equally ruinous and absurd: – and hence the inference may be, that this was not the construction – this was not the meaning in view. But by the same rule, every possible construction which the words employed can admit of, might be proved not to have been the meaning in view: nor is this clause a whit more absurd or ruinous than all that goes before it, and a great deal of what comes after it. And, in short, if this be not the meaning of it, what is? Give it a sense – give it any sense whatever, – it is mischievous: – to save it from that imputation, there is but one course to take, which is to acknowledge it to be nonsense.

Thus much would be clear, if anything were clear in it, that according to this clause, whatever proprietary rights, whatever property a man once has, no matter how, being imprescriptible, can never be taken away from him by any law: or of what use or meaning is the clause? So that the moment it is acknowledged in relation to any article, that such article is my property, no matter how or when it became so, that moment it is acknowledged that it can never be taken away from me: therefore, for example, all laws and all judgments, whereby anything is taken away from me without my free consent – all taxes, for example, and all fines – are void, and, as such, call for resistance and insurrection, and so forth, as before.

3. *Security*. Security stands the third on the list of these natural and imprescriptible rights which laws did not give, and which laws are not in any degree to be suffered to take away.

. . .

Security for person is the branch that seems here to have been understood: – security for each man's person, as against all those hurtful or disagreeable impressions (exclusive of those which consist in the mere disturbance of the enjoyment of liberty,) by which a man is affected in his person; loss of life – loss of limbs – loss of the use of limbs – wounds, bruises, and the like. All laws are null and void, then, which on any account or in any manner seek to expose the person of any man to any risk – which appoint capital or other corporal punishment – which expose a man to personal hazard in the service of the military power against foreign enemies, or in that of the judicial power against delinquents: – all laws which, to preserve the country from pestilence, authorize the immediate execution of a suspected person, in the event of his transgressing certain bounds.

4. *Resistance to oppression.* Fourth and last in the list of natural and imprescriptible rights, resistance to oppression – meaning, I suppose, the right to resist oppression. What is oppression? Power misapplied to the prejudice of some individual. What is it that a man has in view when he speaks of oppression? Some exertion of power which he looks upon as misapplied to the prejudice of some individual – to the producing on the part of such individual some suffering, to which (whether as forbidden by the laws or otherwise) we conceive he ought not to have been subjected.

* * *

Whenever you are about to be oppressed, you have a right to resist oppression: whenever you conceive yourself to be oppressed, conceive yourself to have a right to make resistance, and act accordingly. In proportion as a law of any kind – any act of power, supreme or subordinate, legislative, administrative, or judicial, is unpleasant to a man, especially if, in consideration of such its unpleasantness, his opinion is, that such act of power ought not to have been exercised, he of course looks upon it as oppression: as often as anything of this sort happens to a man – as often as anything happens to a man to inflame his passions, – this article for fear his passions should not be sufficiently inflamed of themselves, sets itself to work to blow the flame and urges him to resistance. Submit not to any decree or other act of power, of the justice of which you are not yourself perfectly convinced.

* * *

Article IV

Liberty consists in being able to do that which is not hurtful to another, and therefore the exercise of the natural rights of each man has no other bounds than those which insure to the other members of the society the enjoyment of the same rights. These bounds cannot be determined but by the law.

In this article, three propositions are included:

Proposition 1. Liberty consists in being able to do that which is not hurtful to another. What! in that, and nothing else? Is not the liberty of doing mischief liberty? If not, what is it? and what word is there for it in the language, or in any language by which it can be spoken of? How childish, how repugnant to the ends of language, is this perversion of language! – to attempt to confine a word in common and perpetual use, to an import to which nobody ever confined it before, or will continue to confine it! And so I am never to know whether I am at liberty or not to do or to omit doing one act, till I see whether or no there is anybody that may be hurt by it – till I see the whole extent of all its consequences? Liberty! What liberty? – as against what power? as against coercion from what source? As against coercion issuing from the law? – then to know whether the law have left me at liberty in any respect in relation to any act, I am to consult not the words of the law, but my own conception of what would be the consequences of the act. If among these consequences there be a single one by which anybody would be hurt, then, whatever the law says to me about it, I am not at liberty to do it. I am an officer of justice, appointed to superintend the execution of punishments ordered by justice: – if I am ordered to cause a thief to be whipped, – to know whether I am at liberty to cause the sentence to be executed, I must know whether whipping would hurt the thief: if it would, then I am not at liberty to whip the thief – to inflict the punishment which it is my duty to inflict.

Proposition 2. And therefore the exercise of the natural rights of each man has no other bounds than those which insure to the other members of the society the enjoyment of those same rights. Has no other bounds? Where is it that it has no other bounds? In what nation – under what government? If under any government, then the state of legislation under that government is in a state of absolute perfection. If there be no such government, then, by a confession necessarily implied, there is no nation upon earth in which this definition is conformable to the truth.

Proposition 3. These bounds cannot be determined but by the law. More contradiction, more confusion. What then? – this liberty, this right, which is one of four rights that existed before laws, and will exist in spite of all that laws can do, owes all the boundaries it has, all the extent it has, to the laws. Till you know what the laws say to it, you do not know what there is of it, nor what account to give of it: and yet it existed, and that in full force and vigour, before there were any such things as laws; and so will continue to exist, and that for ever, in spite of anything which laws can do to it. Still the same inaptitude of expressions – still the same confusion of that which it is supposed *is*, with that which it is conceived ought to be.

What says plain truth upon this subject? What is the sense most approaching to this nonsense?

The liberty which the law *ought* to allow of, and leave in existence – leave uncoerced, unremoved – is the liberty which concerns those acts only, by which, if exercised, no damage would be done to the community upon the whole; that is, either no damage at all, or none but what promises to be compensated by at least equal benefit.

Accordingly, the exercise of the rights allowed to and conferred upon each individual, ought to have no other bounds set to it by the law, than those which are necessary to enable it to maintain every other individual in the possession and exercise of such rights as it is consistent with the greatest good of the community that he should be allowed. The marking out of these bounds ought not to be left to anybody but the legislator acting as such – that is, to him or them who are acknowledged to be in possession of the sovereign power: that is, it ought not to be left to the occasional and arbitrary declaration of any individual, whatever share he may possess of subordinate authority.

The word *autrui* – another, is so loose, – making no distinction between the community and individuals, – as, according to the most natural construction, to deprive succeeding legislators of all power of repressing, by punishment or otherwise, any acts by which no individual sufferers are to be found; and to deprive them beyond a doubt of all power of affording protection to any man, woman, or child, against his or her own weakness, ignorance, or imprudence.

*   *   *

Article X

No one ought to be molested [meaning, probably, by government] *for his opinions, even in matters of religion, provided that the manifestation of them does not disturb* [better expressed perhaps by saying, except in as far as the manifestation of them disturb, or rather tends to the disturbance of] *the public order established by the law.*

Liberty of publication with regard to opinions, under certain exceptions, is a liberty which it would be highly proper and fit to establish, but which would receive but a very precarious establishment from an article thus worded. Disturb the public order? – what does that mean? Louis XIV need not have hesitated about receiving an article thus worded into his code. The public order of things in this behalf, was an order in virtue of which the exercise of every religion but the Catholic, according to his edition of it, was proscribed. A law is enacted, forbidding men to express a particular opinion, or set of opinions, relative to a particular point in religion: forbidding men to express any of those opinions, in the expression of which the Lutheran doctrine, for example, or the Calvinistic doctrine, or the Church of England doctrine consists: – in a prohibition to this effect, consists the public order established by the law. Spite of this, a man manifests an opinion of the number of those which thus stand prohibited as belonging to the religion thus proscribed. The act by which this opinion is manifested, is it not an act of disturbance with relation to the public order thus established? Extraordinary indeed must be the assurance of him who could take upon him to answer in the negative.

Thus nugatory, thus flimsy, is this buckler of rights and liberties, in one of the few instances in which any attempt is made to apply it to a good purpose.

What should it have done, then? To this question an answer is scarcely within the province of this paper: the proposition with which I set out is, not that the Declaration of Rights should have been worded differently, but that nothing under any such name, or with any such design, should have been attempted.

A word or two, however, may be given as a work of supererogation: – that opinions of all sorts might be manifested without fear of punishment; that no publication should be deemed to subject a man to punishment on account of any opinions it may be found to contain, considered as mere opinions; but at the same time, that the plea of manifesting religious opinions, or the practising certain acts supposed to be enjoined or recommended in virtue of certain religious opinions as proper or necessary to be practised, should not operate as a justification for either exercising, or prompting men to exercise, any act which the legislature, without any view or reference to religion, has already thought fit, or may hereafter think fit, to insert into the catalogue of prohibited acts or offences.

To instance two species of delinquency, – one of the most serious, the other of the slightest nature – acts tending to the violent subversion of the government by force – acts tending to the obstruction of the passage in the street: – An opinion that has been supposed by some to belong to the Christian religion, is, that every form of government but the monarchical is unlawful: an opinion that has been supposed by some to belong to the Christian religion – by some at least of those that adhere to that branch of the Christian religion which is termed the Roman Catholic – is, that it is a duty, or at least a merit, to join in processions of a certain description, to be performed on certain occasions.

What, then, is the true sense of the clause in question, in relation to these two cases? What ought to be the conduct of a government that is neither monarchical nor Catholic, with reference to the respective manifestation of these two opinions?

First, as to the opinion relative to the unlawfulness of a government not monarchical. The falsity or erroneousness which the members of such a government could not but attribute in their own minds to such an opinion, is a consideration which, according to the spirit and intent of the provision in question, would not be sufficient to authorize their using penal or other coercive measures for the purpose of preventing the manifestation of them. At the same time, should such manifestation either have already had the effect of engaging individuals in any attempt to effect a violent subversion of the government by force, or appear to have produced a near probability of any such attempt – in such case, the engagement to permit the free manifestation of opinions in general, and of religious opinions in particular, is not to be understood to preclude the government from restraining the manifestation of the opinion in question, in every such way as it may deem likely to promote or facilitate any such attempt.

Again, as to the opinion relative to the meritoriousness of certain processions. By the principal part of the provision, government stands precluded from prohibiting publications manifesting an opinion in favour of the obligatoriness or meritoriousness of such processions. By the spirit of the same engagement, they stand precluded from prohibiting the performance of such processions, unless a persuasion of a political inconvenience as resulting from such practice – a persuasion not grounded on any notions of their unlawfulness in a religious view – should come to be entertained: as if, for example, the multitude of the persons joining in the procession, or the crowd of persons flocking to observe them, should fill up the streets to such a degree, or for such a length of time, and at intervals recurring with such frequency, as to be productive of such a degree of obstruction to the free use of the streets for the purposes of business, as in the eye of government should constitute a body of inconvenience worth encountering by a prohibitive law.

It would be a violation of the spirit of this part of the engagement, if the government – not by reason of any view it entertained of the political inconveniences of these processions (for example, as above,) but for the purpose of giving an ascendency to religious opinions of an opposite nature (determined, for example, by a Protestant antipathy to Catholic processions) – were to make use of the real or pretended obstruction to the free use of the streets, as a pretence for prohibiting such processions.

These examples, while they serve to illustrate the ground and degree and limits of the liberty which it may seem proper, on the score of public tranquillity, and peace, to leave to the manifestation of opinions of a religious nature, may serve, at the same time, to render apparent the absurdity and perilousness of every attempt on the part of the government for the time being, to tie up the hands of succeeding governments in relation to this or any other spot in the field of legislation. Observe how nice, and incapable of being described beforehand by any particular marks, are the lines which mark the limits of right and wrong in this behalf – which separate the useful from the pernicious – the prudent course from the imprudent! – how dependent upon the temper of the times – upon the events and circumstances of the day! – with how fatal a certainty persecution and tyranny on the one hand, or revolt and civil war on the other, may follow from the slightest deviation from propriety in the drawing of such lines! – and what a curse to any country a legislator may be, who, with the purest intentions, should set about settling the business to all eternity by inflexible and adamantine rules, drawn from the sacred and inviolable and imprescriptible rights of man, and the primeval and everlasting laws of nature!

• • •

Article XVI

Every society in which the warranty of rights is not assured ('la garantie des droits n'est pas assurée,') nor the separation of powers determined, has no constitution.

Here we have an exhibition: self-conceit inflamed to insanity – legislators turned into turkey-cocks – the less important operation of constitution-making, interrupted for the more important operation of bragging. Had the whole human species, according to the wish of the tyrant, but one neck, it would find in this article a sword designed to sever it.

This constitution, – the blessed constitution, of which this matchless declaration forms the base – the constitution of France – is not only the most admirable constitution in the world, but the only one. That no other country but France has the happiness of possessing the sort of thing, whatever it be, called a constitution, is a meaning sufficiently conveyed. This meaning the article must have, if it have any: for other meaning, most assuredly it has none.

Every society in which the warranty of rights is not assured (*toute société dans laquelle la garantie des droits n'est pas assurée,*) is, it must be confessed, most rueful nonsense; but if the translation were not exact, it would be unfaithful: and if not nonsensical, it would not be exact.

Do you ask, has the nation I belong to such a thing as a constitution belonging to it? If you want to know, look whether a declaration of rights, word for word the same as this, forms part of its code of laws; for by this article, what is meant to be insinuated, not expressed (since by nonsense nothing is expressed,) is the necessity of having a declaration of rights like this set by authority in the character of an introduction at the head of the collection of its laws.

As to the not absolutely nonsensical, but only very obscure clause, about a society's having 'the separation of powers determined,' it seems to be the result of a confused idea of an intended application of the old maxim, *Divide et impera*: the governed are to have the governors under their governance, by having them divided among themselves. A still older maxim, and supposing both maxims applied to this one subject, I am inclined to think a truer one, is, that a house divided against itself cannot stand.

Yet on the existence of two perfectly independent and fighting sovereignties, or of three such fighting sovereignties (the supposed state of things in Britain seems here to be the example in view,) the perfection of good government, or at least of whatever approach to good government can subsist without the actual adoption *in terminis* of a declaration of rights such as this, is supposed to depend. Hence, though Britain have no such thing as a constitution belonging to it at present, yet, if during a period of any length, five or ten years for example, it should ever happen that neither House of Commons nor House of Lords had any confidence in the King's Ministers, nor any disposition to endure their taking the lead in legislation (the House of Commons being all the while, as we must suppose, peopled by universal suffrage,) possibly in such case, for it were a great deal too much to affirm, Britain might be so far humoured as to be allowed to suppose herself in possession of a sort of thing, which, though of inferior stuff, might pass under the name of a constitution, even without having this declaration of rights to stand at its head.

That Britain possesses at present anything that can bear that name, has by Citizen Paine, *following*, or *leading* (I really remember not, nor is it worth remembering,) at any rate *agreeing* with this declaration of rights, been formally denied.

According to general import, supported by etymology, by the word *constitution,* something *established,* something *already* established, something possessed of *stability,* something that has given *proofs* of stability, seems to be implied. What shall we say, if of this most magnificent of all boasts, not merely the simple negative, but the direct converse should be true? and if instead of France being the only country which has a constitution, France should be the only country that has none! Yet if government depend upon obedience – the stability of government upon the permanence of the disposition to obedience, and the permanence of that disposition upon the duration of the habit of obedience – this most assuredly must be the case.

* * *

Conclusion

On the subject of the fundamental principles of government, we have seen what execrable trash the choicest talents of the French nation have produced.

On the subject of chemistry, Europe has beheld with admiration, and adopted with unanimity and gratitude, the systematic views of the same nation, supported as they were by a series of decisive experiments and conclusive reasonings.

Chemistry has commonly been reckoned, and not altogether without reason, among the most abstruse branches of science. In chemistry, we see how high they have soared above the sublimest knowledge of past times; in legislation, how deep they have sunk below the profoundest ignorance: – how much inferior has the maturest design that could be furnished by the united powers of the whole nation proved, in comparison of the wisdom and felicity of the chance-medley of the British Constitution.

Comparatively speaking, a select few applied themselves to the cultivation of chemistry – almost an infinity, in comparison, have applied themselves to the science of legislation.

In the instance of chemistry, the study is acknowledged to come within the province of science: the science is acknowledged to be an abstruse and difficult one, and to require a long course of study on the part of those who have had the previous advantage of a liberal education; whilst the cultivation of it, in such manner as to make improvements in it, requires that a man should make it the great business of his life; and those who have made these improvements have thus applied themselves.

In chemistry there is no room for passion to step in and to confound the understanding – to lead men into error, and to shut their eyes against knowledge: in legislation, the circumstances are opposite, and vastly different.

What, then, shall we say of that system of government, of which the professed object is to call upon the untaught and unlettered multitude (whose existence depends upon their devoting their whole time to the acquisition of the means of supporting it,) to occupy themselves without ceasing upon all questions of government (legislation and administration included) without exception – important and trivial, – the most general and the most particular, but more especially upon the most important and most general – that is, in other words, the most scientific – those that require the greatest measures of science to qualify a man for deciding upon, and in respect of which any want of science and skill are liable to be attended with the most fatal consequences?

What should we have said, if, with a view of collecting the surest grounds for the decision of any of the great questions of chemistry, the French Academy of Sciences (if its members had remained unmurdered) had referred such questions to the Primary Assemblies?

If a collection of general propositions, put together with the design that seems to have given birth to this performance – propositions of the most general and extensive import, embracing the whole field of legislation – were capable of being so worded and put together as to be of use, it could only be on the condition of their being deduced in the way of abridgment from an already formed and existing assemblage of less general propositions, constituting the tenor of the body of the laws. But for these more general propositions to have been abstracted from that body of particular ones, that body must have been already in existence: the general and introductory part, though placed first, must have been constructed last; – although first in the order of communication, it should have been last in the order of composition. For the framing of the propositions which were to be included, time, knowledge, genius, temper, patience, everything was wanting. Yet the system of propositions which were to include them, it was determined to have at any rate. Of time, a small quantity indeed might be made to serve, upon the single and very simple condition of not bestowing a single thought upon the propositions which they were to include: and as to knowledge, genius, temper, and patience, the place of all these trivial requisites was abundantly supplied by effrontery and self-conceit. The business, instead of being performed in the way of abridgment, was performed in the way of anticipation – by a loose conjecture of what the particular propositions in question, were they to be found, might amount to.

What I mean to attack is, not the subject or citizen of this or that country – not this or that citizen – not citizen Sieyes or citizen anybody else, but all anti-legal rights of man, all declarations of such rights. What I mean to attack is, not the execution of such a design in this or that instance, but the design itself.

It is not that they have failed in their execution of the design by using the same word promiscuously in two or three senses – contradictory and incompatible senses – but in undertaking to execute a design which could not be executed at all without this abuse of words. Let a man distinguish the senses – let him allot, and allot invariably a separate word for each, and he will find it impossible to make up any such declaration at all, without running into such nonsense as must stop the hand even of the maddest of the mad.

•   •   •

It is in England, rather than in France, that the discovery of the *rights of man* ought naturally to have taken its rise: it is we – we English, that have the better *right* to it. It is in the English language that the transition is more natural, than perhaps in most others: at any rate, more so than in the French. It is in English, and not in French, that we may change the sense without changing the word, and, like Don Quixote on the enchanted horse, travel as far as the moon, and farther, without ever getting off the saddle. One and the same word, right – right, that most enchanting of words – is sufficient for operating the fascination. The word is ours, – that magic word, which, by its single unassisted powers, completes the fascination. In its adjective shape, it is as innocent as a dove: it breathes nothing but morality and peace. It is in this shape that, passing in at the heart, it gets possession of the understanding: – it then assumes its substantive shape, and joining itself to a band of suitable associates, sets up the banner of insurrection, anarchy, and lawless violence.

It is right that men should be as near upon a par with one another in every respect as they can be made, consistently with general security: here we have it in its adjective form, synonymous with desirable, proper, becoming, consonant to general utility, and the like. I have a right to put myself upon a par with everybody in every respect: here we have it in its *substantive* sense, forming with the other words a phrase equivalent to this, – wherever I find a man who will not let me put myself on a par with him in every respect, it is right, and proper, and becoming, that I should knock him down, if I have a mind to do so, and if that will not do, knock him on the head, and so forth.

The French language is fortunate enough not to possess this

mischievous abundance. But a Frenchman will not be kept back from his purpose by a want of words: the want of an adjective composed of the same letters as the substantive *right*, is no loss to him. Is, has been, ought to be, shall be, can, – all are put for one another – all are pressed into the service – all made to answer the same purposes. By this inebriating compound, we have seen all the elements of the understanding confounded, every fibre of the heart inflamed, the lips prepared for every folly, and the hand for every crime.

Our right to this precious discovery, such as it is, of the rights of man, must, I repeat it, have been prior to that of the French. It has been seen how peculiarly rich we are in materials for making it. *Right*, the substantive *right*, is the child of law: from *real* laws come *real* rights; but from *imaginary* laws, from laws of nature, fancied and invented by poets, rhetoricians, and dealers in moral and intellectual poisons, come *imaginary* rights, a bastard brood of monsters, 'gorgons and chimæras dire.' And thus it is, that from *legal rights*, the offspring of law, and friends of peace, come *anti-legal rights*, the mortal enemies of law, the subverters of government, and the assassins of security.

Will this antidote to French poisons have its effect? – will this preservative for the understanding and the heart against the fascination of sounds, find lips to take it? This, in point of speedy or immediate efficacy at least, is almost too much to hope for. Alas! how dependent are opinions upon sound! Who shall break the chains which bind them together? By what force shall the associations between words and ideas be dissolved – associations coeval with the cradle – associations to which every book and every conversation give increased strength? By what authority shall this original vice in the structure of language be corrected? How shall a word which has taken root in the vitals of a language be expelled? By what means shall a word in continual use be deprived of half its signification? The language of plain strong sense is difficult to learn; the language of smooth nonsense is easy and familiar. The one requires a force of attention capable of stemming the tide of usage and example; the other requires nothing but to swim with it.

It is for education to do what can be done; and in education is, though unhappily the slowest, the surest as well as earliest resource. The recognition of the nothingness of the laws of nature and the rights of man that have been grounded on them, is a branch of knowledge of as much importance to an Englishman, though a negative one, as the most perfect acquaintance that can be formed with the existing laws of England.

* * *

Supply Without Burthen or Escheat *Vice* Taxation:

being a proposal for a saving of taxes
by an extension of the law of escheat:
including strictures on the taxes on
collateral succession, comprised in
the budget on 7th December, 1795

• • •

*What is that mode of supply, of which the twentieth part is a tax, and
that a heavy one, while the whole would be no tax, and would not be felt
by anybody?*

The question has the air of a riddle; but the proposition it involves,
paradoxical as it may appear, is not more strikingly paradoxical than
strictly true.

The answer is, an extension of the existing *law of Escheat* – a law
coeval with the very first elements of the constitution; to which I
would add, as an aid to its operation, a correspondent *limitation*, not
an *extension* of the power of *bequest*.

Of the extended law of escheat, according to the degree of
extension here proposed, the effect would be, the appropriating to the
use of the public all vacant successions, property of every denomina-
tion included, on the failure of near relations, will or no will, subject
only to the power of bequest, as hereinafter limited.

• • •

[After outlining the details and the advantages of his proposal,
Bentham goes on to anticipate a number of objections that he
believes are likely to be raised against it.]

(Objection V. The measure would be an infringement upon the law of nature.)

An infringement this, it may be said, of natural rights: of which the right of property is one: a right which it is the business of law not to infringe but to secure. Among the rights of property is the natural right of inheritance. This right has no other limits than the stock of natural heirs.

Succession to kinsmen a natural right? How can that be? when the enjoyment of it, wherever it is enjoyed, depends altogether upon the dispositions and operations of the law! – Succession a natural, an univeral right? How can that be? – when in no two nations it is the same! If natural right had any place in the subject, if the doctrine of natural right had any truth in it at all, or were to the purpose in respect of any branch of the matter of succession, it should surely be that which respects the succession of children to parents. Yet what becomes of natural right even here? In one and the same nation – not to speak of various nations – in one and the same nation – in our own nation – among men of landed property in most instances the eldest son gets every thing – in a few instances it is the youngest son gets every thing, and here the eldest nothing – and in both cases what becomes of the natural right of the daughters?* Among moneyed men, all the children, sons and daughters, take alike.

Whence this astonishing disparity? Whence this invasion upon the very vitals of natural right? – From a reason that existed once – a feudal reason – a reason that for ages has been gone. – To keep one individual member of a family in pay, in expectation of his contributing one soldier upon occasion for the defence of the state, all the other members, to every one of whom nature had given equal necessities and equal claims – all the other members were to be starved: to keep one individual in pay, whether the whole of the succession was wanted for the purpose, or whether a hundredth part would have sufficed. Which then shall meet with greatest deference? a dead and antiquated reason – a reason long time perished, not only in point of use and benefit, but except in a few speculative minds, perished even as a remembrance – or a reason in full vigour – a reason which now is all that the other ever was and infinitely more – a reason

---

*If one child may be thus cut off, why not another? if nine children, why not the tenth? If natural law, instead of being a chimera, were a really existing law, and as such capable of being violated, what violations could be more flagrant than those which it has all along sustained, and is now sustaining every day, from the existing law of England?

as gentle in its operation as that was iniquitous and harsh: a reason that would find the country a hundred defenders where that would have found one?

The infinite diversity of the footing on which the business of succession stands in different nations is a happy incident for the present purpose. What can be a more demonstrative or a more striking proof how perfectly all these pretended natural rights, or to speak what is at once more material and more intelligible, how perfectly *expectation* in all these instances is at the command of law! Where is the hardship upon me, what do I suffer in England by not having an estate which would have been mine had I belonged to Russia or France?

I know of no natural rights except what are created by general utility: and even in that sense it were much better the word were never heard of. All such language is at any rate false: all such language is either pernicious, or at the best an improper and fallacious way of indicating what is true.

In starting this topic or rather this expression I am full well aware what a deluge of nonsense I am treading up. But as this sort of nonsense is not one of the readiest of arguments, but perhaps the most formidable opponent which a useful and rational proposal can have to struggle with, I know not how to get altogether clear of mentioning it: but what I do say of it shall be as little and as short as possible.

Relations have a natural right to succeed to one: and as no one can say where this right ends, this is as much as to say that it ends no where. To set bounds to the right of succession any where is therefore to violate natural rights. But a law by which any natural right is violated is a grievance and an act of tyranny: and tyranny ought to be risen up against and resisted: the right of resistance to oppression is one of these natural rights which are indefeasible and have not been given up and cannot be, &c. &c. &c.

To this head of argument I have two answers. One is that it is mere nonsense: to say nothing of its being such mischievous nonsense – a topic which is not to the present purpose.

The other is that it is inconsistent nonsense: in as much as, if it be intelligible and just, it does not apply with any greater force against the arrangement here proposed to be made than against every other arrangement that can be named, actual or possible.

First then it is stark nonsense: it is a contradiction in terms.

Of a natural right who has any idea? I, for my part, I have none: a natural right is a round square, – an incorporeal body. What a legal right is I know. I know how it was made. I know what it means when made. To me a right and a legal right are the same thing, for I know no other. Right and law are correlative terms: as much so as son and father. Right is with me the child of law: from different operations of the law result different sorts of rights. A natural right is a son that never had a father.* By natural right is meant a sort of a thing which is to have the effect of law, which is to have an effect paramount to that of law, but which subsists not only without law, but against law: and its characteristic property, as well as sole and constant use, is the being the everlasting and irreconciliable enemy of law. As scissors were invented to cut up cloth, so were natural rights invented to cut up law, and legal rights. A natural right is a species of cold heat, a sort of dry moisture, a kind of resplendent darkness.

Name me any right, name me what I mean by a right, the only sort that with me has either meaning or existence, name me a legal right either actual or possible, a right existing in this country or in any other, a right past, present, or future, I will shew by what it was made and how it was made. I will point out whatever laws have concurred in its formation. But of these natural rights the boasted property is to exist before laws were made, to exist in the teeth of them, and to exist for ever, though laws should be no more.

If natural rights came not from the law, from any sort of law – whence did it [sic] come? I will tell you – It is the spawn of despotism, begot upon incapacity. It is the effusion of a hard heart operating upon a cloudy mind. When a man is bent upon having things his own way and give no reason for it, he says: I have a right to have them so. When a man has a political caprice to gratify, and is determined to gratify it, if possible, at any price, when he feels an ardent desire to see it gratified but can give no reason why it should be gratified, when he

---

*I can conceive indeed another sort of right, distinct from political, and even of superior force: but still not without the aid of law. From a divine law comes a divine right just as intelligibly as from a political human law comes a political human right. Thus from a supposed divine law in favour of monarchy came the Jus divinum, the divine right, of Kings. This sort of right is certainly as intelligible as that which every body understands of course who has any understanding about the matter from the word: this is perfectly intelligible, though, as the existence of the law for the purpose is always denied and never can be proved, it is as perfectly useless. But the natural rights we hear so much of under that name are of all things the farthest from being divine rights. For in no mouths are they so frequent nor so much insisted upon as in the mouths of those by whom the existence of a divine law and of a divine lawgiver are equally denied.

finds it necessary to get the multitude to join with him, but either stoops not to enquire whether they would be the better or the happier for so doing, or feels himself at a loss to prove it, he sets up a cry of rights. I have a right to have it so: you have all a right to have it so: none but tyrants can refuse us. Give us then our rights. The dictates of reason and utility are the result of circumstances which require genius to discover, strength of mind to weigh, and patience to investigate: the language of natural rights require nothing but a hard front, a hard heart and an unblushing countenance. It is from the beginning to the end so much flat assertion: it neither has any thing to do with reason not will endure the mention of it. It lays down as a fundamental and inviolable principle whatever is in dispute: admitt it, you are an honest fellow, a true patriot: question it, or so much as ask for a proof of it, you are whatever is most odious, sinning equally against truth and against conscience.

The strength of this argument is in proportion to the strength of lungs in those who use it. The principle of utility, with the united powers of Bacon, Locke, Hume, Smith, Paley to develop it, would be nothing against one Danton bawling out natural rights. The strength of this argument lies in the strength of lungs: I mean in the first instance: for ultimately it depends upon the sharpness of the daggers which he who uses it has in his pocket. I will speak daggers, says Hamlet, but I will use none: here the distinction has no place. To speak these verbal daggers is to promise upon the first occasion to use real ones, and in that promise consists its force. Weak as it is in the character of an argument, it is proportionably strong as an insult and a menace: and indeed, the plain and simple version of it is a menace and nothing else. List yourself under my banner, join in my howl, swallow my nonsense – or you are a tyrant, or a slave, an accomplice of tyrants: and as to what ought to be done with tyrants and their abettors – who does not know? Remember the ides of March, said one to Caesar to warn him of his fate. Remember the ides of September is a memento I always conceive as given when I hear of natural rights: where this is the imagery displayed in front, I always see in the back ground a cluster of daggers or of pikes introduced in the National Assembly with the applause of the President Condorcet for the avowed purpose of exterminating the King's friends. Of late these pikes and these daggers have been exhibited in broad day, and pointed out to reasonable and reasoning men, as gibbets used to be to murderers and thieves. But though till lately kept behind the curtain, they were always at hand, and but too close to the elbow of many a well-meaning man who hardly suspected how near he was to use them, or how void of all meaning his discourse, his politics, or fancied philosophy was, except in as far as he meant to use them.*

It may be said, and certainly with great truth, that this doctrine, however new in complection and effect, is old enough in point of language: that it has been the language of all sorts of men in all sorts of times – of the quiet as well as of the violent – of the dull as well as the sprightly, of the Grotius's and the Puffendorffs as well as of the Condorcets and Brissots and Robertspierres. True it is that it has been the result not only of the superabundance of zeal, but that, even without a spark of zeal, it has flowed from mere penury of argument: a mere way of speaking and a pretence for talking when a man had nothing to say. Not only quiet and dull men and men who have owed their quietness to their dulness, but many an excellent and many a well-meaning man, who in other points has shewn himself by no means destitute of intelligence: a man who, in other points, has shewn himself not only conspicuous but really useful to mankind.

This, I confess, is not to be disputed, but how close together stand truth and error, littleness and greatness, accuteness and stupidity, clearness and confusion in the minds of the wisest of mankind! In roads infested with epidemic nonsense the traveller has but one alternative, to confute it or to adopt it: to oppose himself to, or to be confounded with, the crowd.

---

*A book in which the object was to enquire, not what are our natural rights, but what in each instance *ought* to be our legal ones upon the principle of utility, that is, what are the rights which, in each instance, it would be for the happiness of the community that the law should create, and what means it should employ to secure us in the possession of them, a book in which incidentally a few of the inconsistencies which never fail to attend the language of natural rights were exposed, was once put into the hands of that coldblooded instigator of promiscuous assassination, who now lurks somewhere in a state of well-merited degradation and distress, a fugitive from men superior, if possible, to himself in wickedness. From the passage above mentioned he turned with an instinctive and as it were a prophetic and presaging horror, for without mentioning or thinking of him it unmasked him and was in effect one of the severest satyres on the whole tenor of his language and complexion of his thoughts. No, such enquiries were not to be countenanced – utility was a dangerous and delusive enquiry: it was treachery to the great cause of natural right and natural justice. Natural rights were not to be doubted of or to be made the subject of investigation: to engage in any such discussions was to desert the cause. It was endeavouring to open the eyes of the multitudes, and their steadiness depended upon their blindness.

Nonsense it always was from the beginning, but those upon whom it pressed, and who suffered themselves to be imposed upon while its malignity lay concealed, may, now that its malignity has shewn itself in all its full blackness, perhaps suffer themselves to be weaned from it.

◈ 4 ◈
Edmund Burke's
Reflections on the
Revolution in France

I

Edmund Burke embodied a category of person he himself regarded as most threatening to the established social order – the category of those who had ability but no property. He was born in 1741, the son of an Irish attorney, and studied philosophy at Trinity College, Dublin, and law in London. He was not, however, called to the Bar but chose a life devoted to political activity and writing (he published a number of philosophical works including *A Philosophical Inquiry into the Origin of Our Idea of the Sublime and the Beautiful* which had some influence in contemporary aesthetics). Though his background was humble, he placed his ability, from an early stage, at the service of men of rank and property, becoming private secretary to the Marquess of Rockingham, and pursuing a parliamentary career under Rockingham's patronage and with his financial support. Burke was never untroubled by money worries and he was always sensitive on the subject of his background in a parliament that was still (Burke thought quite properly) dominated by the landed interest.[1] His purchase of a house and estate at Beaconsfield in 1768 left him heavily mortgaged for the rest of his life. His brothers were involved in shady financial dealings, and Burke was sufficiently close to them to be tainted by their dishonour.[2] He held office as paymaster of the forces in the period 1782–4 but his attempts to reform that office redounded to his own pecuniary disadvantage. And in 1793 one of Burke's most eloquent pieces, 'A Letter to a Noble Lord', was written as a diatribe against an aristocrat who had dared to oppose a parliamentary proposal to award Burke a pension. It was only in his final years that he achieved anything like financial security.

Apart from his unpropertied background, Burke's Irish origins contributed to his feeling himself to be, and being perceived as, an outsider. He rarely visited Ireland after coming to England, but he remained a partisan of Irish interests. More importantly his Irish background gave him some experience of a country whose level of development was somewhat lower than England's and therefore a sense of how contingent and fragile the achievements of civilization were. Conor Cruise O'Brien has aruged that this is the key to the urgency of Burke's concern about the contagion of the French Revolution: he was baffled by those in England who thought complacently, 'It couldn't happen here.' As O'Brien puts it, 'an Irishman could not be so sceptical, or so placid; revolt was in fact imminent in Ireland, and broke out in 1798, the year after Burke's death.'[3]

Connected with this, there is one other aspect of Burke's background that may be relevant. His mother was a Catholic and his father perhaps also an adherent of that faith. Burke campaigned often against the Popery Laws and appeared to detest the Protestant ascendancy which was, of course, the established order in his native land. Part of this stems from the same brand of religious conservatism that also explained his hostility to British oppression in India: the people of a country should not be prevented from practising their traditional religions. But in other respects, Burke in his thinking on Ireland is at his most liberal.[4] He regarded toleration (perhaps implausibly) as part of the English spirit and regretted that it was not expressed in the government of England's dominions. In Ireland, he noted, the Protestant ascendancy had the effect of dividing the nation into utterly opposed classes: 'One of these bodies was to possess *all* the franchises, *all* the property, *all* the education: the other was to be composed of the drawers of water and cutters of turf for them.'[5] The effect of this exploitation, he believed, could not be other than to foment discontent, and to produce on the basis of justified grievances the sort of upheaval which the French had contrived on the basis of coffee-house philosophy and no real grievances at all.

Burke's political career was served in the House of Commons on and off from 1765 to 1794. His views about the duties of a Member of Parliament *vis-à-vis* his constituency are set out in his famous 'Speech to the Electors of Bristol' in 1774. There he argued against the doctrine that a representative must be mandated by his electors:

> If government were a matter of will upon any side, yours without question ought to be superior. But government and legislation are matters of reason and judgement, and not of inclination; and what sort of reason is that, in which the determination precedes the discussion . . . ?[6]

Learned, always well briefed and an excellent orator, Burke cut an impressive figure in Commons debate: in his years in the chamber, he is recorded as having made well over 600 speeches.[7] But though he was identified with Rockingham's (and later Charles James Fox's) Whig faction all his parliamentary life, Burke was often isolated and unpopular in politics. His own brand of conservative wisdom and the cutting edge of his oratory tended to alienate friends and opponents alike.

His greatest isolation came in the period immediately preceding and during the French Revolution when he was embarked on a long and lonely campaign to impeach Warren Hastings for his mal-administration of India. For Burke the charges against Hastings revolved around his exploitation of Indian natives and the East India Company's insensitivity to a civilization that was older and in many ways more complicated than that of England. In other words, the Hastings campaign involved many of the main themes of Burkean politics: respect for existent social traditions; opposition to imposing alien ways of life on existing folkways; suspicion of the pretensions of administrative reason, and so on. There are places in his oratory against Hastings where he seems even to be involved in an appeal to the *natural rights* of the victims of exploitation – something that would not sit easily with his attack on such appeals in the French context. Certainly he did invoke what seemed to be simple and universal principles of transcendent justice in this campaign. But the apparent inconsistency is mitigated by noting that there is a considerable difference between indicting an administrator whose conduct has been evidently wrong and actually seeking to administer a society on the basis of the simple principles that might be employed in such an indictment. It was the second of these, not the first, that he criticized in the French revolutionary declarations.[8]

If the Hastings campaign places a question mark over Burke's attitude to natural justice, his support for the cause of the American colonists in the 1770s poses an even greater paradox. From 1775 Burke and his allies in Parliament lost no opportunity to attack the North administration for its conduct of American affairs: they urged conciliation with the colonists and openly supported the rebellion when it broke out. Yet in 1789, when a revolution erupted in France apparently embodying the same causes and certainly spouting the same rhetoric, there was not anyone in England more immediately and ferociously opposed to it than Burke. The paradox is not dissolved by alleging a sell-out on Burke's part (though there were many, including Thomas Paine and Karl Marx, who made this allegation).[9]

Burke had a reputation for consistency – or rather, since the philosophy he clung to all his adult life was marred by tensions and contradictions, he had a reputation for sticking to the same set of (sometimes inconsistent) principles throughout his career. The answer lies rather in his different perception of the two events. He never saw the American colonists as revolutionaries in a radical sense. They had a way of life, established commercial practices and a local administration of their own which they took themselves to be defending against the novel impositions, fiscal and political, of the North regime in England. Moreover many of the particular grievances of the Americans related to restrictions on freedom of trade. There is a strand of *laissez-faire* 'free market' philosophy in Burke's speeches which stems in part from his convictions about the necessity of property in a stable society, and in part from the same sort of suspicion of government interference – 'the zealots of the sect of regulation'[10] – in otherwise self-regulating economic activity that motivated liberal writers like Adam Smith. By contrast the French Jacobins were rising against an *ancien régime*, and in circumstances where the established order was by no means intolerable to them. They were attacking property and commerce, not defending it; and they were proposing novelty in politics, not resisting it. In France, as far as Burke could tell, it was the monarchy that stood for custom and ancient principle while the people attacked it with newfangled metaphysical ideas. In America it was almost the reverse: George III and his ministers were dreaming up new ideas about sovereignty and pushing them to a logical extreme. As Burke put it, 'if intemperately, unwisely, fatally, you sophisticate and poison the very source of government, by urging subtle deductions, and consequences odious to those you govern, from the unlimited and illimitable nature of supreme sovereignty, you will teach them by those means to call that sovereignty itself in question.'[11]

In 1777 Burke was a member of a powerful faction centred around Fox who were able to exert considerable influence by their policy of boycotting the House on all questions relating to America. The 1780s, by contrast, were lean years. In the election of 1780 he lost his parliamentary seat and had to scramble to secure another: this experience of electioneering left him with a quite comprehensive distaste for the English electorate.[12] In 1782 Rockingham died, and though Burke secured his post as paymaster in the subsequent administration, he was in opposition again after the election of 1784. The ultimately unsuccessful campaign against Hastings led to his vilification in the press. By 1789 whatever independent influence he had in his party (independent, that is, of Rockingham and Fox) had faded and Burke was back in his familiar role of defender of the English establishment from an outsider's position.

Reflections on the Revolution in France has the form of a reply to a letter from a young Frenchman calling for Burke's 'thoughts on the late proceedings in France'. He had in fact received such a letter and had replied to it in November 1789 and again in January 1790. Those letters were moderate in their comments on events in Paris: disapproving but distanced.[13] Nevertheless, unlike many of his contemporaries (including at this time Jeremy Bentham), Burke contemplated 'the portentous state of France – where the Elements which compose Human Society seem all to be dissolved' with deep foreboding.[14] In a way, it was not unexpected as far as he was concerned. Burke had made a study of the French financial system and had concluded as early as 1769 that one should 'look hourly for some extraordinary convulsion in that system'.[15] He was certainly convinced that the *ancien régime* was in much greater difficulty and needed more urgent reform than its counterpart in England. Still, he believed that intelligent and careful reform might bring the system round, and it was his sense that the opportunity for this had been missed in 1789 that explains some of his subsequent hostility: 'You might have repaired those walls; you might have built on those old foundations.'[16]

Burke's concern became more urgent and more practical when he realized an attempt was being made to export revolutionary sentiments to England. The opening pages of the book refer to a sermon by Richard Price, a Nonconformist minister and moralist, to the Revolution Society in London entitled 'A Discourse on the Love of our Country'. Price enraged Burke by arguing that the spirit of 1688 was embodied in the French Revolution and that true Englishmen should accordingly seize the chance for radical political reform. Burke's response to that was to maintain that 1688 represented an agreement by the people to submit themselves to the House of Orange and its successors for ever – an argument Thomas Paine had no difficulty in ridiculing in *Rights of Man*.[17] History apart, it was the spirit of Price's speech and the evident danger that it might have some influence – Price and his society were known to be in correspondence with the National Assembly – that prompted Burke to write the *Reflections*. In February 1790, when both Fox and Pitt expressed enthusiasm in the Commons for the French achievement, Burke answered that if necessary he would 'abandon his best friends, and join with his worst enemies' to oppose the spread of democratic principles to England.[18]

The book was started in February and finished by the summer. Published on 1 November 1790, it was an immediate success, selling more than 17,000 copies by the end of the year. The fact that a number of books and pamphlets (of which Paine's was the most prominent) were published to oppose it was evidence of how widely it was read and how seriously it was taken.[19] That reputation increased, of course, as events in France unfolded in a way that confirmed Burke's most extreme predictions. (In order to gauge the extent of Burke's apprehension about revolution as such, we have to remember that the book was written long before the Terror of the 1790s turned most people away from the Jacobin cause.) And its author's fortunes rose accordingly: he was publicly congratulated by the king and other political leaders, and his parliamentary oratory in the last years of his career – mainly on French and Irish affairs – had considerably more impact than it did in the 1780s.

Still, the success of a book like this – the confirmation of one's worse fears – was not a basis for happiness. The failure of his case against Hastings in 1794, the death of his son in the same year, the apparent victory of the revolution in France and apprehensions about revolution in Ireland all meant that Burke was still a bitter and troubled man when he died in 1797.

II

The task of understanding Burke's attack on the Declaration of Rights is complicated, first by his own insistence that his intention was not to attack human rights as such but to vindicate what he called 'the *real* rights of man' against 'the pretended rights of these theorists' (p. 104), and second, by the fact that in recent years a number of writers have tried to interpret Burke as a proponent of natural law and Lockean philosophy in a way that would be congenial to his presentation as a 'conservative' in the American style.[20] Since Burke wrote quickly, passionately and somewhat carelessly, with an orator's rhetoric rather than a philosopher's deliberation, and since his style combined argument with irony, description with sarcasm, and reason with diatribes *ad hominem*, there is ample opportunity for inter-pretation and re-interpretation, for and against almost any reading of the text.

It is probably not worth trying to settle the question of whether his philosophy should be located in the natural law tradition or not. It is clear enough that his beliefs about hierarchy and hubris were related to some conception of a natural order ordained by a creator with normative implications for human politics, and in this respect at least his writing can be put in a category that includes the work of John Locke as well as that of Cicero, Aquinas and Pufendorf. But to accommodate Locke *and* Burke, the category has to be very wide indeed, and probably too wide to be of much use in the campaign to identify him as true believer in natural rights in the tradition, say, of the Founding Fathers of the American republic. Though he was not averse to the rhetorical deployment of the language of rights and even, on occasion, the language of the social contract, Burke appears to have rejected the substance of many of the ideas that, for us at least, mark out the natural rights movement as an interesting and distinct philosophical and political tradition. Thus, for instance, he rejected the idea that the mere fact of our humanity endowed us with rights which were of serious significance for the evaluation of current political arrangements; in fact he rejected the whole approach which based our present rights on considerations in principle independent of the evolved political and social system of the society in which we live. Though he shared with Locke a view that political philosophy rested on theological foundations, he resisted all inferences of political or juridical equality from the premise that we were all equally creatures of the Almighty. For Burke our equality in the eyes of God was our equal taint of original sin, our common abjection before the mysteries of His priesthood and our equal capacity for some modicum of contentment in that condition. He certainly rejected any political theory that made individual reason and interest a touchstone of political legitimacy; instead he counselled individual humility in the face of tradition and awe in response to mystification – an approach quite alien either to early modern conceptions of the social contract or to Enlightenment conceptions of political understanding. Finally, on the basis of this repudiation of individual reason, he rejected the idea that natural law provided a perspective from which the common people could embark on large-scale evaluation or criticism of their social arrangements, and on the basis of which renovation or even revolution could be justified. He believed fervently that nothing but chaos and disorder would result from individuals' trying to find out for themselves what the law of nature required of them and basing their conduct on the answers they came up with. These were the central ideas of natural right in the American and French Revolutions and Burke would have none of them.

But I do not want to deny there was *some* normative edge to Burke's political philosophy: it was not merely a counsel of submission to established authority no matter how those authorities conducted themselves. As we have seen, Burke cheered the rebels in America (though on grounds quite other than those asserted in their Declaration of Independence), and he fought passionately to bring an end to oppression and exploitation in Ireland and India. In the *Reflections* he even went so far as to countenance the possibility that the overthrow and punishment of an established monarch is sometimes justified. 'The punishment of real tyrants is a noble and awful act of justice', he wrote, but he insisted that it must always be 'the very last resource of the thinking and the good' in response not only to cruelty and oppression in the past but to the otherwise unavoidable prospect of their continuation in the future.[21] It would always be difficult to determine when such a course was justified, and that indicated, in Burke's opinion, that just as the overthrow of a king 'was not made for common abuses, so it is not to be agitated by common minds'.

> The nature of the disease is to indicate the remedy to those whom nature has qualified to administer in extremities this critical, ambiguous, bitter portion to a distempered state. Times and occasions and provocations will teach their own lessons.[22]

Such a course will always be a matter of the deepest and wisest consultation 'of dispositions, and of means, and of probable consequences, rather than of positive rights'. Passages like these indicate the distance that there was between even the cutting edge of Burke's normative theory of politics and the more egalitarian Lockean theories of right and revolution.

The 'natural rights' interpretation of Burke is perhaps a reaction to the more popular view that his political philosophy is straightforwardly utilitarian (in the style, for example, of David Hume). But the fact is that there are a number of themes and arguments in the *Reflections* which make most sense when they are read in opposition, not only to natural rights, but also to *all* rational and intellectualist approaches to politics and political reform. Still it cannot be denied that there are utilitarian strands in Burke's writing and aspects of his critique of rights which do overlap with those of Bentham. It may be worth starting by looking at these in a little more detail, before going on to consider other aspects of Burke's approach which Bentham would have joined forces with Jefferson and Rousseau in repudiating.

III

As much as any utilitarian, Burke deplored the substitution of easy slogans like 'Liberty, Equality, and Fraternity' for the business of detailed and considered thought in politics. Statements of moral principle, he suggested, could never be justified at that level of generality:

> Circumstances (which with some gentlemen pass for nothing) give in reality to every political principle its distinguishing colour, and discriminating effect. The circumstances are what render every civil and political scheme beneficial or noxious to mankind. (p. 97)

One great trouble with the rights of man was that they defied this circumstantial evaluation. The charge that Burke laid again and again was one of 'metaphysical abstraction' (p. 97). For the sake of intellectual clarity or verbal precision, theories of rights lay aside all the 'infinite modifications' of time and circumstance which deter-mine the practicability of a proposal. It is, he said, as though these theorists consider 'their speculative designs as of infinite value, and the actual arrangement of the state as of no estimation' (p.109). Burke gave many examples of the sort of consideration proponents of rights failed to take into account:

> The effect of liberty to individuals is, that they may do what they please: We ought to see what it will please them to do before we risk congratulations, which may soon be turned into complaints. . . . What is the use of discussing a man's abstract right to food or medicine? The question is upon the method of procuring and administering them. In that deliberation I shall always advise to call in the aid of the farmer and the physician, rather than the professor of metaphysics. (pp. 85 and 106)

Above all, they fail to take into account the differences between one society and another. Here Burke is a follower of Montesquieu. Different climates, conditions, geography and history make all the difference to the workings of a given set of legal and political arrangements. This is no doubt one of the reasons why Burke is inclined to favour the liberties of Englishmen rather than the rights of man 'as an estate specially belonging to the people of this kingdom without any reference whatever to any other more general or prior right' (p. 100). The universality of the Declaration suggested its proponents were recklessly unconcerned with any of the national distinctions that might make a difference to its application in effect.

According to Burke there were no simple answers in politics, and certainly none that could be expressed in the axiomatic form, allegedly valid for all times and places, that was favoured in the Declaration. What was needed is what one might call an Aristotelian sense of moderation in each society 'incapable of definition, but not impossible to be discerned': 'Political reason is a computing principle: adding, subtracting, multiplying, and dividing, morally and not metaphysically or mathematically, true moral denominations' (p. 107).

That passage suggests that Burke favoured something like an informal version of Bentham's 'felicific calculus'. Certainly whenever Burke reflected on the function of government, he used phraseology to which no utilitarian could ever take exception. 'Power', he said, 'has no other rational end than that of the general advantage.'[23] And elsewhere: 'Government is a contrivance of human wisdom to provide for human *wants*' (p. 105). But the similarities between Burke and Bentham must not be exaggerated. For one thing, Burke's conception of well-being was not straightforwardly hedonistic in the way that Bentham's was. It was more like Aristotelian *eudaimonia* – 'the happiness that is found by virtue in all conditions'.[24] As such it was a conception which presupposed an independent account of moral virtue and moral duty (which for Burke was theologically grounded) as well as providing a teleological basis for political duty and political morality. Secondly, Burke's creed was not the formulaic utilitarianism of the Benthamic calculus. The passage quoted above does suggest some commitment to maximization, with the summing and the trade-offs that that usually involves. But the preference for 'moral' over 'mathematical' computation suggests something much closer to Aristotelian *phronesis* – implicit and informal practical judgement – than to the formal and articulate calculations that Bentham recommended. Thirdly, in at least one passage in the *Reflections*, Burke simply repudiated the whole utilitarian idea of trade-offs between the suffering of some and the advantage of others – an idea he described as 'weighing, as it were, in scales hung in a shop of horrors, – so much actual crime against so much contingent advantage, – and after putting in and out weights, declaring that the balance was on the side of the advantages.'[25]

Above all, Burke differed from Bentham in his doubts about the practical application of utilitarian reformism. Where Bentham was forever drawing up new schemes, Burke was counselling the greatest caution in the deployment of the utilitarian standard in politics:

The science of constructing a commonwealth, or renovating it, or reforming it, is, like every other experimental science, not to be taught à priori. Nor is it a short experience that can instruct us in that practical science; because the real effects of moral causes are not always immediate; but that which in the first instance is prejudicial may be excellent in its remoter operation; and its excellence may arise even from the ill effects it produces in the beginning. The reverse also happens; and very plausible schemes, with very pleasing commencements, have often shameful and lamentable conclusions. In states there are often some obscure and almost latent causes, things which appear at first view of little moment, on which a very great part of its prosperity or adversity may most essentially depend. (p.106)

This means that if Burke *was* a utilitarian, he was, in our modern terms, an 'indirect utilitarian' – someone who believed that the best results are often or most likely produced by people who are not trying consciously to produce them.[26] He spoke in several places of the importance of moral 'prejudice' as opposed to calculation in political affairs. Acting on prejudice has the advantage of removing hesitation; it is, as Burke puts it, 'of ready application in the emergency' (p. 116). It can lead to greater resolution and 'steadiness' in conduct because the prescriptions of a prejudice are likely to engage the affections in the way that the outcome of a calculation may not. And it makes action more predictable and therefore makes it easier for people to co-ordinate and plan their activity.

Of course, in all theories of this kind, everything depends on what prejudices we decide to treat in this way, for there must surely be some prejudices and traditions whose unhesitating application would be even less likely to promote the general good than leaving individual reason to its own devices. But here Burke is at his most conservative – a conservatism that borders on irrationalism: 'We know that *we* have made no discoveries; and we think that no discoveries are to be made, in morality; nor many in the great principles of government' (p. 114). But elsewhere, in a less obdurate mood, his point is that those prejudices that have stood the test of time are likely to be of the greatest utility. Burke believed that the science of government required not only experience but also probably 'more experience than any person can gain in his whole life, however sagacious and observing he may be' (p. 106):

We are afraid to put men to live and trade each on his own private stock of reason; because we suspect that this stock in each man is small, and that the individuals would do better to avail themselves of the bank and capital of ages. (p. 115)

If there were no great risk involved, maybe we could afford to embark on consequentialist calculations of our own in politics. But Burke was convinced that the consequences of a wrong move, in the way of political renovation could be catastrophic, and saw no comparable catastrophe in the continued existence of the *anciens régimes* in the countries – England and France – that he was writing about. Utilitarian caution, then, was on the side of the prejudices embodied in the existing institutions of those regimes.

Conservatism, caution and respect for establishment were the dispositions to be cultivated in Burke's indirect utilitarianism. On the other side of things, he was quite clear about the disposition of those who based their politics on natural rights. Like Bentham he lambasted them for their selfishness and arrogance, and regretted the hardening of the spirit of those who held themselves ready at all times for permanent revolution. They were intoxicated, he thought, with their own powers of abstract thought, and their pride in the products of that thought – its clarity and systematicity – leads them to grossly underestimate the actual prerequisites for practical political thinking. 'The nature of man is intricate', he insisted, and 'the objects of society are of the greatest possible complexity'. So when the designers of right-based constitutions pride themselves on their 'simplicity of contrivance', Burke expresses his conviction 'that the artificers are grossly ignorant of their trade, or totally negligent of their duty' (p. 107). But what could be expected of those whose 'attachment to their country itself, is only so far as it agrees with some of their fleeting projects; it begins and ends with that scheme of polity which falls in with their momentary opinion' (p. 116)?

Besides Burke's conception of political virtue, there was also a commitment in his political philosophy to the idea of a political class: an élite whose privileged position in relation to political action could again be justified by its contribution to the general good. Sometimes, as we saw in his remarks on the justification of regicide, this class was defined by their uncommon wisdom and sensibility; much of what Burke says about aristocracy comes under this heading. But as far as parliaments were concerned, the principle on which Burke distinguished his political élite was that of the ownership of property. In liberal thought, this principle was based on nothing more elevated than the necessity for taxpayers' consent to taxation. For Burke, however, it was suggested by what he called a 'philosophic analogy' between political establishment and the fortunes of a family's property, an analogy that dominated his political writing:

> The idea of inheritance furnishes a sure principle of conservation, and a sure principle of transmission; without at all excluding a principle of improvement. . . . Whatever advantages are obtained by a state proceeding on these maxims, are locked fast as in a sort of family settlement. . . .[W]orking after the pattern of nature, we receive, we hold, we transmit our government and our privileges, in the same manner in which we enjoy and transmit our property and our lives. (p. 100)

But it is more than analogy, for the suggestion is that since only proprietors know anything about permanence and conservation, only proprietors can be relied on to run a country. The shambles of French administration was attributed to the fact that the National Assembly was almost devoid of men of property. The great majority was made up of lawyers, whose livelihood, as Burke put it, 'had always depended upon whatever rendered property questionable, ambiguous and insecure, and country curates, who, immersed in hopeless poverty, could regard all property, whether secular or ecclesiastical, with no other eye than that of envy. Nothing lasting, and therefore in human life nothing useful, could be expected from such men.'[27]

Above all, behind the turmoil of the French Revolution and the chatter about natural rights, Burke saw the spectre of democracy. His distaste for democracy was partly his aversion to Rousseauian doctrines of popular sovereignty and the general will. A democracy, he said, is 'the most shameless thing in the world' if its people are 'suffered to imagine that their will any more than that of kings, is the standard of right and wrong.'[28] Ironically from our perspective, we find him identifying what he took to be the democratic character of natural rights with the danger of majoritarian tyranny: 'In a democracy the majority of the citizens is capable of exercising the most cruel oppressions upon the minority, whenever strong divisions prevail in that kind of polity, as they often must.'[29] The overwhelming worry, though, was about the political ability of the people. Burke was not an élitist in the sense of being unresponsive to the plight of the masses; on the contrary, he asserted in a famous passage, 'If it should come to the last extremity, and to a contest of blood, God forbid! God forbid! – my part is taken; I would take my fate with the poor, and low, and feeble.'[30] He even insisted that the poor alone were the judges of whether they were being oppressed or not. However, if it was a matter of either investigating the cause of the oppression or of remedying it,

> they ought never to be called into council about the one or the other. They ought to be totally shut out; because their reason is weak; because when once aroused, their passions are ungoverned; because they want information; because the smallness of the property, which individually they possess, renders them less attentive to the consequence of the measures they adopt in affairs of moment.[31]

IV

Alongside these utilitarian themes, there is a darker (some would say a richer) aspect to Edmund Burke's critique of natural rights. In the previous section we outlined the charges of imprudence and recklessness that he laid at the proponents of the new constitution: his concern there was for 'sentient beings, by the sudden alteration of whose state, condition, and habits, multitudes may be rendered miserable'.[32] But other charges that he makes are less concerned with the well-being of individuals, than with that of communities and countries – considered as enduring entities apart from the men and women who make them up – and other observations that he makes about political thought seem to call not for an increase in prudence but for the abandonment of prudential thought altogether in favour of other less rationalistic mental attitudes. As always, Burke's thought is ambiguous in these areas. His rhetoric mingles concern for the country with concern for its inhabitants, and respect for tradition with respect for the well-being of those who live under them. And since, even when he is attacking reason, he is always *making an argument* of some sort, however rhetorical it may be, it is very difficult to make any charge of irrationalism stick. In what follows, however, I am less concerned with reaching a *verdict* on Burke than with teasing out those among the many themes of his critique that sit least happily with the utilitarian approach.

I shall begin by considering Burke's critique of reason. We have seen that much of his conservative scepticism about reform and even his cherishing of prejudice in political life can be explained in utilitarian terms. It is rational to be cautious about reason if our reason serves reliably to inform us of how little we can know about society. But often Burke seems to go further than this. It is not just our pretension to knowledge but the whole style of rationalistic thought that he repudiates. The sense one gets time and again in Burke's writing is that contemporary political theorists have become obsessed with what is in fact a rather insignificant mental faculty – the faculty of a priori deductive reasoning – and have applied it quite inappropriately to the great affairs of state when it ought instead to be confined to the operations of petty arithmetic. To the intellectuals this faculty has the satisfying advantage of producing clear and distinct ideas: ideas which are precise and tidily ordered in relation to one another. But for Burke there is nothing clear and distinct about politics, and the later pages of the *Reflections* abound with bitter attacks on the 'geometrical and arithmetical constitution' these logicians want to impose. He contrasts what appears to be the pleasant messiness of the English and *anciens régimes* with the 'ornamental gardens' proposed by the National Assembly where everything is divided neatly into squares and levelled into one form.[33] In passages like these one gets the impression that it is precision, delineation and order in themselves that are being opposed. 'Aristotle, the great master of reasoning, cautions us . . . against this species of delusive geometrical accuracy in moral arguments, as the most fallacious of all sophistries.'[34]

For all his utilitarianism, then, it seems that Burke exulted in the obscurity of the traditional order and its opacity to liberal reason. Our pride, he wrote, is properly humbled 'under the dispensations of a mysterious wisdom'.[35] Remove mystery and the 'pleasing illusions' of political life, and you leave a stark and unattractive array of human bodies.

The sort of a priorism of the Declaration of Rights is also criticized for what Burke calls its 'metaphysical abstraction'. It grounds itself on whatever first principles the 'moral geometer' wishes to posit and leaves him free to pursue them in his speculations wherever they happen to take him. For Burke this is a mode of activity quite inappropriate to politics, where there is no 'Archimedean point' from which an individual's reason can sit in judgement on the folkways of his society and no reliable method of proceeding to such judgement even if there were.

The term he uses to oppose the pretensions and 'pert loquacity' of individual reason is usually 'wisdom'. Though wisdom is a disposition we normally associate with thought, Burke wants to drive a wedge between wisdom and reflection. Wisdom is more a matter of inarticulately following one's prejudices than of thinking anything through: the image we are given is of 'great cattle, reposed beneath the shadow of the English oak, [which] chew the cud and are silent'.[36] The wise man *sees* or *feels* what is to be done (usually little or nothing) rather than trying consciously to work it out.

Turning now to Burke's celebration of *feeling* in politics, again there is much in that which can be accommodated within a broad utilitarian framework. In the long peroration on the French queen and the transportation of her family to Paris, we are told that societies have a need for awe, superstition, ritual and honour for their stability and in order to be able to command the allegiance and loyalty on which they often depend. Ceremony and chivalry – bowing to magistrates, paying homage to princes, the sacredness of the royal person, and so on – are said to be useful because they incorporate into politics some of 'the sentiments which beautify and soften private society' (p. 110). A state which brushed all that aside in the name of rational enlightenment would be a state that in the end rested on nothing but power:

> On the scheme of this barbarous philosophy . . . laws are to be supported only by their own terrors, and by the concern, which each individual may find in them, from his own private specu-lations, or can spare to them from his own private interests. In the groves of *their* academy, at the end of every visto, you see nothing but the gallows. Nothing is left that engages the affections on the part of the commonwealth. On the principles of this mechanic philosophy, our institutions can never be embodied, if I may use the expression, in persons; so as to create in us love, veneration, admiration, or attachment. But that sort of reason which banishes the affections is incapable of filling their place. (p. 111)

In other passages, however, feeling and illusion seem to be valued for their own sake. In the face of great spectacles of state, 'our minds are purified by terror and pity';[37] we can indulge our sentiments and emotions in the theatre of ceremonial statecraft.

> We have not been drawn and trussed, in order that we may be filled, like stuffed birds in a museum, with chaff and rags, and paltry blurred shreds of paper about the rights of man. We preserve the entirety of our feelings native and entire, unsophisticated by pedantry and infidelity. We have real hearts of flesh and blood beating in our bosoms. We fear God; we look up with awe to kings; with affection to parliaments; with duty to magistrates; with reverence to priests; and with respect to nobility. Why? Because when such ideas are brought before our minds, it is *natural* to be affected, because all other feelings are false and spurious. (p. 115)

Now it is important to take this claim about the *naturalness* of feeling in its context. Burke is not here appealing to anything like the sort of conception of human nature that proponents of rights appealed to. The feelings in question are not legitimized by their association with the frame of primitive pre-social man. On the contrary Burke felt that any appeal to human nature in this sense would yield only the rights and sentiments of savages. Without the 'decent drapery' of social and political life, our 'naked shivering nature' commands no respect at all and provides no basis for any norms or principles of politics. Instead the feelings that Burke refers to here as 'natural' are the *'inbred* sentiments' of our socialization. In celebrating *them* as natural, and in extolling them above the liberal intellect which tries to pierce the social garb and look at the residual humanity underneath, Burke is arguing that it is through our socialization and not in our underlying biology that we find the true dignity of the human person.

If he places this emphasis on socialization, to what extent is Burke then a relativist about social norms? There are many suggestions of relativism in Burke's writing. I suppose his predilection for the 'entailed liberties' of Englishmen over the rights of man can be read (as we read it in the previous section) as a utilitarian preoccupation with the detailed circumstances that might make certain things work in England but not elsewhere. But it can also be read as an assertion that the rights we happen to have in England are important (to us) simply because they are English and therefore ours – as Burke puts it, *'without any reference whatever* to any other more general or prior right' (p. 100; my emphasis). There are passages where Burke echoes Rousseau's theory that the entry of primitive man into society produces a new and moralized human nature, quite different from the biological nature that the members of the species have in common.[38] But while Rousseau believed it was possible still to speak in universal terms about the interests, needs and rights of socialized man, Burke writes often as though the entry into society produces a different new man for each society – 'as it were so many different species of animals',[39] each one more or less the embodiment or *Träge* of local mores, institutions and structures. If this is true, the pursuit of *human* rights is *radically* misconceived and not merely foolish or imprudent. As Antony Quinton puts it, 'since human nature is socially determined and thus essentialy various, there can be no specific rights of man as such, only the rights of men who have developed within a particular social and historical setting'.[40]

Certainly something like this is necessary to sustain Burke's belief that we owe allegiance to our society not just because it benefits us, and certainly not because we have promised to obey it, but because we cannot think of ourselves, except in our savage nature, in any way that distinguishes us from this allegiance. We cannot challenge the social structures that in part constitute our being for they leave no foothold on the basis of which genuinely independent moral criticism could be undertaken.

However, if there is relativism in Burke's political philosophy, it is quite a limited relativism. He himself is happy to offer advice to people in other societies, and even to hold out English arrangements as a model to the French despite the very different historical experience that leads him to repudiate all offers from the other direction.[41] Above all, in its background moral premises, Burke's thought is theological and quite unrelativistic. The basic tenets of morality, imposed by divine command, are clear, universal and absolute. It is only their application in the political sphere that is difficult and conditioned; the mistake of the natural rights theorists is to think that one can treat the precepts of political organization as though they were as clearly revealed as the moral commands of God.

Apart from his challenge to rationalism, there are other aspects of Burke's philosophy that distinguish it from mainstream utilitarianism, however broadly that is conceived. Though Burke is concerned for the men and women who, he believes, will suffer under the new dispensation of natural rights, he appears equally concerned for the fate of their countries, considered organically as structures and entities over and above the people who make them up. The state, we are told, is a 'permanent body composed of transient parts', wherein individual members come and go while the whole remains 'in a condition of unchangeable constancy' (p. 100).

Similarly with the Burkean theme of our responsibility for posterity. Though we may be concerned for the welfare of future generations on humanitarian grounds – 'where the great interests of mankind are concerned through a long succession of generations, that succession ought to be admitted into some share in the councils which are so deeply to affect them'[42] – more often Burke's concern for posterity is expressed in terms that have little to do with individual well-being. It seems often to have been that the generations living in a country should be united by some common, lasting structures, whether that was good for the individual members of those generations or not. The concern was lest the commonwealth 'be disconnected into the dust and powder of individuality':

By this unprincipled facility of changing the state as often, and as much, and in as many ways as there are floating fancies or fashions, the whole chain and continuity of the commonwealth would be broken. No one generation could link with another. Men would become little better than the flies of a summer. (p. 117)

Whatever its individual advantages, the resolution of society into its constituent parts and its reconstitution as a partnership of equals violates what Burke called the *real* social contract – 'the great partnership' not only between those who are living, but between those who are dead, and those who are to be born' (p. 118). The passage goes on to develop the conceit in a way that makes it almost impossible to distinguish argument from rhetorical embellishment:

Each contract of each particular state is but a clause in the great primeval contract of eternal society, linking the lower with the higher natures, connecting the visible and invisible world, according to a fixed compact sanctioned by the inviolable oath which holds all physical and all moral natures, each in their appointed place. (p. 118)

Though Burke is quick to deny the Divine Right of Kings (a doctrine he identifies with 'exploded fanatics of slavery'[43]), he subscribes wholeheartedly to Cicero's dictum that nothing is more pleasing to God than the existence of human *civitates*. In this context he talks of the public ceremonial that modern philosophers would destroy, as an 'oblation of the state' in homage to the deity.[44] It turns out that the theorists of rights are guilty not merely of imprudence and intellectual arrogance but of blasphemy and impiety as well.

My aim in this introduction has not been to argue for or against the utilitarian reading of Burke. It is clear that there are themes in his critique which overlap with those in Bentham's, and indeed – for all the untheoretical character of his work – there are insights in his utilitarianism which are more sophisticated than Bentham's ever were. But I hope I have been able to indicate the aspects of Burke's utilitarianism – if that is what it is – which give it its distinctively conservative flavour, and which lead to his confronting the theory of natural rights with a set of attitudes that differ in the end quite markedly from those deployed by either of our other two critics.[45]

Reflections on the Revolution in France

and on the proceedings in certain societies in London relative to that event

*In a letter intended to have been sent to
a gentleman in Paris by
the right honourable Edmund Burke*

DEAR SIR,
You are pleased to call again, and with some earnestness, for my thoughts on the late proceedings in France. I will not give you reason to imagine that I think my sentiments of such value as to wish myself to be solicited about them. They are of too little consequence to be very anxiously either communicated or withheld. It was from attention to you, and to you only, that I hesitated at the time, when you first desired to receive them. In the first letter I had the honour to write to you, and which at length I send, I wrote neither for nor from any description of men; nor shall I in this. My errors, if any, are my own. My reputation alone is to answer for them.

You see, Sir, by the long letter I have transmitted to you, that, though I do most heartily wish that France may be animated by a spirit of rational liberty, and that I think you bound, in all honest policy, to provide a permanent body, in which that spirit may reside, and an effectual organ, by which it may act, it is my misfortune to entertain great doubts concerning several material points in your late transactions.

* * *

I flatter myself that I love a manly, moral, regulated liberty as well as any gentleman of that society, he be who he will; and perhaps I have given as good proofs of my attachment to that cause, in the whole course of my public conduct. I think I envy liberty as little as they do, to any other nation. But I cannot stand forward, and give praise or blame to any thing which relates to human actions, and human concerns, on a simple view of the object as it stands stripped of every relation, in all the nakedness and solitude of metaphysical abstraction. Circumstances (which with some gentlemen pass for nothing) give in reality to every political principle its distinguishing colour, and discriminating effect. The circumstances are what render every civil and political scheme beneficial or noxious to mankind. Abstractedly speaking, government, as well as liberty, is good; yet could I, in common sense, ten years ago, have felicitated France on her enjoyment of a government (for she then had a government) without enquiry what the nature of that government was, or how it was administered? Can I now congratulate the same nation upon its freedom? Is it because liberty in the abstract may be classed amongst the blessings of mankind, that I am seriously to felicitate a madman, who has escaped from the protecting restraint and wholesome darkness of his cell, on his restoration to the enjoyment of light and liberty? Am I to congratulate an highwayman and murderer, who has broke prison, upon the recovery of his natural rights? This would be to act over again the scene of the criminals condemned to the gallies, and their heroic deliverer, the metaphysic Knight of the Sorrowful Countenance.

When I see the spirit of liberty in action, I see a strong principle at work; and this, for a while, is all I can possibly know of it. The wild *gas*, the fixed air, is plainly broke loose: but we ought to suspend our judgment until the first effervescence is a little subsided, till the liquor is cleared, and until we see something deeper than the agitation of a troubled and frothy surface. I must be tolerably sure, before I venture publicly to congratulate men upon a blessing, that they have really received one. Flattery corrupts both the receiver and the giver; and adulation is not of more service to the people than to kings. I should therefore suspend my congratulations on the new liberty of France, until I was informed how it had been combined with government; with public force; with the discipline and obedience of armies; with the collection of an effective and well-distributed revenue; with morality and religion; with the solidity of property; with peace and order; with civil and social manners. All these (in their way) are good things too; and, without them, liberty is not a benefit whilst it lasts, and is not likely to continue long. The effect of liberty to individuals is, that they may do what they please: we ought to see what it will please them to do, before we risque congratulations, which may be soon turned into complaints. Prudence would dictate this in the case of separate insulated private men; but liberty, when men act in bodies, is *power*. Considerate people, before they declare themselves, will observe the use which is made of *power*; and particularly of so trying a thing as *new* power in *new* persons, of whose principles, tempers and dispositions, they have little or no experience, and in situations where those who appear the most stirring in the scene may possibly not be the real movers.

All these considerations however were below the transcendental diginity of the Revolution Society. Whilst I continued in the country, from whence I had the honour of writing to you, I had but an imperfect idea of their transactions. On my coming to town, I sent for an account of their proceedings, which had been published by their authority, containing a sermon of Dr. Price, with the Duke de Rochefoucault's and the Archbishop of Aix's letter, and several other documents annexed. The whole of that publication, with the manifest design of connecting the affairs of France with those of England, by drawing us into an imitation of the conduct of the National Assembly, gave me a considerable degree of uneasiness. The effect of that conduct upon the power, credit, prosperity, and tranquillity of France, became every day more evident. The form of constitution to be settled, for its future polity, became more clear. We are now in a condition to discern, with tolerable exactness, the true nature of the object held up to our imitation. If the prudence of reserve and decorum dictates silence in some circumstances, in others prudence of an higher order may justify us in speaking our thoughts. The beginnings of confusion with us in England are at present feeble enough; but with you, we have seen an infancy still more feeble, growing by moments into a strength to heap mountains upon mountains, and to wage war with Heaven itself. Whenever our neighbour's house is on fire, it cannot be amiss for the engines to play a little on our own. Better to be despised for too anxious apprehensions, than ruined by too confident a security.

• • •

The very idea of the fabrication of a new government is enough to fill us with disgust and horror. We wished at the period of the Revolution, and do now wish, to derive all we possess as *an inheritance from our forefathers*. Upon that body and stock of inheritance we have taken care not to inoculate any cyon alien to the nature of the original plant. All the reformations we have hitherto made, have proceeded upon the principle of reference to antiquity; and I hope, nay I am persuaded, that all those which possibly may be made hereafter, will be carefully formed upon analogical precedent, authority, and example.

Our oldest reformation is that of Magna Charta. You will see that Sir Edward Coke, that great oracle of our law, and indeed all the great men who follow him, to Blackstone, are industrious to prove the pedigree of our liberties. They endeavour to prove, that the antient charter, the Magna Charta of King John, was connected with another positive charter from Henry I. and that both the one and the other were nothing more than a re-affirmance of the still more ancient standing law of the kingdom. In the matter of fact, for the greater part, these authors appear to be in the right; perhaps not always: but if the lawyers mistake in some particulars, it proves my position still the more strongly; because it demonstrates the powerful prepossession towards antiquity, with which the minds of all our lawyers and legislators, and of all the people whom they wish to influence, have been always filled; and the stationary policy of this kingdom in considering their most sacred rights and franchises as an *inheritance*.

In the famous law of the 3rd of Charles I. called the *Petition of Right*, the parliament says to the king, 'Your subjects have *inherited* this freedom,' claiming their franchises, not on abstract principles as the 'rights of men,' but as the rights of Englishmen, and as a patrimony derived from their forefathers. Selden, and the other profoundly learned men, who drew this petition of right, were as well acquainted, at least, with all the general theories concerning the 'rights of men,' as any of the discoursers in our pulpits, or on your tribune; full as well as Dr. Price, or as the Abbé Sieyes. But, for reasons worthy of that practical wisdom which superseded their theoretic science, they preferred this positive, recorded, *hereditary* title to all which can be dear to the man and the citizen, to that vague speculative right, which exposed their sure inheritance to be scrambled for and torn to pieces by every wild litigious spirit.

The same policy pervades all the laws which have since been made for the preservation of our liberties. In the Ist of William and Mary, in the famous statute, called the Declaration of Right, the two houses utter not a syllable of 'a right to frame a government for themselves.' You will see, that their whole care was to secure the religion, laws, and liberties, that had been long possessed, and had been lately endangered. 'Taking into their most serious consideration the *best* means for making such an establishment, that their religion, laws, and liberties might not be in danger of being again subverted,' they auspicate all their proceedings, by stating as some of those *best* means, 'in the *first place*' to do, 'as their *ancestors in like cases have usually done* for vindicating their *antient* rights and liberties, to *declare*;' – and then they pray the king and queen, 'that it may be *declared* and enacted, that *all and singular* the rights and liberties *asserted and declared* are the true *antient* and indubitable rights and liberties of the people of this kingdom.'

You will observe, that from Magna Charta to the Declaration of Right, it has been the uniform policy of our constitution to claim and assert our liberties, as an *entailed inheritance* derived to us from our forefathers, and to be transmitted to our posterity; as an estate specially belonging to the people of this kingdom without any reference whatever to any other more general or prior right. By this means our constitution preserves an unity in so great a diversity of its parts. We have an inheritable crown; an inheritable peerage; and an house of commons and a people inheriting privileges, franchises, and liberties, from a long line of ancestors.

This policy appears to me to be the result of profound reflection; or rather the happy effect of following nature, which is wisdom without reflection, and above it. A spirit of innovation is generally the result of a selfish temper and confined views. People will not look forward to posterity, who never look backward to their ancestors. Besides, the people of England well know, that the idea of inheritance furnishes a sure principle of conservation, and a sure principle of transmission; without at all excluding a principle of improvement. It leaves acquisition free; but it secures what it acquires. Whatever advantages are obtained by a state proceeding on these maxims, are locked fast as in a sort of family settlement; grasped as in a kind of mortmain for ever. By a constitutional policy, working after the pattern of nature, we receive, we hold, we transmit our government and our privileges, in the same manner in which we enjoy and transmit our property and our lives. The institutions of policy, the goods of fortune, the gifts of Providence, are handed down, to us and from us, in the same course and order. Our political system is placed in a just correspondence and symmetry with the order of the world, and with the mode of existence decreed to a permanent body composed of transitory parts; wherein, by the disposition of a stupenduous wisdom, moulding together the great mysterious incorporation of the human race, the whole, at one time, is never old, or middle-aged, or young, but in a condition of unchangeable constancy, moves on through the varied tenour of perpetual decay, fall, renovation, and progression. Thus, by preserving the method of nature in the conduct of the state, in what we improve, we are never wholly new; in what we retain we are never wholly obsolete. By adhering in this manner and on those principles to our forefathers, we are guided not by the superstition of antiquarians, but by the spirit of philosophic analogy. In this choice of inheritance we have given to our frame of polity the image of a relation in blood; binding up the constitution of our country with our dearest domestic ties; adopting our fundamental laws into the bosom of our family affections; keeping inseparable, and cherishing with the warmth of all their combined and mutually reflected charities, our state, our hearths, our sepulchres, and our altars.

Through the same plan of a conformity to nature in our artificial institutions, and by calling in the aid of her unerring and powerful instincts, to fortify the fallible and feeble contrivances of our reason, we have derived several other, and those no small benefits, from considering our liberties in the light of an inheritance. Always acting as if in the presence of canonized forefathers, the spirit of freedom, leading in itself to misrule and excess, is tempered with an awful gravity. This idea of a liberal descent inspires us with a sense of habitual native dignity, which prevents that upstart insolence almost inevitably adhering to and disgracing those who are the first acquirers of any distinction. By this means our liberty becomes a noble freedom. It carries an imposing and majestic aspect. It has a pedigree and illustrating ancestors. It has its bearings and its ensigns armorial. It has its gallery of portraits; its monumental inscriptions; its records, evidences, and titles. We procure reverence to our civil institutions on the principle upon which nature teaches us to revere individual men; on account of their age; and on account of those from whom they are descended. All your sophisters cannot produce any thing better adapted to preserve a rational and manly freedom than the course that we have pursued, who have chosen our nature rather than our speculations, our breasts rather than our inventions, for the great conservatories and magazines of our rights and privileges.

* * *

I see that your example is held out to shame us. I know that we are supposed a dull sluggish race, rendered passive by finding our situation tolerable; and prevented by a mediocrity of freedom from ever attaining to its full perfection. Your leaders in France began by affecting to admire, almost to adore, the British constitution; but as they advanced they came to look upon it with a sovereign contempt. The friends of your National Assembly amongst us have full as mean an opinion of what was formerly thought the glory of their country. The Revolution Society has discovered that the English nation is not free. They are convinced that the inequality in our representation is a 'defect in our constitution so *gross and palpable*, as to make it excellent chiefly in *form and theory*'. That a representation in the legislature of a kingdom is not only the basis of all constitutional liberty in it, but of '*all legitimate government*; that without it a *government* is nothing but an *usurpation*;' – that 'when the representation is *partial*, the kingdom possesses liberty only *partially*; and if extremely partial it gives only a *semblance*; and if not only extremely partial, but corruptly chosen, it becomes a *nuisance*.' Dr. Price considers this inadequacy of representation as our *fundamental grievance*; and though, as to the corruption of this semblance of representation, he hopes it is not yet arrived to its full perfection of depravity; he fears that 'nothing will be done towards gaining for us this *essential blessing*, until some *great abuse of power* again provokes our resentment, or some *great calamity* again alarms our fears, or perhaps till the acquisition of a *pure and equal representation by other countries*, whilst we are *mocked* with the *shadow*, kindles our shame.' To this he subjoins a note in these words. 'A representation, chosen chiefly by the Treasury, and a *few* thousands of the *dregs* of the people, who are generally paid for their votes.'

You will smile here at the consistency of those democratists, who, when they are not on their guard, treat the humbler part of the community with the greatest contempt, whilst, at the same time, they pretend to make them the depositories of all power. It would require a long discourse to point out to you the many fallacies that lurk in the generality and equivocal nature of the terms 'inadequate representation.' I shall only say here, in justice to that old-fashioned constitution, under which we have long prospered, that our representation has been found perfectly adequate to all the purposes for which a representation of the people can be desired or devised. I defy the enemies of our constitution to show the contrary. To detail the particulars in which it is found so well to promote its ends, would demand a treatise on our practical constitution, I state here the doctrine of the Revolutionists, only that you and others may see, what an opinion these gentlemen entertain of the constitution of their country, and why they seem to think that some great abuse of power, or some great calamity, as giving a chance for the blessing of a constitution according to their ideas, would be much palliated to their feelings; you see why they are so much enamoured of your fair and equal representation, which being once obtained, the same effects might follow. You see they consider our house of commons as only 'a semblance,' 'a form,' 'a theory,' 'a shadow,' 'a mockery,' perhaps 'a nuisance.'

These gentlemen value themselves on being systematic; and not without reason. They must therefore look on this gross and palpable defect of representation, this fundamental grievance (so they call it), as a thing not only vicious in itself, but as rendering our whole government absolutely *illegitimate*, and not at all better than a downright *usurpation*. Another revolution, to get rid of this illegitimate and usurped government, would of course be perfectly justifiable, if not absolutely necessary. Indeed their principle, if you observe it with any attention, goes much further than to an alteration in the election of the house of commons; for, if popular representation, or choice, is necessary to the *legitimacy* of all government, the house of lords is, at one stroke, bastardized and corrupted in blood. That house is no representative of the people at all, even in 'semblance' or in 'form.' The case of the crown is altogether as bad. In vain the crown may endeavour to screen itself against these gentlemen by the authority of the establishment made on the Revolution. The Revolution which is resorted to for a title, on their system, wants a title itself. The Revolution is built, according to their theory, upon a basis not more solid than our present formalities, as it was made by an house of lords not representing any one but themselves; and by an house of commons exactly such as the present, that is, as they term it, by a mere 'shadow and mockery' of representation.

Something they must destroy, or they seem to themselves to exist for no purpose. One set is for destroying the civil power through the ecclesiastical; another for demolishing the ecclesiastick through the civil. They are aware that the worst consequencess might happen to the public in accomplishing this double ruin of church and state; but they are so heated with their theories, that they give more than hints, that this ruin, with all the mischiefs that must lead to it and attend it, and which to themselves appear quite certain, would not be unacceptable to them, or very remote from their wishes. A man amongst them of great authority, and certainly of great talents, speaking of a supposed alliance between church and state, says, 'perhaps *we must wait for the fall of the civil powers* before this most unnatural alliance be broken. Calamitous no doubt will that time be. But what convulsion in the political world ought to be a subject of lamentation, if it be attended with so desirable an effect?' You see with what a steady eye these gentlemen are prepared to view the greatest calamities which can befall their country!

It is no wonder therefore, that with these ideas of everything in their constitution and government at home, either in church or state, as illegitimate and usurped, or, at best as a vain mockery, they look abroad with an eager and passionate enthusiasm. Whilst they are possessed by these notions, it is vain to talk to them of the practice of their ancestors, the fundamental laws of their country, the fixed form of a constitution, whose merits are confirmed by the solid test of long experience, and an increasing public strength and national prosperity. They despise experience as the wisdom of unlettered men; and as for the rest, they have wrought under-ground a mine that will blow up at one grand explosion all examples of antiquity, all precedents, charters, and acts of parliament. They have 'the rights of men.' Against these there can be no prescription; against these no agreement is binding: these admit no temperament, and no compromise: any thing withheld from their full demand is so much of fraud and injustice. Against these their rights of men let no government look for security in the length of its continuance, or in the justice and lenity of its administration. The objections of these speculatists, if its forms do not quadrate with their theories, are as valid against such an old and beneficent government as against the most violent tyranny, or the greenest usurpation. They are always at issue with governments, not on a question of abuse, but a question of competency, and a question of title. I have nothing to say to the clumsy subtilty of their political metaphysics. Let them be their amusement in the schools. – 'Illa *se jactet in aula – Æolus, et clauso ventorum carcere regnet*' – But let them not break prison to burst like a Levanter, to sweep the earth with their hurricane, and to break up the fountains of the great deep to overwhelm us.

Far am I from denying in theory; full as far is my heart from withholding in practice, (if I were of power to give or to withhold,) the *real* rights of men. In denying their false claims of right, I do not mean to injure those which are real, and are such as their pretended rights would totally destroy. If civil society be made for the advantage of man, all the advantages for which it is made become his right. It is an institution of beneficence; and law itself is only beneficence acting by a rule. Men have a right to live by that rule; they have a right to justice; as between their fellows, whether their fellows are in politic function or in ordinary occupation. They have a right to the fruits of their industry; and to the means of making their industry fruitful. They have a right to the acquisitions of their parents; to the nourishment and improvement of their offspring; to instruction in life, and to consolation in death. Whatever each man can separately do, without trespassing upon others, he has a right to do for himself; and he has a right to a fair portion of all which society, with all its combinations of skill and force, can do in his favour. In this partnership all men have equal rights; but not to equal things. He that has but five shillings in the partnership, has as good a right to it, as he that has five hundred pound has to his larger proportion. But he has not a right to an equal dividend in the product of the joint stock; and as to the share of power, authority, and direction which each individual ought to have in the management of the state, that I must deny to be amongst the direct original rights of man in civil society; for I have in my contemplation the civil social man, and no other. It is a thing to be settled by convention.

If civil society be the offspring of convention, that convention must be its law. That convention must limit and modify all the descriptions of constitution which are formed under it. Every sort of legislative, judicial, or executory power are its creatures. They can have no being in any other state of things; and how can any man claim, under the conventions of civil society, rights which do not so much as suppose its existence? Rights which are absolutely repugnant to it? One of the first motives to civil society, and which becomes one of its fundamental rules, is, *that no man should be judge in his own cause.* By this each person has at once divested himself of the first fundamental right of uncovenanted man, that is, to judge for himself, and to assert his own cause. He abdicates all right to be his own governor. He inclusively, in a great measure, abandons the right of self-defence, the first law of nature. Men cannot enjoy the rights of an uncivil and of a civil state together. That he may obtain justice he gives up his right of determining what it is in points the most essential to him. That he may secure some liberty, he makes a surrender in trust of the whole of it.

Government is not made in virtue of natural rights, which may and do exist in total independence of it; and exist in much greater clearness, and in a much greater degree of abstract perfection: but their abstract perfection is their practical defect. By having a right to every thing they want every thing. Government is a contrivance of human wisdom to provide for human *wants.* Men have a right that these wants should be provided for by this wisdom. Among these wants is to be reckoned the want, out of civil society, of a sufficient restraint upon their passions. Society requires not only that the passions of individuals should be subjected, but that even in the mass and body as well as in the individuals, the inclinations of men should frequently be thwarted, their will controlled, and their passions brought into subjection. This can only be done *by a power out of themselves*; and not, in the exercise of its function, subject to that will and to those passions which it is its office to bridle and subdue. In this sense the restraints on men, as well as their liberties, are to be reckoned among their rights. But as the liberties and the restrictions vary with times and circumstances, and admit of infinite modifications, they cannot be settled upon any abstract rule; and nothing is so foolish as to discuss them upon that principle.

The moment you abate any thing from the full rights of men, each to govern himself, and suffer any artificial positive limitation upon those rights, from that moment the whole organization of government becomes a consideration of convenience. This it is which makes the constitution of a state, and the due distribution of its powers, a matter of the most delicate and complicated skill. It requires a deep knowledge of human nature and human necessities, and of the things which facilitate or obstruct the various ends which are to be pursued by the mechanism of civil institutions. The state is to have recruits to its strength, and remedies to its distempers. What is the use of discussing a man's abstract right to food or to medicine? The question is upon the method of procuring and administering them. In that deliberation I shall always advise to call in the aid of the farmer and the physician, rather than the professor of metaphysics.

The science of constructing a commonwealth, or renovating it, or reforming it, is, like every other experimental science, not to be taught à priori. Nor is it a short experience that can instruct us in that practical science; because the real effects of moral causes are not always immediate; but that which in the first instance is prejudicial may be excellent in its remoter operation; and its excellence may arise even from the ill effects it produces in the beginning. The reverse also happens; and very plausible schemes, with very pleasing commencements, have often shameful and lamentable conclusions. In states there are often some obscure and almost latent causes, things which appear at first view of little moment, on which a very great part of its prosperity or adversity may most essentially depend. The science of government being therefore so practical in itself, and intended for such practical purposes, a matter which requires experience, and even more experience than any person can gain in his whole life, however sagacious and observing he may be, it is with infinite caution that any man ought to venture upon pulling down an edifice which has answered in any tolerable degree for ages the common purposes of society, or on building it up again, without having models and patterns of approved utility before his eyes.

These metaphysic rights entering into common life, like rays of light which pierce into a dense medium, are, by the laws of nature, refracted from their straight line. Indeed in the gross and complicated mass of human passions and concerns, the primitive rights of men undergo such a variety of refractions and reflections, that it becomes absurd to talk of them as if they continued in the simplicity of their original direction. The nature of man is intricate; the objects of society are of the greatest possible complexity; and therefore no simple disposition or direction of power can be suitable either to man's nature, or to the quality of his affairs. When I hear the simplicity of contrivance aimed at and boasted of in any new political constitutions, I am at no loss to decide that the artificers are grossly ignorant of their trade, or totally negligent of their duty. The simple governments are fundamentally defective, to say no worse of them. If you were to contemplate society in but one point of view, all these simple modes of polity are infinitely captivating. In effect each would answer its single end much more perfectly than the more complex is able to attain all its complex purposes. But it is better that the whole should be imperfectly and anomalously answered, than that, while some parts are provided for with great exactness, others might be totally neglected, or perhaps materially injured, by the overcare of a favourite member.

The pretended rights of these theorists are all extremes; and in proportion as they are metaphysically true, they are morally and politically false. The rights of men are in a sort of *middle*, incapable of definition, but not impossible to be discerned. The rights of men in governments are their advantages; and these are often in balances between differences of good; in compromises sometimes between good and evil, and sometimes, between evil and evil. Political reason is a computing principle; adding, subtracting, multiplying, and dividing, morally and not metaphysically or mathematically, true moral denominations.

By these theorists the right of the people is almost always sophistically confounded with their power. The body of the community, whenever it can come to act, can meet with no effectual resistance; but till power and right are the same, the whole body of them has no right inconsistent with virtue, and the first of all virtues, prudence. Men have no right to what is not reasonable, and to what is not for their benefit; for though a pleasant writer said, *Liceat perire poetis*, when one of them, in cold blood, is said to have leaped into the flames of a volcanic revolution, *Ardentem frigidus Ætnam insiluit*, I consider such a frolic rather as an unjustifiable poetic licence, than as one of the franchises of Parnassus; and whether he were poet, or divine, or politician, that chose to exercise this kind of right, I think that more wise, because more charitable thoughts would urge me rather to save the man, than to preserve his brazen slippers as the monuments of his folly.

*   *   *

I confess to you, Sir, I never liked this continual talk of resistance and revolution, or the practice of making the extreme medicine of the constitution its daily bread. It renders the habit of society dangerously valetudinary: it is taking periodical doses of mercury sublimate, and swallowing down repeated provocatives of cantharides to our love of liberty.

This distemper of remedy, grown habitual, relaxes and wears out, by a vulgar and prostituted use, the spring of that spirit which is to be exerted on great occasions. It was in the most patient period of Roman servitude that themes of tyrannicide made the ordinary exercise of boys at school – *cum perimit sœvos classis numerosa tyrannos.* In the ordinary state of things, it produces in a country like ours the worst effects, even on the cause of that liberty which it abuses with the dissoluteness of an extravagant speculation. Almost all the high-bred republicans of my time have, after a short space, become the most decided, thorough-paced courtiers; they soon left the business of a tedious, moderate, but practical resistance, to those of us whom in the pride and intoxication of their theories, they have slighted, as not much better than tories. Hypocrisy, of course, delights in the most sublime speculations; for, never intending to go beyond speculation, it costs nothing to have it magnificent. But even in cases where rather levity than fraud was to be suspected in these ranting speculations, the issue has been much the same. These professors, finding their extreme principles not applicable to cases which call only for a qualified, or, as I may say, civil and legal resistance, in such cases employ no resistance at all. It is with them a war or a revolution, or it is nothing. Finding their schemes of politics not adapted to the state of the world in which they live, they often come to think lightly of all public principle; and are ready, on their part, to abandon for a very trivial interest what they find of very trivial value. Some indeed are of more steady and persevering natures; but these are eager politicians out of parliament, who have little to tempt them to abandon their favourite projects. They have some change in the church or state, or both, constantly in their view. When that is the case, they are always bad citizens, and perfectly unsure connexions. For, considering their speculative designs as of infinite value, and the actual arrangement of the state as of no estimation, they are at best indifferent about it.

They see no merit in the good, and no fault in the vicious management of public affairs; they rather rejoice in the latter, as more propitious to revolution. They see no merit or demerit in any man, or any action, or any political principle, any further than as they may forward or retard their design of change: they therefore take up, one day, the most violent and stretched prerogative, and another time the wildest democratic ideas of freedom, and pass from the one to the other without any sort of regard to cause, to person, or to party.

In France you are now in the crisis of a revolution, and in the transit from one form of government to another – you cannot see that character of men exactly in the same situation in which we see it in this country. With us it is militant; with you it is triumphant; and you know how it can act when its power is commensurate to its will. I would not be supposed to confine those observations to any description of men, or to comprehend all men of any description within them – No! far from it. I am as incapable of that injustice, as I am of keeping terms with those who profess principles of extremes; and who under the name of religion teach little else than wild and dangerous politics. The worst of these politics of revolution is this; they temper and harden the breast, in order to prepare it for the desperate strokes which are sometimes used in extreme occasions. But as these occasions may never arrive, the mind receives a gratuitous taint; and the moral sentiments suffer not a little, when no political purpose is served by the depravation. This sort of people are so taken up with their theories about the rights of man, that they have totally forgot his nature. Without opening one new avenue to the understanding, they have succeeded in stopping up those that lead to the heart. They have perverted in themselves, and in those that attend to them, all the well-placed sympathies of the human breast.

.   .   .

It is now sixteen or seventeen years since I saw the queen of France, then the dauphiness, at Versailles; and surely never lighted on this orb, which she hardly seemed to touch, a more delightful vision. I saw her just above the horizon, decorating and cheering the elevated sphere she just began to move in; glittering like the morning star, full of life, and splendor, and joy. Oh! what a revolution! and what an heart must I have, to contemplate without emotion that elevation and that fall! Little did I dream when she added titles of veneration to those of enthusiastic, distant, respectful love, that she should ever be obliged to carry the sharp antidote against disgrace concealed in that bosom; little did I dream that I should have lived to see such disasters fallen upon her in a nation of gallant men, in a nation of men of honour and of cavaliers. I thought ten thousand swords must have leaped from their scabbards to avenge even a look that threatened her with insult. – But the age of chivalry is gone. That of sophisters, œconomists, and calculators, has succeeded; and the glory of Europe is extinguished for ever. Never, never more, shall we behold that generous loyalty to rank and sex, that proud submission, that dignified obedience, that subordination of the heart, which kept alive, even in servitude itself, the spirit of an exalted freedom. The unbought grace of life, the cheap defence of nations, the nurse of manly sentiment and heroic enterprize, is gone! It is gone, that sensibility of principle, that chastity of honour, which felt a stain like a wound, which inspired courage whilst it mitigated ferocity, which ennobled whatever it touched, and under which vice itself lost half its evil, by losing all its grossness.

This mixed system of opinion and sentiment had its origin in the antient chivalry; and the principle, though varied in its appearance by the varying state of human affairs, subsisted and influenced through a long succession of generations, even to the time we live in. If it should ever be totally extinguished, the loss I fear will be great. It is this which has given its character to modern Europe. It is this which has distinguished it under all its forms of government, and distinguished it to its advantage, from the states of Asia, and possibly from those states which flourished in the most brilliant periods of the antique world. It was this, which, without confounding ranks, had produced a noble equality, and handed it down through all the gradations of social life. It was this opinion which mitigated kings into companions, and raised private men to be fellows with kings. Without force, or opposition, it subdued the fierceness of pride and power; it obliged sovereigns to submit to the soft collar of social esteem, compelled stern authority to submit to elegance, and gave a domination vanquisher of laws, to be subdued by manners.

But now all is to be changed. All the pleasing illusions, which made power gentle, and obedience liberal, which harmonized the different shades of life, and which, by a bland assimilation, incorporated into politics the sentiments which beautify and soften private society, are to be dissolved by this new conquering empire of light and reason. All the decent drapery of life is to be rudely torn off. All the super-added ideas, furnished from the wardrobe of a moral imagination, which the heart owns, and the understanding ratifies, as necessary to cover the defects of our naked shivering nature, and to raise it to dignity in our own estimation, are to be exploded as a ridiculous, absurd, and antiquated fashion.

On this scheme of things, a king is but a man; a queen is but a woman; a woman is but an animal; and an animal not of the highest order. All homage paid to the sex in general as such, and without distinct views, is to be regarded as romance and folly. Regicide, and parricide, and sacrilege, are but fictions of superstition, corrupting jurisprudence by destroying its simplicity. The murder of a king, or a queen, or a bishop, or a father, are only common homicide; and if the people are by any chance, or in any way gainers by it, a sort of homicide much the most pardonable, and into which we ought not to make too severe a scrutiny.

On the scheme of this barbarous philosophy, which is the offspring of cold hearts and muddy understandings, and which is as void of solid wisdom, as it is destitute of all taste and elegance, laws are to be supported only by their own terrors, and by the concern which each individual may find in them from his own private speculations, or can spare to them from his own private interests. In the groves of *their* academy, at the end of every visto, you see nothing but the gallows. Nothing is left which engages the affections on the part of the commonwealth. On the principles of this mechanic philosophy, our institutions can never be embodied, if I may use the expression, in persons; so as to create in us love, veneration, admiration, or attachment. But that sort of reason which banishes the affections is incapable of filling their place. These public affections, combined with manners, are required sometimes as supplements, sometimes as correctives, always as aids to law. The precept given by a wise man, as well as a great critic, for the construction of poems, is equally true as to states. *Non satis est pulchra esse poemata, dulcia sunto.* There ought to be a system of manners in every nation which a well-formed mind would be disposed to relish. To make us love our country, our country ought to be lovely.

But power, of some kind or other, will survive the shock in which manners and opinions perish; and it will find other and worse means for its support. The usurpation which, in order to subvert antient institutions, has destroyed antient principles, will hold power by arts similar to those by which it has acquired it. When the old feudal and chivalrous spirit of *Fealty*, which, by freeing kings from fear, freed both kings and subjects from the precautions of tyranny, shall be extinct in the minds of men, plots and assassinations will be anticipated by preventive murder and preventive confiscation, and that long roll of grim and bloody maxims, which form the political code of all power, not standing on its own honour, and the honour of those who are to obey it. Kings will be tyrants from policy when subjects are rebels from principle.

When antient opinions and rules of life are taken away, the loss cannot possibly be estimated. From that moment we have no compass to govern us; nor can we know distinctly to what port we steer. Europe undoubtedly, taken in a mass, was in a flourishing condition the day on which your Revolution was compleated. How much of that prosperous state was owing to the spirit of our old manners and opinions is not easy to say; but as such causes cannot be indifferent in their operation, we must presume, that, on the whole, their operation was beneficial.

We are but too apt to consider things in the state in which we find them, without sufficiently adverting to the causes by which they have been produced, and possibly may be upheld. Nothing is more certain, than that our manners, our civilization, and all the good things which are connected with manners, and with civilization, have, in this European world of ours, depended for ages upon two principles; and were indeed the result of both combined; I mean the spirit of a gentleman, and the spirit of religion. The nobility and the clergy, the one by profession, the other by patronage, kept learning in existence, even in the midst of arms and confusions, and whilst governments were rather in their causes than formed. Learning paid back what it received to nobility and to priesthood; and paid it with usury, by enlarging their ideas, and by furnishing their minds. Happy if they had all continued to know their indissoluble union, and their proper place! Happy if learning, not debauched by ambition, had been satisfied to continue the instructor, and not aspired to be the master! Along with its natural protectors and guardians, learning will be cast into the mire, and trodden down under the hoofs of a swinish multitude.

If, as I suspect, modern letters owe more than they are always willing to own to antient manners, so do other interests which we value full as much as they are worth. Even commerce, and trade, and manufacture, the gods of our œconomical politicians, are themselves perhaps but creatures; are themselves but effects, which, as first causes, we choose to worship. They certainly grew under the same shade in which learning flourished. They too may decay with their natural protecting principles. With you, for the present at least, they all threaten to disappear together. Where trade and manufacturers are wanting to a people, and the spirit of nobility and religion remains, sentiment supplies and not always ill supplies their place; but if commerce and the arts should be lost in an experiment to try how well a state may stand without these old fundamental principles, what sort of a thing must be a nation of gross, stupid, ferocious, and at the same time, poor and sordid barbarians, destitute of religion, honour, or manly pride, possessing nothing at present, and hoping for nothing hereafter?

I wish you may not be going fast, and by the shortest cut, to that horrible and disgustful situation. Already there appears a poverty of conception, a coarseness and vulgarity in all the proceedings of the assembly and of all their instructors. Their liberty is not liberal. Their science is presumptuous ignorance. their humanity is savage and brutal.

It is not clear, whether in England we learned those grand and decorous principles, and manners, of which considerable traces yet remain, from you, or whether you took them from us. But to you, I think, we trace them best. You seem to me to be '*gentis incunabula nostrœ.*' France has always more or less influenced manners in England; and when your fountain is choaked up and polluted, the stream will not run long, or not run clear with us, or perhaps with any nation. This gives all Europe, in my opinion, but too close and connected a concern in what is done in France. Excuse me, therefore, if I have dwelt too long on the atrocious spectacle of the sixth of October 1789, or have given too much scope to the reflections which have arisen in my mind on occasion of the most important of all revolutions, which may be dated from that day, I mean a revolution in sentiments, manners, and moral opinions. As things now stand, with every thing respectable destroyed without us, and an attempt to destroy within us every principle of respect, one is almost forced to apologize for harbouring the common feelings of men.

. . .

If it could have been made clear to me, that the king and queen of France (those I mean who were such before the triumph) were inexorable and cruel tyrants, that they had formed a deliberate scheme for massacring the National Assembly (I think I have seen something like the latter insinuated in certain publications) I should think their captivity just. If this be true, much more ought to have been done, but done, in my opinion, in another manner. The punishment of real tyrants is a noble and awful act of justice; and it has with truth been said to be consolatory to the human mind. But if I were to punish a wicked king, I should regard the dignity in avenging the crime. Justice is grave and decorous, and in its punishments rather seems to submit to a necessity, than to make a choice. Had Nero, or Agrippina, or Louis the Eleventh, or Charles the Ninth, been the subject; if Charles the Twelfth of Sweden, after the murder of Patkul, or his predecessor Christina, after the murder of Monaldeschi, had fallen into your hands, Sir, or into mine, I am sure our conduct would have been different.

* * *

I almost venture to affirm, that not one in a hundred amongst us participates in the 'triumph' of the Revolution Society. If the king and queen of France, and their children, were to fall into our hands by the chance of war, in the most acrimonious of all hostilities (I deprecate such an event, I deprecate such hostility) they would be treated with another sort of triumphal entry into London. We formerly have had a king of France in that situation; you have read how he was treated by the victor in the field; and in what manner he was afterwards received in England. Four hundred years have gone over us; but I believe we are not materially changed since that period. Thanks to our sullen resistance to innovation, thanks to the cold sluggishness of our national character, we still bear the stamp of our forefathers. We have not, as I conceive, lost the generosity and dignity of thinking of the fourteenth century; nor as yet have we subtilized ourselves into savages. We are not the converts of Rousseau; we are not the disciples of Voltaire; Helvetius has made no progress amongst us. Atheists are not our preachers; madmen are not our lawgivers. We know that we have made no discoveries, and we think that no discoveries are to be made, in morality; nor many in the great principles of government, nor in the ideas of liberty, which were understood long before we were born, altogether as well as they will be after the grave has heaped its mould upon our presumption, and the silent tomb shall have imposed its law on our pert loquacity. In England we have not yet been completely embowelled of our natural entrails; we still feel within us, and we cherish and cultivate, those inbred sentiments which are the faithful guardians, the active monitors of our duty, the true supporters of all liberal and manly morals. We have not been drawn and trussed, in order that we may be filled, like stuffed birds in a museum, with chaff and rags, and paltry blurred shreds of paper about the rights of man. We preserve the whole of our feelings still native and entire, unsophisticated by pedantry and infidelity. We have real hearts of flesh and blood beating in our bosoms. We fear God; we look up with awe to kings; with affection to parliaments; with duty to magistrates; with reverence to priests; and with respect to nobility*. Why? Because when such ideas are brought before our minds, it is *natural* to be so affected; because all other feelings are false and spurious, and tend to corrupt our minds, to vitiate our primary morals, to render us unfit for rational liberty; and by teaching us a servile, licentious, and abandoned insolence, to be our low sport for a few holidays, to make us perfectly fit for, and justly deserving of slavery, through the whole course of our lives.

You see, Sir, that in this enlightened age I am bold enough to confess, that we are generally men of untaught feelings; that instead of casting away all our old prejudices, we cherish them to a very considerable degree, and, to take more shame to ourselves, we cherish them because they are prejudices; and the longer they have lasted, and the more generally they have prevailed, the more we cherish them. We are afraid to put men to live and trade each on his own private stock of reason; because we suspect that this stock in each man is small, and that the individuals would do better to avail themselves of the general bank and capital of nations, and of ages. Many of our men of speculation, instead of exploding general prejudices, employ their sagacity to discover the latent wisdom which prevails in them. If they find what they seek, (and they seldom fail) they think it more wise to continue the prejudice, with the reason involved, than to cast away the coat of prejudice, and to leave nothing but the naked reason; because prejudice, with its reason, has a motive to give action to that reason, and an affection which will give it permanence. Prejudice is of ready application in the emergency; it previously engages the mind in a steady course of wisdom and virtue, and does not leave the man hesitating in the moment of decision, sceptical, puzzled, and unresolved. Prejudice renders a man's virtue his habit; and not a series of unconnected acts. Through just prejudice, his duty becomes a part of his nature.

Your literary men, and your politicians, and so do the whole clan of

*The English are, I conceive, misrepresented in a Letter published in one of the papers, by a gentleman thought to be a dissenting minister. – When writing to Dr. Price, of the spirit which prevails at Paris, he says, 'The spirit of the people in this place has abolished all the proud *distinctions* which the king and *nobles* had usurped in their minds; whether they talk of *the king, the noble, or the priest*, their whole language is that of the most *enlightened and liberal amongst the English.*' If this gentleman means to confine the terms *enlightened and liberal* to one set of men in England, it may be true. It is not generally so.

the enlightened among us, essentially differ in these points. They have no respect for the wisdom of others; but they pay it off by a very full measure of confidence in their own. With them it is a sufficient motive to destroy an old scheme of things, because it is an old one. As to the new, they are in no sort of fear with regard to the duration of a building run up in haste; because duration is no object to those who think little or nothing has been done before their time, and who place all their hopes in discovery. They conceive, very systematically, that all things which give perpetuity are mischievous, and therefore they are at inexpiable war with all establishments. They think that government may vary like modes of dress, and with as little ill effect. That there needs no principle of attachment, except a sense of present conveniency, to any constitution of the state. They always speak as if they were of opinion that there is a singular species of compact between them and their magistrates, which binds the magistrate, but which has nothing reciprocal in it, but that the majesty of the people has a right to dissolve it without any reason, but its will. Their attachment to their country itself, is only so far as it agrees with some of their fleeting projects; it begins and ends with that scheme of polity which falls in with their momentary opinion.

. . .

But one of the first and most leading principles on which the commonwealth and the laws are consecrated, is lest the temporary possessors and life-renters in it, unmindful of what they have received from their ancestors, or of what is due to their posterity, should act as if they were the entire masters; that they should not think it amongst their rights to cut off the entail, or commit waste on the inheritance, by destroying at their pleasure the whole original fabric of their society; hazarding to leave to those who come after them, a ruin instead of an habitation, and teaching these successors as little to respect their contrivances, as they had themselves respected the institutions of their forefathers. By this unprincipled facility of changing the state as often, and as much, and in as many ways, as there are floating fancies or fashions, the whole chain and continuity of the commonwealth would be broken. No one generation could link with the other. Men would become little better than the flies of a summer.

And first of all, the science of jurisprudence, the pride of the human intellect, which, with all its defects, redundancies, and errors, is the collected reason of ages, combining the principles of original justice with the infinite variety of human concerns, as a heap of old exploded errors, would be no longer studied. Personal self-sufficiency and arrogance, the certain attendants upon all those who have never experienced a wisdom greater than their own, would usurp the tribunal. Of course, no certain laws, establishing invariable grounds of hope and fear, would keep the actions of men in a certain course, or direct them to a certain end. Nothing stable in the modes of holding property, or exercising function, could form a solid ground on which any parent could speculate in the education of his offspring, or in a choice for their future establishment in the world. No principles would be early worked into the habits. As soon as the most able instructor had completed his laborious course of institution, instead of sending forth his pupil, accomplished in a virtuous discipline, fitted to procure him attention and respect, in his place in society, he would find everything altered; and that he had turned out a poor creature to the contempt and derision of the world, ignorant of the true grounds of estimation. Who would insure a tender and delicate sense of honour to beat almost with the first pulses of the heart, when no man could know what would be the test of honour in a nation, continually varying the standard of its coin? No part of life would retain its acquisitions. Barbarism with regard to science and literature, unskilfulness with regard to arts and manufactures, would infallibly succeed to the want of a steady education and settled principle; and thus the commonwealth itself would, in a few generations, crumble away, be disconnected into the dust and powder of individuality, and at length dispersed to all the winds of heaven.

To avoid therefore the evils of inconstancy and versatility, ten thousand times worse than those of obstinacy and the blindest prejudice, we have *consecrated* the state; that no man should approach to look into its defects or corruptions but with due caution; that he should never dream of beginning its reformation by its subversion; that he should approach to the faults of the state as to the wounds of a father, with pious awe and trembling solicitude. By this wise prejudice we are taught to look with horror on those children of their country who are prompt rashly to hack that aged parent in pieces, and put him into the kettle of magicians, in hopes that by their poisonous weeds, and wild incantations, they may regenerate the paternal constitution, and renovate their father's life.

Society is indeed a contract. Subordinate contracts, for objects of mere occasional interest, may be dissolved at pleasure; but the state ought not to be considered as nothing better than a partnership agreement in a trade of pepper and coffee, callico or tobacco, or some other such low concern, to be taken up for a little temporary interest, and to be dissolved by the fancy of the parties. It is to be looked on with other reverence; because it is not a partnership in things subservient only to the gross animal existence of a temporary and perishable nature. It is a partnership in all science; a partnership in all art; a partnership in every virtue, and in all perfection. As the ends of such a partnership cannot be obtained in many generations, it becomes a partnership not only between those who are living, but between those who are living, those who are dead, and those who are to be born. Each contract of each particular state is but a clause in the great primæval contract of eternal society, linking the lower with the higher natures, connecting the visible and invisible world, according to a fixed compact sanctioned by the inviolable oath which holds all physical and all moral natures, each in their appointed place. This law is not subject to the will of those, who by an obligation above them, and infinitely superior, are bound to submit their will to that law. The municipal corporations of that universal kingdom are not morally at liberty at their pleasure, and on their speculations of a contingent improvement, wholly to separate and tear asunder the bands of their subordinate community, and to dissolve it into an unsocial, uncivil, unconnected chaos of elementary principles. It is the first and supreme necessity only, a necessity that is not chosen but chooses, a necessity paramount to deliberation, that admits no discussion, and demands no evidence, which alone can justify a resort to anarchy. This necessity is no exception to the rule; because this necessity itself is a part too of that moral and physical disposition of things to which man must be obedient by consent or force. But if that which is only submission to necessity should be made the object of choice, the law is broken; nature is disobeyed; and the rebellious are outlawed, cast forth, and exiled, from this world of reason, and order, and peace, and virtue, and fruitful penitence, into the antagonist world of madness, discord, vice, confusion, and unavailing sorrow.

* * *

∽ 5 ∾

Karl Marx's
'On the Jewish Question'

I

It is perhaps worth recording that the author of 'On the Jewish Question' was himself born into a Jewish family, in the Rhineland town of Trier in 1818. The beginning of the nineteenth century was a difficult time for German Jews. Though there was a measure of civil equality, there was still considerable discrimination against Jews in the professions: Marx's father was obliged to undergo a nominal conversion to Protestant Christianity in order to retain his position as a legal official. It is unclear to what extent Jewish customs were practised in the household Marx grew up in and how much influence either the rabbinical tradition of his family or the experience of discrimination had on the young Marx. Certainly anti-Semitic jibes were often flung at him by opponents in later controversies. And since Marx himself was not above using the rhetoric of anti-Semitism when it suited his polemic purposes – 'What is the secular cult of the Jew? Haggling. What is his secular god? Money.'[1] – there is at least some evidence for the suggestion that he suffered from the pathological Jewish self-hate typical of many of the victims of that prejudice.[2]

In other respects Marx's upbringing was that of the privileged son of an educated bourgeois family. He read for a degree in law first at the University of Bonn, then at Berlin, and it was at Berlin that he came under the influence of Hegelian philosophy. The effect of that influence cannot be overestimated: though from an early stage Marx defined his own thought in conscious opposition to the detail of Hegelian social theory, he remained transfixed by Hegel's overall project of charting history as the development, transformation and resolution of mankind into an organic whole, self-consciously in control of a world of its own making. Throughout the 1830s Marx involved himself in the regular discussions of a group of Hegel's followers in Berlin – the group we know as the 'Young Hegelians'. As

Marx's interest turned towards philosophy, he abandoned the idea of a legal career (like Bentham and Burke, he never practised the law he studied), embarking instead on the doctoral dissertation that would be necessary to secure an academic post. The completed dissertation (on the philosophy of Epicurus) was submitted to the University of Jena, and Marx was duly rewarded with his doctorate. But he was never able to use it as a professional qualification. In 1842 he embarked on a career as a journalist; the increasingly radical content of his writing made it necessary for him to live in more or less perpetual exile, and quite impossible for him to obtain a faculty position in a university.

The focus of the Young Hegelian movement was largely on the question of how religion was to be understood in the development of the human spirit. Not content with the conservative reading of Hegel that regarded the mere existence of organized religion as a guarantee of its rationality, many of the Young Hegelians viewed religion in secular and critical terms, attacking it as a transitory, inadequate and obsolescent product of human consciousness.[3] That in turn led to political criticism: to a critique of the conditions that generated religious belief, and of the legal and political structures by which Christianity was sustained. Prominent among Marx's Young Hegelian friends was Bruno Bauer, a university lecturer in theology. Bauer collaborated with Marx on a number of projects in the early 1840s, mostly attempts to demonstrate the mythic character of Christianity, to excoriate readings of Hegel that purported to lend philosophical credibility to those myths, and to attack the Prussian ideology of 'a Christian state'.[4]

However, as the distinctively materialist and socialist sides of Marx's thought developed, he began to distance himself increasingly from his Young Hegelian colleagues. At Bauer's suggestion he started writing for a progressive Rhineland newspaper, the *Rheinische Zeitung*, and later became its editor. He wrote on political matters and increasingly on social and economic questions in a way that led in 1843 to the suppression of the paper. But though his own articles had this effect, Marx was often critical of what he took to be the politically naive and irresponsible behaviour of the Berlin members of the Young Hegelian circle. The social criticism of this group – 'Die Freien' or the Free Thinkers – was, he believed, an immoderate and ungrounded form of intellectual élitism, out of touch with the concerns of the mass of the people and the social realities that might lend some credibility to political criticism. Whereas the Free Thinkers affected a communist posture, Marx declared 'that to introduce, as contraband as it were, socialist and communist ideas . . . into incidental theatre reviews was indecent and even immoral'.[5] And when they sneered at the political endeavours of the bourgeois, it was Marx who reminded them of the importance of those 'liberals . . . who have assumed the thankless and painful task of conquering liberty, step by step, within the limits imposed by the constitution'.[6]

At the same time as he was pressing for a more realistic and practical politics of radicalism, Marx was developing an account of the relation between politics and society that would lead eventually to his repudiation (as opposed to reinterpretation) of Hegel's political philosophy. His experience as a journalist in the early 1840s covering, first, the deliberations of the Rhineland Parliament on property laws, and second, the impoverishment of Mosel winegrowers convinced him that law and politics could not be regarded as autonomous activities but should be seen as something determined and conditioned by relations in the social and economic sphere. This led Marx to rethink the Hegelian emphasis on the state: 'My investigation led to the conclusion . . . that legal relations as well as forms of state are to be understood neither in themselves nor from the so-called general development of the human mind, but rather had their roots in the material conditions of life.'[7] It followed that the success of the struggle for political freedom depended not on the cleverness of radical argument, nor even on the *realpolitik* of revolutionaries versus policemen, but in the last resort on the necessity for political freedom in relation to the development of economic forces. The materialism of this approach also had other corollaries which were likely to be unpalatable to idealistic intellectuals like Bauer. If it was the sphere of material activity that determined the reality of human life, then any plausible account of human freedom and human fulfilment would have to be given primarily in material and economic terms, and any plausible account of alienation and oppression should be focused primarily on the conditions of labour rather than on the frustration of the life of the mind.

It is against this background that we should read Marx's critique of Bruno Bauer in 'On the Jewish Question'. Bauer had written a series of articles on Jewish emancipation for the periodical *Deutsche Jahrbücher* – a periodical that Marx had been associated with and which he was to revive briefly in Paris in the form of the *Deutsche-französische Jahrbücher* in 1844.

The issue was the vexed one of how strenuously one should campaign for political and civil rights to be accorded to Jews in what purported, in Prussia at any rate, to be a Christian st e. Both Marx and Bauer were, of course, opposed to the latter idea. But Bauer argued that as long as Jews retained and flaunted the distinctiveness of their Jewishness, they were unlikely to achieve true emancipation. If a people 'does not progress with History, . . . if it keeps aloof from political passions, then it lacks one of the most important incentives to exalted and pure morality.'[8] To this Marx replied in his essay that political emancipation, for what it was worth in the bourgeois state, was perfectly compatible with the persistence of religious distinctions; but this, he thought, showed how far short of true human freedom political emancipation fell. True emancipation could only be achieved by people taking control of the material conditions of their lives. Though Bauer's intention in the original paper had been in fact quite limited, Marx was obviously taking the opportunity to articulate a much broader position in his review article – in fact it set out the whole basis of his developing view of the nature of human fulfilment in the context of the liberal state.

The bulk of 'On the Jewish Question' had been written while Marx was in the Rhineland, but he brought it with him to Paris and published it in the *Deutsche-französische Jahrbücher* in 1844. He also published another piece in the same issue of the journal – 'Towards a Critique of Hegel's *Philosophy of Right*: An Introduction'. Hegel, too, had been sceptical about the rights of man as an expression of true human freedom. He regarded them as empty, abstract and fanatical, reducing 'the union of individuals in the state to a contract and therefore to something based on their arbitrary wills, their opinion, and their capriciously given express consent'. The effect of trying to reconstruct a state on this basis, 'after the destruction of all existing and given material', ended inevitably 'in the maximum of frightfulness and terror'.[9] What was lacking, according to Hegel, was any substantial basis of ethical life in a rights-based state: *Sittlichkeit*, a collective ethical way of life, something over and above the individual in which the individual could orient his otherwise meagre subjective consciousness. Now though Marx agreed with Hegel in taking 'the individual in isolation' as the guiding thread of theories of natural rights, he was impatient with the view that what was needed to remedy this individualism was great participation in ethical life. What was needed, he said, was something which turned the Hegelian philosophy upside-down: greater involvement with the messy business of man's natural life of labour, production, interaction with nature, industry and material consumption. Human emancipation was retarded not by lack of ethics, but by poverty and exploitation. The essay on Hegel introduced for the first time into Marx's writing the idea of the revolutionary overthrow of the existing order by the proletariat – 'a class with radical chains'[10] – and this was the direction that all Marx's subsequent political writing took.

The double number that contained these essays was the first and last issue of the *Deutsche-französische Jahrbücher*. It ceased publication in 1844 due to a combination of factors: financial difficulties, difficulties with censorship and distribution, ideological disagreements among the contributors, and so on. Marx by this time was working closely with Friedrich Engels, heir to a bourgeois manufacturing fortune, and the two of them marked the extent of their break with the rump of the Young Hegelians in the publication of works like *The Holy Family*, which was an onslaught on (a caricature of) the ideas of the Bauer brothers, and later *The German Ideology*, which articulated their materialist view of history and, in Engels's words, 'settled accounts with our former philosophical views'.[11]

Early in 1845 the French government responding to Prussian pressure expelled Marx and other German radicals from Paris, and Marx and Engels left for Brussels. There they founded an international Communist League – the direct ancestor of most modern Communist parties – and drafted *The Communist Manifesto*. That work spoke of 'a spectre . . . haunting Europe' – the spectre of proletarian uprising.[12] It contained an analysis of history, a characterization of the 'contradictions' of bourgeois society, a vilification of other communist movements, and a call for universal suffrage to enable workers to gain power and implement a programme based on the abolition of landed and industrial property.

The year of failed revolution in Europe, 1848–9, saw Marx in Paris once more, expelled from Brussels, and then in Cologne and London. He took a deep interest in the revolutionary movements that convulsed Europe during his life, in 1848 and in 1871. In this the point of reference for him, as for all contemporary thinkers, was of course the French Revolution of 1789. Marx returned to that theme many times, but though he celebrated the fall of the *ancien régime*, he never characterized it as anything other than a bourgeois revolution. Historically its task was 'the unchaining and setting up modern bourgeois society' and breaking down the feudal impediments to capitalist industry and national unity.[13] In that the bourgeoisie succeeded: 'The Revolution was a "failure" only for the mass . . . whose real conditions for emancipation were substantially different from the conditions within which the bourgeoisie could emancipate itself and society.'[14] Subsequent upheavals in France were even less significant: mere *coups d'état*, on Marx's account: but 'the next attempt of the French Revolution will be no longer, as before, to transfer the bureaucratic-military machine from one hand to another, but to smash it, and this is the preliminary condition for every real people's revolution on the Continent'.[15]

As well as his political agitation, Marx was working all this time towards his greatest achievement – a systematic account in economic terms of the rise of modern capitalism, the nature of capitalist production, the laws of commodity exchange, the determination of wages and the length of the working day, the effects of mechanization, and the shape and likely results of the successive crises that he believed would eventually wrack the capitalist economic order. Marx's economics was embodied above all in *Capital*, written in London, the first volume of which was published in 1867. (The second and third volumes exist only in an incomplete form.) The nature and scale of this economic project represent in many ways a break with the spread of Marx's philosophical and cultural endeavours in earlier years. Some commentators have suggested that there is a decisive rupture between the concerns of the author of *Capital* and the later works and those of the early Marx.[16] On this account the early Marx was concerned with humanistic themes – alienation, exploitation, and so on – while the later Marx was concerned more with the natural history of social structures and with human individuals only to the extent that they could be regarded as *Träge* of social relations defined independently of them.[17] 'On the Jewish Question' would certainly fall on the earlier, humanistic side of this gap. But the rupture itself is probably exaggerated. The *Capital* project required an enormous concentration of effort on just a few of the themes that had been developed in the early writings. But very few of the other early themes disappear altogether from view. Though there is apparently less explicit discussion in Marx's later work about human emancipation and the nature of alienation in the modern world, and though the *terms* 'freedom' and 'alienation' are not used so often, it is arguable that the effect of much of the Marxian economics is to give serious and sustained *substance* to those ideas rather than to pass them by.

Though Marx foretold the end of capitalism, he never wrote much about the shape or structure of the socialist society he expected to take its place. Some of his later writings on events in the 1870s have been treated by commentators as though they contained an implicit theory of politics. In *The Civil War in France* his enthusiastic discussion of the Commune of 1871 is taken to indicate a belief that its 'pyramidal' democratic structure of revocable delegates prefigured the political structures Marx believed would (or should) exist under socialism.[18] But the fact is that Marx said very little on the subject, and what little he did write about post-capitalist political structures – *Critique of the Gotha Programme* is the best example – was usually occasioned by his fury at some half-baked scheme put forward by other people who called themselves communists.

There seem to have been two reasons for this reticence. On the one hand, Marx claimed to repudiate all forms of Utopian speculation as unscientific. He believed that socialist organization was inevitable, on social and economic grounds, and saw no point in, as he put it, 'writing recipes for the cookshops of the future'.[19] The point was to involve oneself in the social processes that were leading to the change, not to try and anticipate it in speculative thought. The other reason is more complicated. Marx seems to have believed (and certainly Engels and later Lenin did) that under socialism the need for state forms and politics as we know it would gradually disappear. The state, as Engels put it, would 'wither away' and 'the government of men would be replaced by the administration of things'.[20] This belief develops one of the main themes of 'On the Jewish Question' – the denial of the intrinsic importance of politics, considered as a sphere apart from material life. In his later work Marx appears to have believed that politics and the state were necessitated by class conflict, either as a direct coercive agency of the dominant class or as a power standing apart from the classes which prevented class conflict from becoming internecine. Once the capitalist state was overthrown, residual class conflict would persist for a while, and there would be a need for what he called 'a dictatorship of the proletariat'.[21] But that would be a transitional period, for the proletariat distinguished itself from other ruling classes by standing for all the oppressed and not rising on the basis of the oppression of any other group. Gradually, then, the need for its political dominance of other segments of society would diminish, while at the same time the prosperity that socialist production involved would increasingly free humanity from the need to rely on coercive mechanisms of distribution.

Marx's silence on issues of political organization, then, from the publication of 'On the Jewish Question' in 1844 to his death in London nearly forty years later, is not difficult to explain. But it has left a very significant lacuna in modern socialist thought, a tradition which is still largely dominated by the Marxian legacy. There is a widespread conviction amongst Marxist-Leninists that it is unnecessary to address issues of power, right and political freedom in the way that other political theorists have. Under capitalism, civil and political freedoms are an empty sham; under socialism, any preoccupation with them will turn out to be redundant. Unfortunately, however, government and politics, the power of man over man, have not so far withered away with the demise of class conflict in the socialist societies of China, the USSR and Eastern Europe. Though the oldest of these states has been governed now by a communist party for seventy years, it still regards itself as a 'transitional' form, and takes that as a justification for avoiding (and banning) any serious theoretical work on how the power of state agencies may be limited and controlled in 'the higher phase of socialism'.[22] Over the last thirty years or so, there have been attempts by many socialists to come to grips with the idea of human rights and to consider whether it could be given a distinctively socialist content.[23] Opinions about the point and success of that enterprise vary. What is clear, though, is that it finds precious little basis in Marx's work subsequent to 1844, and precious little support in the writings of his immediate followers.

II

The vulgar Marxist line on human rights is well known. It is that, in their traditional formulations, doctrines of rights present the pre-occupations of the bourgeois capitalist individual as though they were universal and compelling principles of human nature. In their content, the alleged rights of man are said to reflect the wish of the capitalist entrepreneur to be free from social restriction and responsibility, and free of any concern for the welfare (or even the freedom) of those whom he exploits. The right to liberty, the right to property, the right to personal security, and the right to resist any government that gets in the way of bourgeois activity – these are all rights whose fundamental orientation is towards the selfish desires of the acquisitive individual. Marxists will also argue that bourgeois ideology permeates not just the content but the very *form* of rights. The form is individualistic: it presupposes that the potential for conflict between individuals in the society will always be so great that each person needs some coercively maintained guarantee that the acts of others will not imperil the pursuit and fulfilment of her interests. Furthermore, the abstraction of rights-principles commits us to an artificial and legalistic myopia: it allows us to neglect the differences and inequalities that matter in the world, between those who have and those who do not have control over the means of production. With this form and this content, human rights may be fit for the life of capitalist society; but, it is maintained, they will have no place in the harmonious communism to which capitalism and the lower phase of socialism will eventually give way.

Many of Karl Marx's arguments in 'On the Jewish Question' appear to support this version of the Marxist view of rights. When he discusses what the French Declaration of 1793 had taken as the fundamental rights of man – liberty, property, security and equality – Marx commented that 'the so-called rights of man . . . are nothing but the rights of the member of civil society, i.e. egoistic man, separated from other men and from the community' (p. 145). According to Marx, man as a member of civil society is man acting within the forms of capitalist industry and capitalist economy – a private individual pursuing material gain in a context where all his relations with others are mediated by the market and commodity exchange. The suggestion is that the rights of man, though they purport to be universal or even 'natural' in character, are rights which make sense only in relation to that particular phase of social and economic organization.

In his book *Marx and Justice* Allen Buchanan has argued that in saying the rights of man were 'nothing but' the rights of egoistic man, Marx meant that such rights were *valuable only for* egoists in this social context.[24] There are, I think, slight problems with this interpretation. It is true that Marx believed rights would be pursued only by people of that sort and in that context: other people in other forms of society would not see the point of these concerns. But Buchanan's 'valuable only for' says more than that. It seems to suggest an objective relation of value which makes little sense in the context of Marx's historicism. The stronger claim that Marx *is* making is, I think, about the identity and constitution of the members of civil society and their self-interest. He is suggesting that the concerns articulated by these rights are constitutive of the mentality of the member of capitalist civil society and correspondingly that one cannot have a genuine capitalist economy in which these guarantees are not juridically provided.

On the particular rights themselves, Marx's comments are crude and predictable. (It is quite impossible to agree with Ernst Bloch that Marx exposes the bourgeois content of these rights 'with unsurpassable sharpness'.[25]) Noting that the right to liberty is defined as 'the power of doing anything that does not harm others', Marx suggests it leads each person to see in others the limitation of his freedom. Each individual is to have a fenced-off domain of freedom from which others are excluded, so that the freedom in question involves only what Mill was later to call 'self-regarding action'. 'The freedom in question', says Marx, 'is that of a man treated as an isolated monad and withdrawn into himself' (p. 146).

Once property comes into the picture, the fences around each individual are presented, not just as negative guarantees of isolation, but as positive obstacles to the individual's responsibility to others. Though the private property owner is still withdrawn into himself, his actions are no longer innocuous: 'The right of man to property is the right to enjoy his possessions and dispose of the same arbitrarily without regard for other men, independent of society, the right of selfishness' (p. 146). Equality and security add little to the picture in Marx's opinion. Equality secures this anti-social freedom to each individual without discrimination. And security constitutes these rights as *guarantees*, as 'the assurance of egoism' (p. 147).

Other less fundamental aspects of the rights of man are viewed as equally atomistic in character. Freedom of conscience or religious freedom means that, in modern society, religion is no longer a state institution but becomes a purely private matter:

> It has become the expression of the separation of man from his common essence, from himself and from other men, as it was originally. It is still only the abstract recognition of a particular perversion, private whim, and arbitrariness. . . . It is shoved away into the crowd of private interests and exiled from the common essence as such. (p. 142)

Of course, Marx is not suggesting the idea of civic religion be resurrected; merely that we should not be surprised when the religious impulse surfaces in the form of privatized conscience and a plurality of sects in a society dominated by human rights.

What Marx says about these rights, then, is bound up with his general view of man in capitalist society. Such a society fosters an illusion of self-sufficient atomism – of individuals free of any essential dependence on others. But their needs and the real basis of their life make the illusion of individualism transparent.

> The egotistic individual in civil society may in his non-sensuous imagination and lifeless abstraction inflate himself to the size of an atom, i.e. to an unrelated, self sufficient, wantless, absolutely full, blessed being. Unblessed sensuous reality does not bother about his imagination; each of his senses compels him to believe in the existence of the world and the individuals outside him, and even his profane stomach reminds him that the world outside him is not empty but is what really fills. Every activity and property of his being, every one of his vital urges becomes a need, a necessity,

which his self seeking transforms into seeking for other things and human beings outside him.[26]

The natural individual was therefore a fantasy of political economy. As Marx put it in the *Grundrisse*: 'Man is in the most literal sense of the word a *zoon politikon*, not only a social animal, but an animal which can develop into an individual only in society.'[27] Though these truths were evident, Marx believed, they were implicitly denied in the culture and consciousness of civil society. The price was high. The individual in that society was pictured by Marx in the most piteous terms: 'Uncultivated and unsocial, . . . corrupted by the whole organization of society, lost to himself, sold, given over to the domination of inhuman conditions and elements, . . . [he] treats other men as means, degrades himself to a means, and becomes the plaything of alien powers' (p. 140).

The rights of man, then, symbolized for Marx the alienation of the human from what he called in his early writings 'species being' – the manifestation of life in and through social activity and social enjoyment.[28] Though they appeared to be oriented towards freedom, they ignore the aspects of social life that would be necessary for true emancipation. Instead they presented social life 'as a framework exterior to individuals, a limitation of their original self-sufficiency'. And this preoccupation with the rights of man arose in the context of, and was bound up with, processes which 'tear asunder all the species-bonds of man, put egoism and selfish need in the place of those species-bonds and dissolve man into a world of atomistic individuals with hostile attitudes towards each other' (p. 147).

III

According to some commentators, this is more or less *all* Marx has to say about human rights.[29] If that were true, then socialist hostility to human rights in the Marxist tradition would have an obvious canonical explanation. In fact Marx's position is much more subtle than the account so far suggests.

Marx took very seriously the distinction in the title of the French Declaration between the rights of *man* and the rights of *the citizen*. The former, 'as different from the rights of the citizen', are to Marx nothing but the rights of egoistic man (p. 145). But citizens' rights, as such, cannot be so easily dismissed. The right to participate in shaping the general will (Article III), the free communication of thoughts and opinions (Article XI), the right to demand an account from public officials (Article XV), and democratic rights in general: none of these can be made sense of as the rights of 'an isolated monad withdrawn into himself' or even as the right to do something 'without regard for other men' (p. 146). On the contrary such rights are explicitly constitutive of certain forms of action in common with others, and Marx recognizes that. In political community, he writes, man 'counts as a species being' (p. 141) and 'is valued as a communal being' (p. 140), as 'a moral person' (p. 150). Political rights, he goes on, are 'rights that are only exercised in community with other men' (p. 144). The suggestion seems to be that, in their form at least, these rights help to constitute the sort of community that Marx expects to see in the final phases of human emancipation.

But though political rights are taken seriously in this way, political freedom and the creation of a political community in a capitalist society are also said to have serious limitations. 'Political emancipation is of course a great progress. Although it is not the final form of human emancipation in general, it is nevertheless the final form of human emancipation inside the present world order' (p. 141). There seem to be several things Marx is getting at when he expresses these doubts and qualifications about the impact of universal citizens' rights.

To begin with, he points out that the dismantling of religious and proprietary disqualifications from the franchise does not count as full emancipation, because people's private lives continue to be dominated by religious and proprietary considerations. 'The state', he says, 'can liberate itself from a limitation without man himself being truly free of it' (p. 139). In the USA, for example, where there is a rigid separation of church and state, 'the overwhelming majority of people is still religious' (p. 138). Similarly, even though socio-economic differences may have no formal political status, they still 'have an effect in their own manner' (p. 140). Buchanan interprets this last remark as a Marxian allusion to the idea that 'inequalities in social position continue to exert a pernicious influence through both legal and illegal channels'.[30] But Marx's suggestion is deeper than that familiar allegation of the corruption of politics and political equality by inequalities of wealth. He is alluding to the idea that religion and private property are both alienated forms of life, and that their removal from the political sphere does not remove – indeed it may enhance – their expression of man's basic self-alienation. It does not prevent them from acting as obstacles to genuine social understanding.

Secondly, Marx toys with the view that liberal political equality is not religiously neutral but is itself a Christian idea (just as he toys in Part II of the essay with the apparently anti-Semitic view that haggling over money is the secular expression of Judaism): 'What makes a political democracy Christian is the fact that in it man, not only a single man but every man, counts as a sovereign being' (p. 143). The view is not developed much further than this, and it is simply impossible to tell from the immediate context whether or not this is regarded as a progressive aspect of Christianity.

A third point, however, is the most important. The most powerful criticism that Marx makes is that political emancipation, in a bourgeois context, lacks the substantive content that alone could qualify it as complete human freedom. In its *form*, political life in a liberal democracy is the species-life of man: we live explicitly in and through our relations with all others in our society. But as a matter of *substance*, Marx's view is that the species-life of man is primarily material – it is man's life as a producer working with others on nature and on the means of production society has created. Full-blooded emancipation, therefore, requires not just the existence of a political community, but the involvement of that community in the democratic organization and running of productive economic life. The material connections between human beings, veiled at present by the illusions of the market-place, will reveal themselves explicitly as people begin participating consciously in social control of the means of production. But for the time being, in a capitalist society, however liberal, the political community has nothing of this sort to do. As Marx put it in an essay written later in 1844:

> The administration [of a capitalist state] must . . . limit itself to a formal and negative activity, for its power ceases just where civil life and work begin. Indeed, in the face of the consequences that spring from the unsocial nature of this civil life, this private property, this reciprocal plundering of different civil groups, in the face of these consequences, impotence is the natural law of the administration.[31]

Under capitalism, man's material life is organized on an atomized and egoistic basis. The result of this dissonance between the form and content of political community is the schizophrenia of a double life for man, what Marx refers to as a 'dualism' between species-life and individual life: 'He has a life both in the political community, where he is valued as a communal being, and in civil society, where he is active as a private individual' (p. 140). This leads to what Marxists call a 'contradiction' between the communal character of the rights of the citizen and the atomistic character of the rights of man; the contradiction is an internal one because the latter constitute the autonomy of the economic domain which in reality ought to be the proper concern of the former. To this extent Marx argues that the rights of the citizen are hollow and the sovereignty of citizenship 'imaginary' (p. 141).

The contradiction takes an additional ironic twist in the way the rights of the citizen are presented by theorists of rights. They are presented, Marx alleged, as though their role were to serve and uphold the fundamental rights of man. If we say, as philosophers of natural rights often say, that the point of political community is the better protection of life, liberty and property, then 'the political community is degraded by the political emancipators to a mere means for the preservation of these so-called rights of man, [and] the citizen is declared to be the servant of egoistic man' (p. 147). The rights of man, connected as they are with the material aspects of human existence, are declared 'natural', and the rights of the citizen are functionally subordinated to them. Marx does note one or two occasions when, in the heat of revolution, political actors have asserted the primacy of their communal life, attacking inequality, for example, in the way Rousseau and later the Jacobins suggested (p. 147). But unless they are prepared to foster an atmosphere of permanent revolution, the old priorities will reassert themselves: selfishness retains power over community, for under capitalism it is selfishness that is associated with the natural, material life of man.

IV

It is difficult to say what we should conclude from this complex critique about Marx's view of rights as such in 1844. The easy option is simply to say that, so far as Marx is concerned, the rights of man and the rights of the citizen are so closely tied together in the human rights tradition that the egoism of the former taints and overwhelms whatever communalism there is in the concept of the latter. This is Buchanan's interpretation:

> Marx is apparently saying that the rights of man and the rights of the citizen are *correlatives* which mark a division between man's existence as an independent egoist in civil society and his idealized life as a citizen, a moral agent concerned with the common good rather than his own narrow self interest. The implication is that in communism, where the concept of the egoistic, isolated individual

is no longer applicable, the correlative concept of man as citizen, along with the notion of the rights of the citizen will no longer apply.[32]

Now, if 'citizen' means 'citizen-*as-opposed-to-real-man*', Buchanan's view is undoubtedly correct. But it does not follow that a communist community will not be constituted in part by rights *rather like* those of the rights of the citizen (in this special sense) under capitalism. Marx does insist in a number of places that, come the revolution, socialism will cast aside its political cloak and *a fortiori* its concern with political rights. But again there is a problem with words. In this context the term 'political' may mean involvement in the practice of a coercive power, separated in its concerns from real life; and it is certainly the aim of Marx's communism to repudiate that. It need not mean politics in the broader sense of people's participation in articulate decision-making.[33] Indeed, in the few (the *very* few) passages of his later works where Marx talked about socialist democracy, he hinted that it would continue to exhibit at least some of the forms of the practices that would be constituted by (say) an application of Articles VI and XV of the 1789 Declaration.[34] It is too swift, therefore, to say that the correlativity of egoistic man and merely political citizen commits Marx to a repudiation of human rights. And certainly the fact that he believed citizens' rights were a hollow mockery under capitalism provides in itself no reason for interpreting Marx as thinking rights as such have no part to play in the constitution of communist society.

But perhaps the very idea of rights has features which are uncongenial to a socialist. Buchanan suggests that rights are essentially *coercive* and usually *legalistic* guarantees, and that the socialist contention is that with the abolition of scarcity and class conflict the necessity for that sort of assurance will disappear.[35] Under communism people will still speak freely, participate democratically in the control of production and enjoy a portion of the social product; however, the sources of conflict and insecurity will be so diminished that no one will feel the need to *demand* these as matters of *right* or look for *guarantees* in these respects.[36]

Another suggestion focuses on the *individualism* of rights – not just the egoism evinced in the particular content of the bourgeois rights of man, but the individualism of the idea of rights itself. Rights, it is often said, are claims that individuals make one-by-one, each on his own account.[37] *Together* a set of individual rights (to free speech, to vote, or whatever) may help constitute a form of community, but the idea still evinces a reductionist and atomistic approach to human practice.

Marx indicated some sympathy for this sort of view when he wrote, in an early piece on Hegel, that voting in a liberal democracy still only brings people together on an abstract and individualistic basis: 'This formation into a legislative power requires that all members of civil society regard themselves as individuals, that they actually face one another as individuals.'[38]

The theme of rights did not figure prominently in Marx's writings after 1843. But he returned to it briefly at the end of his career in the pamphlet *Critique of the Gotha Programme*. Here Marx found it necessary to attack the claim of Lasallian socialists that the proceeds of labour belong undiminished with equal right to all members of society. His main objection to this claim was that it attempted to set up a purely distributive standard in abstraction from any consideration of the basis on which the means of production were to be controlled. But, along the way, he made some comments about the formula of 'equal right' which have led many to believe he wanted to repudiate the idea of rights altogether. As a matter of fact, the picture that emerges from this brief pamphlet is far from clear. Marx does insist that all talk of equality in this area is illusory because individuals are equal and unequal in different respects:

> Right by its very nature can consist only in the application of an equal standard; but unequal individuals (and they would not be different individuals if they were not unequal) are measurable only by an equal standard in so far as they are brought under an equal point of view, are taken from one definite side only, for instance, in the present case, are regarded only as workers and nothing more is seen in them, everything else being ignored. Further, one worker is married, another not; one has more children than another, and so on and so forth. Thus with an equal performance of labour, and hence an equal share in the social consumption fund, one will in fact receive more than another, and so on. To avoid all these defects, right instead of being equal would have to be unequal.[39]

Buchanan thinks Marx makes it clear in this passage that he is offering 'a criticism of rights as such'.[40] But that is by no means *clear*; that is it is unclear whether Marx is repudiating rights or the idea of equal income as a subject matter for rights. Certainly if one is an extreme egalitarian with regard to the content of rights, then the conclusions about the unequal effects of equal rights imply the repudiation of rights-talk. But Marx's own words indicate that he was not an egalitarian in that sense. The passage is simply inconclusive on the wider issue.

The fact is that Marx's views on rights were never formulated with the clarity or unequivocality that modern analysis presupposes. Sometimes it seems that right as such is identified with bourgeois right. But elsewhere in the same work, we are told that only certain *formulas* of right are 'stigmatized by a bourgeois limitation'.[41] Sometimes the suggestion is that rights are characteristic only of capitalist and perhaps immediately post-capitalist society; elsewhere we are told that, in the higher phase of communist society, it is 'the narrow horizon of *bourgeois* right' that is transcended.[42]

The only firm conclusions hostile to the idea of rights that we can draw are these. First, Marx was impatient with all distributive slogans in the communist movement, whether they were expressed in the language of rights or not; he dismissed them all as 'obsolete verbal rubbish'.[43] Second, he was convinced that the rights of man were bourgeois and egoistic, and that the rights of the citizen considered apart from then were empty and considered alongside them were tainted to a considerable extent by the atomistic flavour of capitalism. Third and most importantly, Marx was convinced that although the advent of citizens' rights did constitute a form of community, still the political revolution in which they culminated was immeasurably less important than the economic and social revolution he looked forward to. Each revolution promised in its way to end *some* aspects of human alienation.

> But the common essence from which the worker is isolated is a common essence of quite a different reality and compass from the political collectivity. This collectivity from which his own work separates him is life itself, physical and intellectual life, human morality, human activity, human enjoyment, human essence. The human essence is the true collectivity of man. And since isolation from this essence is out of all proportion more universal, insupportable, terrifying and full of contradictions than isolation from the political collectivity, the abolition of this isolation or even a partial reaction or revolt against it is the more immeasurable as man is more immeasurable than the citizen and human life than political life. An industrial revolt can therefore be as partial as it likes; it contains within it a universal soul: a political revolt can be as universal as it likes, even under the most colossal form it conceals a narrow spirit.[44]

It is the attitude evinced in passages like this, rather than the detailed interpretation of 'On the Jewish Question' or *Critique of the Gotha Programme*, that explains the lack of emphasis on rights in the

Marxian tradition.

Perhaps in the end what Karl Marx, the historical individual, did or did not think, or would or would not have said, about rights is unimportant. He is, after all, just one social theorist among others. All the same, it is interesting to look at these works – first, because Marx's writings are still taken seriously as part of the ideology of existing and powerful parties and movements, and second, because his thoughts on the matter provide us with a substantial clue – though not necessarily the last word – on the compatibility of the ideal of rights and other characteristically socialist concerns. Just as Burke's and Bentham's pieces reveal the tensions between human rights on the one hand and, respectively, the foundations of technocratic liberalism and traditional conservatism on the other, so Marx's early writings provide reasons for doubting whether a commitment to human rights can sit happily with socialist conceptions of the relation between man and community. The fact that those reasons are complicated and by no means unqualified is a teasing indication of how vague and unarticulated those socialist conceptions really are.

'On the Jewish Question'

The German Jews seek emancipation. What sort of emancipation do they want? Civil, political emancipation. Bruno Bauer answers them: No one in Germany is politically emancipated. We ourselves are not free. How then could we liberate you? You Jews are egoists if you demand a special emancipation for yourselves as Jews. You ought to work as Germans for the political emancipation of Germany, and as men for the emancipation of mankind, and consider your particular sort of oppression and ignominy not as an exception to the rule but rather as a confirmation of it.

· · ·

The Jewish question always presents itself differently according to the state in which the Jew lives. In Germany, where there is no political state, no state as such, the Jewish question is a purely theological one. The Jew finds himself in religious opposition to the state which recognizes Christianity as its foundation. This state is a professed theologian. Criticism is here criticism of theology, a two-sided criticism of Christian and of Jewish theology. But we are still always moving inside theology however critically we may be moving.

In France, which is a constitutional state, the Jewish question is a question of constitutionalism, a question of the incompleteness of political emancipation. Since here the appearance of a state religion is retained although in an empty and self-contradictory formula, namely that of the religion of the majority, the relationship of the Jew to the state contains the appearance of a religious or theological opposition.

It is in the North American states – or at least a part of them – that the Jewish question loses its theological importance for the first time and becomes a really *secular* question. It is only where the political state exists in its complete perfection that the relationship of the Jew and of the religious man in general to the political state, and thus the relationship of religion to the state, can stand out in all its peculiarities and purity. The criticism of this relationship ceases to be a theological criticism as soon as the state ceases to have a theological attitude to religion, as soon as it adopts the attitude of a state towards religion, i.e. a political attitude. Criticism then becomes a criticism of the political state. At this point, where criticism ceases to be theological, Bauer's criticism ceases to be critical. 'There is in America neither state religion nor a religion declared to be that of the majority, nor pre-eminence of any one way of worship over another. The state is stranger to all forms of worship' (G. de Beaumont, *Mary or Slavery in the U.S. . . .* Paris, 1835, p. 214). There are even some North American states where 'the constitution does not impose religious belief and practice as a condition of political rights' (loc. cit., p. 225). And yet 'people in the U.S. do not believe that a man without religion can be an honest man' (loc. cit., p. 224). Yet North America is the land of religiosity *par excellence* as Beaumont, Tocqueville, and the English-man Hamilton all aver with one voice. But the North American states are serving here only as an example. The question is: what is the relationship of complete political emancipation to religion? The fact that even in the land of completed political emancipation we find not only the existence of religion but a living existence full of freshness and strength furnishes us with the proof that the existence of religion does not contradict or impede the perfection of the state. But since the existence of religion is the existence of a defect, the source of this defect can only be sought in the nature of the state itself. Religion for us no longer has the force of a basis for secular deficiencies but only that of a phenomenon. Therefore we explain the religious prejudice of free citizens by their secular prejudice. We do not insist that they must abolish their religious limitation in order to abolish secular limitations. We insist that they abolish their religious limitations as soon as they abolish their secular limitations. We do not change secular questions into theological ones. We change theological questions into secular ones. History has for long enough been resolved into superstition: we now resolve superstition into history. The question of the relationship of political emancipation to religion becomes for us a question of the relationship of political emancipation to human emancipation. We criticize the religious weakness of the political state by criticizing the secular construction of the political state without regard to its religious weaknesses. We humanize the opposition of the state to a particular religion, Judaism for example, into the opposition of the state to particular secular elements, and the opposition of the state to religion in general into the opposition of the state to its own presuppositions in general.

The political emancipation of the Jew, the Christian, and religious man in general implies the emancipation of the state from Judaism, Christianity, and religion in general. The state as state emancipates itself from religion in the manner peculiar to its own nature by emancipating itself from the state religion, i.e. by not recognizing, as a state, any religion, by affirming itself simply as a state. Political emancipation is not the completed and consistent form of religious emancipation because political emancipation is not the completed and consistent form of human emancipation.

The limitations of political emancipation are immediately evident in the fact that a state can liberate itself from a limitation without man himself being truly free of it and the state can be a free state without man himself being a free man. Bauer himself tacitly admits this when he poses the following condition for political emancipation: 'Every single religious privilege, including the monopoly of a privileged church, must be abolished. If several or more or even the overwhelming majority of people still felt obliged to fulfil their religious duties, this practice should be left to them as a completely private matter.' Therefore the state can have emancipated itself from religion, even when the overwhelming majority of people is still religious. And the overwhelming majority does not cease to be religious simply because its religion is private.

But the attitude of the state, especially the free state, to religion is merely the attitude of the men who make up the state to religion. It follows from this that man liberates himself from an impediment through the medium of the state and politically by entering into opposition with himself and getting round this impediment in an abstract, limited, and partial manner. It follows also that when man liberates himself politically, he liberates himself by means of a detour, through the medium of something else, however necessary that medium may be. It follows finally that man, even when he proclaims himself an atheist through the intermediary of the state, i.e. when he proclaims the state to be atheist, still retains his religious prejudice, just because he recognizes himself only by a detour and by the medium of something else. Religion is precisely the recognition of man by detour through an intermediary. The state is the intermediary between man and his freedom. As Christ is the intermediary onto whom man unburdens all his divinity, all his religious bonds, so the state is the mediator onto which he transfers all his Godlessness and all his human liberty.

The political elevation of man above religion shares all the deficiencies and all the advantages of political elevation in general. The state as state annuls private property, for example, as soon as man declares in a political manner that private property is abolished, as soon as he abolishes the requirement of a property qualification for active and passive participation at elections, as has happened in many North American states. Hamilton interprets this fact from the political standpoint quite correctly: 'the masses have thus gained a victory over the property owners and monied classes'. Is private property not abolished ideally speaking when the non-owner has become the lawgiver for the owner? The census is the last political form of recognizing private property.

And yet the political annulment of private property has not only not abolished private property, it actually presupposes it. The state does away with difference in birth, class, education, and profession in its own manner when it declares birth, class, education and profession to be unpolitical differences, when it summons every member of the people to an equal participation in popular sovereignty without taking the differences into consideration, when it treats all elements of the people's real life from the point of view of the state. Nevertheless the state still allows private property, education, and profession to have an effect in their own manner, that is as private property, as education, as profession, and make their particular natures felt. Far from abolishing these factual differences, its existence rests on them as presupposition, it only feels itself to be a political state and asserts its universality by opposition to these elements. Therefore Hegel defines the relationship of the political state to religion quite rightly when he says: 'In order for the state to come into existence as the self-knowing ethical actuality of spirit, it is essential that it should be distinct from the form of authority and of faith. But this distinction emerges only in so far as divisions occur within the ecclesiatical sphere itself. It is only in this way that the state, above the particular churches, has attained to the universality of thought – its formal principle – and is bringing this universality into existence.' Of course! only thus does the state build its universality over and above its particular elements.

The perfected political state is by its nature the species-life of man in opposition to his material life. All the presuppositions of this egoistic life continue to exist in civil society outside the sphere of the state, but as proper to civil society. When the political state has achieved its true completion, man leads a double life, a heavenly one and an earthly one, not only in thought and consciousness but in reality, in life. He has a life both in the political community, where he is valued as a communal being, and in civil society, where he is active as a private individual, treats other men as means, degrades himself to a means, and becomes the plaything of alien powers. The political state has just as spiritual an attitude to civil society as heaven has to earth. It stands in the same opposition to civil society and overcomes it in the same manner as religion overcomes the limitations of the profane world, that is, it must likewise recognize it, reinstate it, and let itself once more be dominated by it. Man in the reality that is nearest to him, civil society, is a profane being. Here where he counts for himself and others as a real individual, he is an illusory phenomenon. In the state, on the other hand, where man counts as a species-being, he is an imaginary participant in an imaginary sovereignty, he is robbed of his real life and filled with an unreal universality.

The conflict with his citizenship and with other men as members of the community in which man as an adherent of a particular religion finds himself can be reduced to the secular division between political state and civil society. For man as a bourgeois 'life in the state is only an apparent and momentary exception to the essential rule'. Of course the bourgeois, like the Jew, only remains in the life of the state sophistically speaking, just as the citizen only sophistically remains a Jew or bourgeois; but this sophism is not a personal matter. It is a sophism of the political state itself. The difference between the religious man and the citizen is the difference between the trader and the citizen, between the labourer and the citizen, between the property owner and the citizen, between the living individual and the citizen. The opposition to the political man in which the religious man finds himself is the same opposition in which the bourgeois finds himself to the citizen and the member of civil society to his political lion's skin.

This secular strife to which the Jewish question can in the last analysis be reduced – the relationship of the political state to its presuppositions, whether these be material elements like private property or intellectual like education, religion, the conflict between general and private interests, the rift between the political state and the civil society – these secular oppositions are left intact by Bauer while he polemicizes against their religious expressions. 'It is precisely the same need which is the basis of civil society, ensures its continued existence, and guarantees its necessity that also exposes its existence to perpetual dangers, sustains an unsure element within it, produces the continuing oscillating mixture of wealth and poverty, need and superfluity, and in general creates change' (p. 8).

Compare the whole section entitled 'Civil Society' (pp. 8–9), which is drafted from the main points of Hegel's 'Philosophy of Right'. Civil society in its opposition to the political state is recognized as necessary because the political state is recognized as necessary.

Political emancipation is of course a great progress. Although it is not the final form of human emancipation in general, it is nevertheless the final form of human emancipation inside the present world order. It is to be understood that I am speaking here of real, practical emancipation.

Man emancipates himself politically from religion by banishing it from the field of public law and making it a private right. Religion is no longer the spirit of the state where man behaves, as a species-being in community with other men albeit in a limited manner and in a particular form and a particular sphere: religion has become the spirit of civil society, the sphere of egoism, the *bellum omnium contra omnes* [war of all against all]. Its essence is no longer in community but in difference. It has become the expression of separation of man from his common essence, from himself and from other men, as it was originally. It is still only the abstract recognition of a particular perversion, private whim, and arbitrariness. For example, the infinite splintering of religion in North America already gives it the exterior form of a purely individual affair. It is shoved away into the crowd of private interests and exiled from the common essence as such. But we should not be deceived about the limitations of political emancipation. The separation of man into a public and a private man, the displacement of religion from the state to civil society is not a stage but the completion of political emancipation, which thus does not abolish or even try to abolish the actual religiosity of man.

The decomposition of man into Jew and citizen, protestant and citizen, religious man and citizen, this decomposition is no trick played upon political citizenship, no avoidance of political emancipation. It is political emancipation itself, the political manner of emancipating oneself from religion. Of course, in times when the political state is born violently as such out of civil society, when man's self-liberation tries to complete itself in the form of political self-liberation, the state must go as far as abolishing, destroying religion, but only in the same way as it goes as far as abolishing private property, at the most, by declaring a maximum, by confiscation or a progressive tax, or in the same way as it abolishes life, by the guillotine. In moments of particular self-consciousness political life tries to suppress its presuppositions, civil society and its elements, and to constitute itself as the real, harmonious life of man. However, this is only possible through violent opposition to its own conditions, by declaring the revolution to be permanent. The political drama therefore ends necessarily with the restoration of religion, private property, and all the elements of civil society, just as war ends with peace.

* * *

In the so-called Christian state it is alienation that is important, not man himself. The man who is important, the king, is a being specifically differentiated from other men (which is itself a religious conception), who is in direct contact with heaven and God. The relationships that hold sway here are ones of faith. The religious spirit is thus not yet really secularized.

But the religious spirit can never really be secularized. For what is it but the unsecular form of a stage in the development of the human spirit? The religious spirit can only be secularized in so far as the stage in the development of the human spirit whose religious expression it is emerges and constitutes itself in its secular form. This happens in the democratic state. The foundation of this state is not Christianity but the human foundation of Christianity. Religion remains as the ideal, unsecular consciousness of its members, because it is the ideal form of the stage of human development that is realized in this state.

What makes the members of the political state religious is the dualism between their individual life and their species-life, between life in civil society and political life, their belief that life in the state is the true life even though it leaves untouched their individuality. Religion is here the spirit of civil society, the expression of separation and distance of man from man. What makes a political democracy Christian is the fact that in it man, not only a single man but every man, counts as a sovereign being; but it is man as he appears uncultivated and unsocial, man in his accidental existence, man as he comes and goes, man as he is corrupted by the whole organization of our society, lost to himself, sold, given over to the domination of inhuman conditions and elements – in a word, man who is no longer a real species being. The fantasy, dream, and postulate of Christianity, the sovereignty of man, but of man as an alien being separate from actual man, is present in democracy as a tangible reality and is its secular motto.

The religious and theological consciousness has all the more religious and theological force in the complete democracy as it is without political significance and earthly aims. It is the affair of minds that are shy of the world, the expression of a limited understanding, the product of arbitrariness and fantasy, a really other-worldly life. Christianity achieves here the practical expression of its significance of a univeral religion in that it groups together the most different opinions in the form of Christianity and even more because it does not lay on others the requirements of Christianity, but only a religion in general, any religion (compare the above mentioned work of Beaumont). The religious consciousness revels in richness of religious opposition and religious diversity.

Thus we have shown that political emancipation from religion leaves religion intact even though it is no longer a privileged religion. The contradiction with his citizenship in which the adherent of a particular religion finds himself is only a part of the general secular contradiction between the political state and civil society. The perfect Christian state is the one that recognizes itself as a state and abstracts from the religion of its members. The emancipation of the state from religion is not the emancipation of actual man from religion.

So we do not say to the Jews, as Bauer does: you cannot be emancipated politically without emancipating yourselves radically from Judaism. Rather we say to them: because you can be politically emancipated without completely and consistently abandoning Judaism, this means that political emancipation itself is not human emancipation. If you Jews wish to achieve political emancipation without achieving human emancipation, then the incompleteness and contradiction does not only lie in you, it lies in the nature and category of political emancipation. If you are imprisoned within this category, then you are sharing in something common to everyone.

. . .

According to Bauer man must sacrifice the 'privilege of belief' in order to be able to receive general human rights. Let us discuss for a moment the so-called human rights, human rights in their authentic form, the form they have in the writings of their discoverers, the North Americans and French! These human rights are partly political rights that are only exercised in community with other men. Their content is formed by participation in the common essence, the political essence, the essence of the state. They fall under the category of political freedom, under the category of civil rights, which, as we have seen, in no way presuppose the consistent and positive abolition of religion, nor, consequently, of Judaism. It remains to discuss the other part of human rights, the rights of man, in so far as they differ from the rights of the citizen.

Among them are freedom of conscience, the right to exercise a chosen religion. The privilege of belief is expressly recognized either as a human right, or as a conequence of one of the human rights, freedom.

Declaration of the Rights of Man and of the Citizen, 1791, Article 10: 'No one should be molested because of his opinions, not even religious ones'. In the first section of the constitution of 1791 'the liberty of every man to practise the religion to which he adheres' is guaranteed as human right. *The Declaration of the Rights of Man . . . 1793* counts among human rights, in Artcle 7, 'the free exercise of religious practice'. Indeed, concerning the right to publish one's thoughts and opinions, to hold assemblies and practise one's religion, it goes as far as to say: 'the necessity of announcing these rights supposes either the present or the recent memory of despotism'. Compare the constitution of 1795, Section 14, Article 354.

Constitution of Pennsylvania, Article 9, Paragraph 3: 'All men have a natural and indefeasible right to worship Almighty God according to the dictates of their own consciences: no man can of right be compelled to attend, erect or support a place of worship, or to maintain any ministry, against his consent; no human authority can, in any case whatever, control or interfere with the rights of conscience.'

Constitution of New Hampshire, Articles 5 & 6: 'Among the natural rights, some are in their very nature unalienable. . . . Of this kind are rights of conscience'.

The incompatibility of religion with the rights of man is so far from being evident in the concept of the rights of man, that the right to be religious, to be religious in one's own chosen way, to practise one's chosen religion is expressly counted as one of the rights of man. The privilege of faith is a universal right of man.

The rights of man are as such differentiated from the right of the citizen. Who is the 'man' who is different from the 'citizen?' No one but the member of civil society. Why is the member of civil society called 'man', simply man, and why are his rights called the rights of man? How do we explain this fact? From the relationship of the political state to civil society, from the nature of political emancipation.

Above all we notice the fact that the so-called rights of man, the rights of man as different from the rights of the citizen are nothing but the rights of the member of civil society, i.e. egoistic man, man separated from other men and the community. The most radical constitution, the constitution of 1793, can say:

Declaration of the Rights of Man . . . , Article 2. These rights etc. (natural and imprescriptable rights) are: equality, liberty, security, property.

What does liberty consist of?

Article 6: 'Liberty is the power that belongs to man to do anything that does not infringe on the right of someone else' or according to the declaration of the rights of man of 1791 'liberty consists in the power of doing anything that does not harm others'.

Thus freedom is the right to do and perform what does not harm others. The limits within which each person can move without harming others is defined by the law, just as the boundary between two fields is defined by the fence. The freedom in question is that of a man treated as an isolated monad and withdrawn into himself. Why is the Jew, according to Bauer, incapable of receiving the rights of man? 'So long as he is a Jew the limited nature that makes him a Jew will get the upper hand over the human nature that should unite him as a man to other men and will separate him from the non-Jew.' But the right of man to freedom is not based on the union of man with man, but on the separation of man from man. It is the right to this separation, the rights of the limited individual who is limited to himself.

The practical application of the rights of man to freedom is the right of man to private property.

What does the right of man to property consist in?

Article 16 (Constitution of 1793): 'The right of property is the right which belongs to all citizens to enjoy and dispose at will of their goods and revenues, the fruit of their work and industry.'

Thus the right of man to property is the right to enjoy his possessions and dispose of the same arbitrarily, without regard for other men, independently from society, the right of selfishness. It is the former individual freedom together with its latter application that forms the basis of civil society. It leads man to see in other men not the realization but the limitation of his own freedom. Above all it proclaims the right of man 'to enjoy and dispose at will of his goods, his revenues and fruits of his work and industry'.

There still remain the other rights of man, equality and security.

Equality, here in its non-political sense, is simply the counterpart of the liberty described above, namely that each man shall without discrimination be treated as a self-sufficient monad. The constitution of 1795 defines the concept of this equality, in conformity with this meaning, thus:

Article 3 (Constitution of 1795): 'Equality consists of the fact that the law is the same for all, whether it protects or punishes.'

And security?

Article 8 (Constitution of 1793): 'Security consists in the protection afforded by society to each of its members for the conservation of his person, rights, and property.'

Security is the highest social concept of civil society, the concept of the police. The whole of society is merely there to guarantee to each of its members the preservation of his person, rights, and property. It is in this sense that Hegel calls civil society the 'state of need and of reason'.

The concept of security does not allow civil society to raise itself above its egoism. Security is more the assurance of egoism.

Thus none of the so-called rights of man goes beyond egoistic man, man as he is in civil society, namely an individual withdrawn behind his private interests and whims and separated from the community. Far from the rights of man conceiving of man as a species-being, species-life itself, society, appears as a framework exterior to individuals, a limitation of their original self-sufficiency. The only bond that holds them together is natural necessity, need and private interest, the conservation of their property and egoistic person.

It is already paradoxical that a people that is just beginning to free itself, to tear down all barriers between different sections of the people and form a political community, should solemnly proclaim (Declaration of 1791) the justification of egoistic man separated from his fellow men and the community. Indeed, this proclamation is repeated at a moment when only the most heroic devotion can save the nation, and is therefore peremptorily demanded, at a moment when the sacrifice of all interests of civil society is raised to the order of the day and egoism must be punished as a crime (*Declaration of the Rights of Man . . . 1793*). This fact appears to be even more paradoxical when we see that citizenship, the political community, is degraded by the political emancipators to a mere means for the preservation of these so-called rights of man, that the citizen is declared to be the servant of egoistic man, the sphere in which man behaves as a communal being is degraded below the sphere in which man behaves as a partial being, finally that it is not man as a citizen but man as a bourgeois who is called the real and true man.

'The aim of every political association is the preservation of the natural and imprescriptible rights of man' (*Declaration of the Rights of Man... 1791*, Article 2). 'Government is instituted to guarantee man the enjoyment of his natural and imprescriptible rights' (*Declaration of the Rights of Man . . . 1791*, Article 1). So even in the moments of youthful freshness and enthusiasm raised to fever pitch by the pressure of circumstances, political life is declared to be a mere means whose end is the life of civil society. It is true that its revolutionary practice is in flagrant contradiction with its theory. While, for example, security is declared to be a right of man, the violation of the privacy of correspondence is publicly inserted in the order of the day.

While the 'unlimited freedom of the press' (Constitution of 1793, Article 122) is guaranteed as a consequence of the right of man to individual freedom, the freedom of the press is completely destroyed, for 'the liberty of the press must not be permitted when it compromises public liberty' ('The Young Robespierre' in Buchez and Roux, *Parliamentary History of the French Revolution*, vol. 28, p. 159). This means then that the right of man to freedom ceases to be a right as soon as it enters into conflict with political life, whereas, according to the theory, political life is only the guarantee of the rights of man, the rights of individual man, and so must be given up as soon as it contradicts its end, these rights of man. But the practice is only the exception and the theory is the rule. Even though one were to treat the revolutionary practice as the correct version of the relationship, the riddle still remains to be solved of why, in the minds of the political emancipators, the relationship is turned upside-down and the end appears as the means and the means as the end. This optical illusion of their minds would always be the same riddle, although it would then be a psychological and theoretical riddle.

The riddle has a simple solution.

Political emancipation is at the same time the dissolution of the old society on which rests the sovereign power, the essence of the state alienated from the people. Political revolution is the revolution of civil society. What was the character of the old society? One word characterizes it. Feudalism. The old civil society had a directly political character. The elements of civil life, like, for example, property or the family or the type and manner of work, were, in the form of seigniorial right, estates, and corporations, raised to the level of elements of state life. They defined in this form the relationship of the single individual to the state as a whole, that is, his political relationship, the relationship of separation and exclusion from the other parts of society. For this sort of organization of the people's life did not turn property or work into social elements but completed their separation from the state as a whole, and made them into particular societies within society. But the vital functions and conditions of life in civil society were still political even though political in the feudal sense, that is, they excluded the individual from the states as a whole. They turned the particular relationship of the corporation to the totality of the state, into his own general relationship to the life of the people, as it turned his particular civil occupation into his general occupation and situation. As a consequence of this organization the unity of the state – the mind, will, and authority of this state unity, the power of the state in general –

equally appears necessarily as the particular affair of a lord and servants who are cut off from the people.

The political revolution overthrew this feudal power and turned state affairs into affairs of the people; it turned the state into a matter of general concern, i.e. into a true state; it necessarily destroyed all estates, corporations, guilds, privileges which were so many expressions of the separation of the people from the community. The political revolution thus abolished the political character of civil society. It shattered civil society with its simple parts, on the one hand into individuals, on the other hand into the material and spiritual elements that make up the life experience and civil position of these individuals. It unfettered the political spirit that had, as it were, been split, cut up, and drained away into the various cul-de-sacs of feudal society. The political revolution collected this spirit together after its dispersion, freed it from its confusion with civil life, and set it up as the sphere that was common to all, the general affair of the people in ideal independence from the other particular elements of civil life. Particular professions and ranks sank to a merely individual importance. They were no longer the relationship of individuals to the state as a whole. Public affairs as such became the general affair of each individual and politics was a general occupation.

But the perfection of the idealism of the state was at the same time the perfection of the materialism of civil society. The shaking off of the political yoke entailed the shaking off of those bonds that had kept the egoistic spirit of civil society fettered. Political emancipation entailed the emancipation of civil society from politics, from even the appearance of a general content.

Feudal society was dissolved into its basis, into man. But into the man that was its true basis, egoistic man. This man, the member of civil society, is the basis, the presupposition of the political state. He is recognized by it as such in the rights of man.

But the freedom of egoistic man and the recognition of this freedom is the recognition of the unimpeded movement of the spiritual and material elements that go to make up its life.

Man was therefore not freed from religion; he received freedom of religion. He was not freed from property; he received freedom of property. He was not freed from the egoism of trade; he received freedom to trade.

The formation of the political state and the dissolution of civil society into independent individuals, who are related by law just as the estate and corporation men were related by privilege, is completed in one and the same act. Man as member of civil society, unpolitical man, appears necessarily as natural man. The rights of man appear as natural rights, because self-conscious activity is concentrated upon political action. Egoistic man is the passive, given results of the dissolved society, an object of immediate certainty and thus a natural object. Political revolution dissolves civil life into its component parts, without revolutionizing and submitting to criticism these parts themselves. Its attitude to civil society, to the world of need, to work, private interests, private law is that they are the foundation of its existence, its own presupposition that needs no further proof, and thus its natural basis. Finally, man as a member of civil society counts for true man, for man as distinct from the citizen, because he is man in his sensuous, immediate existence, while political man is only the abstract fictional man, man as an allegorical or moral person. This man as he actually is, is only recognized in the form of the egoistic individual, and the true man only in the form of the abstract citizen.

The abstraction of the political man is thus correctly described by Rousseau: 'He who dares to undertake the making of a people's institutions ought to feel himself capable, so to speak, of changing human nature, of transforming each individual, who is by himself a complete and solitary whole, into part of a greater whole from which he in a manner receives his life and being; of altering man's constitution for the purpose of strengthening it; and of substituting a partial and moral existence of the physical and independent existence nature has conferred on us all. He must, in a word, take away from man his own resources and give him instead new ones alien to him, and incapable of being made use of without the help of other men.'

All emancipation is bringing back man's world and his relationships to man himself.

Political emancipation is the reduction of man, on the one hand to a member of civil society, an egoistic and independent individual, on the other hand to a citizen, a moral person.

The actual individual man must take the abstract citizen back into himself and, as an individual man in his empirical life, in his individual work and individual relationships become a species-being; man must recognize his own forces as social forces, organize them, and thus no longer separate social forces from himself in the form of political forces. Only when this has been achieved will human emancipation be completed.

· · ·

ᔥ6᙮

Nonsense upon Stilts?
– a reply

In this final essay I want first to consider briefly the career of the doctrine of human rights in the century or so since the publication of these attacks. How has it fared and how has it changed? At the moment rights have taken on a new importance in politics and political philosophy. But have the objections of Bentham, Burke and Marx been answered? Does the new commitment to rights differ from the old in any way that would make it a safer and more adequate basis for political thought and action? Secondly, I want to concentrate on some of the outstanding themes in the critique of human rights and of the liberal rights tradition, particularly as those themes have been taken up by theorists and philosophers who call themselves the 'new communitarians'.[1] What are their criticisms of liberalism and rights-based philosophy? Are they justified? Or is there something that the liberal can say in response to their indictment?

I

In the years that followed the publication of these works by Bentham, Burke and Marx, the theory of human rights suffered a decline, then a renewal.

Its attractiveness as a touchstone of normative thought about politics suffered a decline in the nineteenth century with the rise of large-scale social theory. The themes of Enlightenment sociology which, as we saw earlier, had always posed at least an implicit threat to the foundations of natural law and natural rights, were now pursued with a new vigour and on a much larger scale to their logical conclusions. The giants of social theory – thinkers like Karl Marx, Emile Durkheim and Max Weber – sought to lay bare the dynamics of social change and to display the life of a society (or, more ambitiously, world history itself) as a process which bore only the most complex and problematic relation to the intentions of those human agents who thought they could fashion it. The myth of the deliberate institution of political society – the social contract – had of course already been exploded. If rights had any relevance at all in society, it was not on account of their being the terms of its foundation. Society was no longer conceived as an artefact or human invention; rather its life was seen as a natural process – a process in which the thoughts and actions of individual men and women were *involved* rather than one over which they had any real control. The images connoted by Declarations of Rights – people asking themselves how their society should be constituted, what terms they would insist on to govern its workings, and how they could retain control of those workings, and so on – these images seemed quite inappropriate to the new naturalistic understanding of social life.

Indeed, not only did nineteenth-century social theory provide an account of social change, but also it linked that to an account of the production of ideology, and more generally to a natural history of thought. Increasingly theories and ideas like the idea of rights were viewed, not as the commitments with which social enquiry should be undertaken, but as *objects* of that enquiry in their own right. (Enthusiasm for the new sociology of ideas obscured the possibility that a theory might occupy *both* roles.) The result of all this was not so much that rights disappeared altogether from view, but that a new set of questions were asked about them. Who believes in rights? Why? Under what historical conditions could that idea be expected to emerge and flourish? Our ability to answer these questions was taken to be conclusive against the importance of exploring the ethical validity of the idea.

None of this meant an end to political activity, or to the business of articulating the concerns underlying that activity. Both ethics and action – including liberal ethics and liberal action – continued. But the spirit of social thought seemed to call for a morality other than the morality of rights. It seemed to call for a morality whose primary referent was *society* – as system, organism, class or people. The displacement of the individual from centre stage in social thought made the theory of the *rights* of the individual uncongenial as a basis for practical politics. If one needed a moral theory, utilitarianism – with its pragmatism and its emphasis on the general good – seemed to offer a better basis for reform and renovation. Even as early as the 1790s a number of French liberals were increasingly beginning to favour the utilitarian side of the revolutionary legacy. The experience of the Terror and the apparent inevitability of the move back through dictatorship to monarchy convinced many that the patient pursuit of

piecemeal reform was to be preferred to the brandishing of revolutionary slogans.[2] Moreover, the impact of the science of political
economy in this period cannot be overestimated: it was political
economy that took up the results of Enlightenment and post-
Enlightenment social theory and anthropology in a form that made
them accessible and useful for the conduct of public affairs. In its
ethical underpinnings, political economy was utilitarian more or less
through and through. Writers like Adam Smith might occasionally
use the rhetoric of the natural right to property or the 'system of
natural liberty'; but whenever they set to defend these ideas, the
defence was always phrased in terms of the social good.[3] In general,
then, the utilitarian concern for the detailed calculation of social
consequences and its repudiation of any absolute commitment of
principle seemed to match the maturity and sophistication of
contemporary social thought. By comparison the morality of rights
seemed naive, simplistic and irrelevant to the complexity of the
problems of nineteenth-century society. The Industrial Revolution
was viewed largely in terms of a play of forces which were to be
understood sociologically, not ethically. And the democratic revolution, in England and elsewhere, was fought for on the basis of the
greatest happiness of the greatest number, rather than individual
human rights. Social determinism, the sociology of ideas, legal
positivism and utilitarianism: in the midst of these theoretical
currents, the rights of man seemed hopelessly out of their depth.

Of course, one should be careful not to exaggerate. There were
those who continued to talk in the idiom of rights about the great
issues facing western society in the nineteenth century and well into
the early twentieth. If the nineteenth century was the era of social
theory, it was also the period of increasing concern about the threat
to individuality implicit in the growth of mass society. The second
part of Alexis de Tocqueville's *Democracy in America* and the
eloquence of John Stuart Mill's essay *On Liberty* were crucial in the
development of contemporary concern about the tyranny of the
majority and modern awareness of the antagonism between rights and
many popular democratic ideas.[4] Moreover, the appending of a Bill of
Rights to the American Constitution in 1787 meant that the idea of
rights continued to dominate the constitutional and administrative
law of that country throughout this period. But even there, the idea
came to be seen by many as an outdated encumbrance on the natural
growth of a form of politics that would be increasingly concerned with
economic efficiency and social justice, rather than with the abstract
rights of the individual.[5]

Certainly the rights of man had nothing like the prominence in international affairs that they have today. The issue of slavery was sometimes addressed in these terms, and so too were the questions of national minorities which afflicted European politics from 1815 to 1945. But the League of Nations, for example, included nothing in its charter about the protection of human rights apart from a vague call to member states for the 'just treatment of the native inhabitants of territories under their control'.[6] It was more concerned with securing peaceful relations between states than with protecting the interests of the citizens of those states (and ultimately of course it had little effect in promoting either concern). There were one or two international organizations set up on a non-official basis to concern themselves with rights-violations: the Paris-based Ligue des Droits de l'Homme was one. But as Hannah Arendt points out,

> All societies formed for the protection of the Rights of Man, all attempts to arrive at a new bill of human rights were sponsored by marginal figures – by a few international jurists without political experience or professional philanthropists supported by the uncertain sentiments of professional idealists. The groups they formed, the declarations they issued, showed an uncanny similarity in language and composition to that of societies for the prevention of cruelty to animals. No statesman, no political figure of any importance could possibly take them seriously; and none of the liberal or radical parties in Europe thought it necessary to incorporate into their program a new declaration of human rights.[7]

It was not until the Second World War that human rights re-entered the mainstream of western thought and politics. The war began as an old-style struggle over territory in Europe. But as it escalated, as the scale of Nazi atrocities became apparent and as American arms and manpower were drawn increasingly into the conflict, it began to be seen as a crusade for basic rights and freedoms. When Churchill and Roosevelt stated their war aims in 1942, they prefaced the Atlantic Charter with their conviction that 'complete victory over their enemies is essential to decent life, liberty, independence and religious freedom, and to preserve human rights and justice, in their own land as well as in other lands'.[8] When Nazi and Japanese leaders were arraigned before Allied tribunals in 1945 they were charged with 'crimes against humanity', and where necessary the tribunals appealed in effect to a consensual conception of natural law to override the defence that those arraigned had been acting in accordance with the laws of the regimes they served. Unlike the League of Nations, the United Nations Organisation committed itself immediately to the rights of man, taking as one of the basic aims of its foundation 'to reaffirm faith in fundamental human rights, in the dignity and worth of the human person, in the equal rights of men and women and of nations large and small'.[9] A Universal Declaration of Human Rights was drafted and, in 1948, adopted by all the member states. In its scope it went far beyond the Declarations of 1776 and 1789, including rights to economic and social security, as well as the traditional civil, political and democratic liberties. (We shall explore the implications of this shortly.) Furthermore the 1945 Declaration has worked much better as a focal point for bringing international political pressure to bear on those countries who persist in violating what are taken to be the rights of their citizens. Of course, there is a limit to what can be done: there is no police force attached to the Declaration. But there are international tribunals and agencies which can investigate and publicize; perhaps the greatest achievement of the post-war consensus in this regard is that there is now scarcely a nation on earth which is not sensitive to or embarrassed by the charge that it is guilty of rights-violations. That may not stop the violations in question, but the sensitivity at least provides a foothold for political and international pressure.

The period of decolonization since 1945 has seen a spate of constitution-making, and again it is notable that most national constitutions now include some sort of Bill of Rights modelled, though often loosely, on the rhetoric of the Universal Declaration. In some of these documents great emphasis is put on the social and economic rights, in others – like the European Convention on Human Rights – the focus is firmly on the traditional liberal agenda. But either way, the concern for rights, and the belief that the rights of human beings ought to be roughly the same all over the world, is no longer a marginal one.

This new consensus on the political importance of human rights has been reflected in political theory. After a long period in which systematic political philosophizing was taken to be obsolete,[10] there has been in recent years a return to 'grand theory', and in Britain and the USA many of the new normative theories of politics are attempts to articulate the basis on which individuals can make claims of right against their society. These theories are systematic, abstract, universalist and comprehensive in their implications for society. Interestingly the abstract rights of the individual are invoked on both sides of the modern debate about economic organization. Philosophers on the right preface their books with assertions like: 'Individuals have rights, and there are things no person or group may do to them (without violating their rights). So strong and far-reaching are these rights that they raise the question of what, if anything, the state and its officials may do.'[11] But philosophers on the left also invoke the idea, claiming that they are the ones who 'take rights seriously' and talking about 'the primacy of welfare rights'.[12] From a position of relative disrepute at the beginning of the century, rights seem to have become the new fashion in modern political philosophy.

II

In what ways does the modern revival of rights differ from its eighteenth-century ancestor?

One difference is apparent from the texts of the Declarations of 1789 and 1948. Like the 'Declaration of the Rights of Man and the Citizen', the Universal Declaration of 1948 affirms abstract principles of freedom and equality, and rights to liberty, democracy, religious toleration, free speech, free association, freedom from arbitrary arrest, a presumption of innocence, and so on. Under the heading of these traditional liberal ideas, the 1948 document goes a little further, applying liberal principles to areas of concern that have become important in the light of our experience since 1789; areas like privacy, freedom of travel, the right to a nationality, sexual freedom, labour organization and non-discrimination. But, as well as this, the 1948 Declaration also promulgates certain principles of social and economic life under the heading of human rights. Article 23, for example, affirms for the individual the right to 'protection against unemployment', and to a 'just and favourable remuneration ensuring for himself and his family an existence worthy of human dignity . . . supplemented if necessary by other means of social protection'. Article 24 enshrines 'the right to rest and leisure, including reasonable limitation of working hours and periodic holidays with pay'. Articles 25, 26 and 27 recognize economic rights to a decent standard of living including 'medical care and necessary social services', to free elementary education, and to the enjoyment of the arts. These articles deviate considerably from the emphasis on civil liberty and political freedom that we find in the 'Declaration of the Rights of Man and the Citizen', as well as in more modest recent charters like the European Convention on Human Rights.

But it is possible perhaps to exaggerate the differences. In a critique of modern views on human rights Maurice Cranston suggests that since the traditional political and civil rights 'are for the most part rights against government interference with a man's activities, a large part of the legislation needed has to do no more than restrain the government's own executive arm'.[13] This is a mistake. The 1789 Declaration was committed to democratic principles as well: the accountability of public officials; no taxation without consultation; and popular participation in law-making. These involve giving citizens not just liberty but *powers*. They therefore involve the institution, maintenance and protection of political frameworks within which those powers are exercised and have their effect. This is not, then, merely a matter of the government restraining itself; it involves a positive and costly effort to keep democratic frameworks in working order. And even with those rights that confer liberties rather than powers, the correlative duties of government go far beyond the negative one of restraining its own arm. In liberal theory, governments are not thought to be instituted merely to *respect* people's rights (what would be the point of that?), but for their better enforcement and protection. Someone's religious liberty is not fully secure unless the government makes a positive effort to protect him from interfering bigots of another persuasion. The fact that the government itself does not persecute him does not mean his rights are being adequately taken care of. Similarly his freedom from arbitrary arrest and imprisonment is not vindicated if the government restrains only the kidnappers in the ranks of its own officials. (Think of the current situation in Beirut!) So it is not true to say that the traditional liberal rights require from governments nothing more than omissions whereas modern socio-economic rights involve costs. *All* rights – even rights to liberty – are costly to uphold.

Still, the 1948 Declaration evinces a substantial change of emphasis, and it is a change that pervades the modern discussion too, not just this particular document. It is no longer widely assumed that human rights must be pinned down to the protection of individual *freedom*. Humans have other needs as well, related to their health, survival, culture, education and ability to work. We all know from our own case how important these needs are. Some theorists have made this concession through recognizing that the satisfaction of these needs is involved in any genuine concern about freedom. But whether one takes this 'positive freedom' approach or not, it is now widely (though not universally) accepted that material needs generate moral imperatives which are as compelling as those related to democracy and civil liberty. If we want a catalogue of what people owe each other as a matter of moral priority, we should look not only to liberty but also to the elementary conditions of material well-being.

In part, these developments are a response to the socialist critique of the rights of man. As we have seen, the socialist complaint was always that the so-called 'human' rights were really *bourgeois* rights – that they paraded as matters of universal concern the fears and preoccupations of a particular sort of acquisitive individual who became common and whose activities were legitimized as the epitome of human excellence only at a particular point in the history of the developed economies. Marx complained in 'On the Jewish Question' that none of the so-called rights of man went much beyond man as he was in capitalist society – an anxious egoist concerned mostly with his own property and his freedom to buy and sell. On the other hand, it was said, the Declarations paid no attention to those concerns that *did* have some claim to be described as 'universal' or 'human': the experience and satisfaction of bodily need; participation in productive activity; involvement in the life processes of others; reproduction, and so on. Concerns like these were brought to the fore in socialist countries, for example, in the rights enshrined in the Constitution of the USSR in 1936. But in fact the basis for their recognition in the west had already been laid with the foundations of modern welfare provision. Social thinkers like T.H. Green, J.A. Hobson and L.T. Hobhouse were able to convince many of their liberal colleagues that freedom was a mockery without the means for social security.[14] A little later, the crisis of the 1930s convinced large sections of the population that the structure of the economy and the fundamental distribution of wealth and of power over the means of production could not be exempted from the sort of urgent moral scrutiny associated with a commitment to human rights. These concerns are reflected in many modern theories of social justice, where it is assumed that setting out a just order for society is not merely a matter of ordering its political institutions but also of determining, on the basis of rights to life and welfare, what structure the economy ought to have as well.[15]

All this remains controversial. From the right there is still some insistence that individual rights to property and protection from aggression 'leave no room' for rights to material security.[16] And many deny that distributive justice is a legitimate political concern at all, let alone a proper subject for the idea of human rights. The politics of rights, they say, have been corrupted by the intrusion of these concerns.[17] On the left, there is considerable apprehension that modern theories of rights do not go, or perhaps are incapable of going, far enough to accommodate social need.[18] For one thing, these rights still proceed at an individual level: 'Every*one* has a right to a standard of living adequate for the health and well-being of *himself and his family*' rather than (say) 'The standard of life in a community is inseparably bound up with the health and well-being of its members'. Thus rights are still seen as the *property* of man, the 'isolated monad . . . withdrawn behind his private interests and whims and separated from the community' (p. 146). For another thing, those socio-economic rights that are invoked are nearly always 'welfarist' in character – focusing their concern on the *consumption* of material goods and services rather than on what socialists regard as 'the real issue', namely power and class in control of the means of production. So though there has been this shift to accommodate new concerns, the theory of human rights has still not freed itself from the charge that it is, at bottom, just a bourgeois excrescence.

Some concerns about the distribution of socio-economic power between the classes, or between rich and poor, can be expressed in the language of rights, and some may not be so easily accommodated. The same is true, I think, for the range of *feminist* concerns. In the past, declarations of human rights (or the rights of '*man*', generously interpreted!) have been seen as holding out a promise of liberation for women as well as men from evils such as oppression, insecurity and political powerlessness. But increasingly it is recognized that the forms of oppression from which women suffer in common with men are only a subset of the forms of oppression from which women suffer. There are types of oppression uniquely connected with sexuality, child-bearing and the family which manifesto writers and philosophers of rights have on the whole failed to address in their general discussion of human rights, but which loom larger in the experience of most women than many of the evils with which human rights are usually preoccupied. Though a lot of recent feminist work addresses questions about 'women's rights', once again there is a controversy about how far an idiom associated with masculine concerns can be adapted to express the demands and aspirations of other genders.

Some issues of concern to women, for example the issue of pornography, are perhaps even distorted if dealt with purely in terms of rights. The rights framework inclines us to think in terms of balancing the rights of pornographers (to free expression, and so on) on the one hand, against the rights of individual women who may suffer tangible harm (the right not to be raped or accosted, for example) on the other. But the most powerful feminist arguments against pornography concern not only the individual harm that can be laid at its door, but also the insult and degradation, concrete and symbolic, suffered by women in general when certain stereotypes are nurtured, certain fantasies played out, and certain forms of violence and domination rehearsed in the public or semi-public realm.[19] It is much easier to articulate these concerns outside a theory of rights than in it, and to that extent a rights-framework can easily seem an ideological straitjacket from a woman's point of view. By the same token, the depth of the cultural critique that has to be undertaken in order to get an adequate sense of what is wrong with pornography is a reason for thinking that, in some sense, the idea of rights may be too *shallow* to do justice to feminist concerns. In traditional liberal theory, rights are concerned with external aspects of behaviour and related to the enforcement of law-like rules of conduct. But the oppression of women by men is not just a matter of externalized power and violence (though it involves that). It goes deep into the personal, the subjective and the phenomenology of the intimate; it resonates throughout the culture, from literature to advertising to grammar; it taints and is bound up with aspects of every institution and practice. There are serious questions to be asked about whether the form of rights can give expression to a social and cultural critique that is this radical and this comprehensive; certainly the feminist critique requires a much subtler and more careful discussion of the levels at which the idea of *respect for persons* impinges on lives and consciousnesses than one generally finds in the literature of political philosophy. Finally, the role of various forms of collectivity in feminist thought and togetherness in the women's movement, the identification of masculine relations with adversarial relations, and the massive problem of bringing the feminist critique into relation with ordinary notions of individual fault and blame – these issues have led many feminists to be sharply supicious of the individualism implicit in the idea of human rights.

Most of the issues we have discussed so far have been issues of content – the way in which theorists of rights have responded to criticism by attempting to accommodate new ideas and new concerns within the language of rights. At the same time there has been – particularly at the level of political theory – a new understanding of the theories and considerations that rights are to be contrasted with. In the rhetoric of 1789 natural law ideas that owed their provenance to writers like Locke were not clearly separated from democratic ideas that found their inspiration in Rousseau, and (for all the criticisms of Bentham and Burke) neither of these sets of ideas was clearly contrasted with considerations of general utility. We have seen already how those themes began to be disentangled in the middle of the nineteenth century, as writers like Mill and de Tocqueville drew attention to the threat posed by mass society to the individuality of the person. Once that antithesis was set up, it became natural to identify rights with individuality and to contrast them with the basis on which democratic decisions were made. This issue of rights versus democracy arose particularly acutely in the USA, where a body whose democratic legitimacy was, at best, indirect – the Supreme Court and the tribunals subordinate to it – had taken on the task of upholding the provisions of the Constitution even in the face of Congressional legislation. Rights in the USA were upheld explicitly as rights against the majority, and many of the greatest battles in this area – for civil rights in the South, for freedom of speech, for the procedural rights of police suspects, and so on – were fought and won against that background. Theoretically the result has been an enormous literature in American constitutional theory seeking to resolve this problematic relationship of apparently non-democratic norms and institutions in what, in other respects, is regarded by its citizens as a paragon among democratic regimes.[20]

Just as democracy has sometimes been regarded as a political expression (albeit a crude one) of utilitarianism – the greatest happiness of the greatest number being reflected in their greater number of votes – so the tyranny of the majority has come to be identified with the ethical problems that surround the application of the utilitarian calculus. The cost–benefit approach that utilitarians take to social problems appears to lend itself to the possibility that the interests of a few may sometimes have to be 'traded off' against the interests of the greater number. In the philosophical literature, this possibility has been explored in terms of 'the punishment of the innocent' – the fact that there is nothing in the logic of utilitarian deterrence, for example, to forbid the execution of an innocent person *pour encourager les autres*.[21] If the sum of utilities gained is great enough, the loss to the unfortunate innocent can always be justified in terms of the social good. Now modern proponents of rights have vehemently opposed this implication of utilitarianism:

> There is no *social entity* with a good that undergoes some sacrifice for its own good. There are only individual people, different individual people, with their own individual lives. Using one of these people for the benefit of others, uses him and benefits the others. Nothing more.[22]

The suggestion is that 'utilitarianism does not take seriously the distinction between persons', and that it does not pay sufficient attention to the intrinsic, not just the instrumental, importance of principles of distribution between persons.[23] With the battle lines drawn up in this way, much of the modern discussion about rights has taken the form of a debate between rights-theorists and utilitarians. To a certain extent the utilitarians repeat the charges that Bentham made; but they have also been made sensitive to the need to examine the possibility of constructing something like the protection that rights offer to individuality within the framework of their own ethical system.[24]

Other important developments that have taken place have more to do with the *form* of the language of rights. They represent a response not to criticisms of substance but to accusations of incoherence.

In modern political philosophy and jurisprudence theorists have tried to be much more precise in their use of the conceptual apparatus associated with rights. Though it had always been vaguely understood that rights were related logically to duties, the classic rights-theorists had made no systematic attempt to explicate the details of that relationship. That has changed in the twentieth century. All philosophers of rights regard themselves as duty-bound nowadays to show off for the benefit of their readers their knowledge of the main differences in the way rights and duties are related, the differences between privileges, claim-rights, powers, immunities, and so on. This has been particularly important in exposing some of the substantive equivocations that were involved in the use of the idea of rights in law and politics. Moreover, the history of the twentieth century has been punctuated by controversies about the nature of that relation which have helped to sharpen modern awareness of what rights involve. In the Preface to this collection I mentioned that Richard Tuck had shown the venerable historical provenance of the great modern debate between 'Choice' and 'Benefit' theories of rights. But though that debate has roots which extend back into the fourteenth century, the analytical tools of modern philosophy have enabled us to be clearer and less easily distracted in our formulation of the exact points at issue.[25] Ironically a lot of the credit for this has to be given to Bentham. Though as we have seen he was utterly opposed to the idea of *natural* rights, he was equally determined to show that the methodology of his analysis of legal fictions could be applied successfully to the idea of legal rights, and could expose the complex and varied relations which the idea of legal right might have to the idea of positive law via the concept of duty. We no longer share Bentham's conviction that talk of rights requires references to *positive* as opposed to some other postulated system of rules, but we are indebted nevertheless to the detail of his analysis of rules, rights and duties.[26]

The final difference between early and recent theories of rights that I want to mention concerns issues of justification. The claims of right that are made in documents like the Universal Declaration of Human Rights are not only controversial but also often very costly for subscribing states to uphold. For example a commitment to human rights seems to require us to uphold someone's freedom of speech even when this undermines political solidarity, or to organize free education even when this strains the resources of the state. What is it that justifies these irksome requirements?

At the level of rhetoric, the shift from 'natural rights' to 'human rights' marks a loss of faith in our ability to justify rights on the basis of truths about human *nature*. To call them *human* rights is now to characterize the scope of the claims being made rather than hint at anything about their justification. The term refers to universality and a commitment to equality and non-discrimination, particularly across races and peoples. But unlike 'natural' it leaves open the question of justification or, worse still, takes the mere existence of a broad consensus on these matters to be a sufficient reason for avoiding the task of justification altogether.

It is true that claims about human nature are still regarded as *relevant* to moral argument. It should make a difference to how we think and act to bear in mind that *all* humans – not just those we love or those of our race or gender – have the capacity to feel pain, fear, affection, loss, and so on; that we are *all* capable of pursuing purposes of our own, from the satisfaction of immediate needs to the prosecution of lifelong projects; and that we have active capacities for abstract thought, imaginative planning, creative problem-solving and sympathetic understanding.[27] It should also make a difference that we are embodied beings, living in an environment of moderate scarcity and limited clemency, not only capable of benefiting from co-operation but also vulnerable to one another in various ways.[28] All that is still relevant. What has changed is that, on the whole, philosophers no longer believe that the mere contemplation of these facts, turning one's reason to consider human nature and the human condition, is sufficient to yield ethical insight and a commitment to moral principles of equal concern and respect.

The view that either reason or science could yield moral principles was, of course, already under pressure in the eighteenth century. We saw earlier how the ethical claims of reason were discredited, and how the idea of God's law as a basis for natural rights was already in disrepute. In the years since 1789 this scepticism has advanced, not retreated. It is based now partly on considerations of logic. Given any beliefs you like about human nature, it seems to be an open question what attitude is to be taken towards them. Indeed the *practical* dispositions that lie at the heart of any moral position seem so different in character from the state of mind that constitutes belief that it is hard to imagine how anything like the former could ever be derived – in a logical sense – from something like the latter. Believing something about human nature and holding oneself ready to act compassionately seem to be such different sorts of experiences that it is hard to imagine a logical bridge between them.

Perhaps it will be argued that what we call our 'beliefs' about human nature are already composed of attitudes as well as propositions, values as well as facts. And indeed it seems quite likely that a range of beliefs as complicated as the ones involved here would have to be shaped and held together by certain practical concerns.[29] For example we form the beliefs we do and make the enquiries we make about the human capacities for planning and purpose at least partly because we cherish a certain purposive and articulate way of living a life. That evaluation is probably bound up with the very concept of agency. But even if this is true, still there is no logical compulsion on anyone to hold just *this* compound of attitudes/beliefs in his dealings with his fellow human beings. He may adopt some other – equally complicated – but ethically contrary conception of human nature. The range of attitudes it is possible to strike in the face of a naked and needy human being is considerable, and only *some* of them involve anything like the recognition that this creature is entitled to make claims on us as a matter of human right.[30] What is more, these are not just theoretic possibilities. Modern scepticism about the 'naturalness' of rights stems also from our historical experience: a greater range of these attitudes have been realized and acted on in the modern world, and among people who had previously led the world in ethical thinking, than most of us would feel comfortable with. The gigantic genocidal experiments of the 1940s and the associated cult of a master race; the oppression, torture and mind control that take place in so many modern countries; the massive indifference of people like us to famine, disease and deprivation in the Third World; and the continued survival – indeed, in some quarters, celebration – of racial and sexual inequality: all this should be enough to shake our confidence that human reason turned on human nature will yield a unique set of ethical conclusions favourable to the rights of man.

Wholesale scepticism about objective values and principles remains a popular position in moral philosophy. But it has not put an end to moral argument or to the enterprise of moral justification. Where a claim about human rights is contested – as many of the socio-economic ones are, for example – there is nothing to do but to work one's way back toward the deeper values and commitments that lie behind it, in the hope of finding premises not too far removed from those that one's opponent wants to use to justify her convictions. Moral justification is no longer the search for knock-down arguments, irresistible to human reason: it is a quest for shared foundations, and so it becomes important to find out what the foundations of our rights-claims really are. Even if the commitment to foundational principles and values is in the end just a matter of attitude, still it is important to uncover the sympathies and concerns that are pre-supposed when people say we should take rights seriously. Articulating our commitment to rights in this way enables us then to establish how much we are divided from our opponents on matters of belief and how much on matters of commitment. The predicaments and difficulties of social life are multiplying at an alarming rate (think of some of the puzzles posed by the new reproductive technology). An *articulated* structure of values – that is a sense of what is deep and what is superficial among our evaluations, how they are connected and which of them rest on what assumptions of fact – helps us to order the moral resources we have at our disposal to deal with these challenges.

This is not the place to review the various attempts that have been made to capture what one might call the 'deep structure' of our thinking about rights. But it is important to note that in response to the common challenge 'What are rights based upon?' philosophers are developing complex and interesting theories which relate them to the values implicit in our commitment to human agency – the human capacity for free action, the value of a sense of purpose, the material conditions for individual initiative and the importance for each person of his own pursuit of what he takes to be a good way of living. The recent work of John Rawls, John Finnis, Alan Gewirth, Carl Wellman, Ronald Dworkin and others may be insufficient to square the old philosophers' circle – to conjure values out of facts, demonstrate the existence of natural law, or compel us from beliefs about human nature to commitments to human rights.[31] But their work is helping to lay bare for consideration the foundations of the concept. To that extent the theory of rights is participating fully in what is undoubtedly the great achievement of modern moral philosophy – to show how argument and justification are possible and may proceed, even while the meta-ethics of realism and objectivity remain controversial, problematic and unclear.

III

Though there have been these developments, four of the charges that have been made against the idea of rights by our critics remain unanswered. These are: (1) the charge that human rights are unduly *abstract* in their formulation – that they abstract too much from locality, history and the detailed circumstances of human life; (2) the charge that theories of rights are too *rationalistic* – they exaggerate what can be achieved by reason in political philosophy; (3) the charge that these theories are too *individualistic* in their approach to social life; and (4), a charge that needs to be carefully distinguished from the third, that the idea of human rights introduces an unjustified element of *egoism* into moral argument. These are the most damning of the allegations made by Bentham, Burke and Marx, and they are the ones that have persisted in the modern discussion. The movement in political theory known as 'the new communitarianism' brings together all four of these themes in a comprehensive assault on the pretensions of rights-based liberalism.[32] In what follows I want to see whether anything can be said in response to this indictment; in doing so, I will be addressing not only the particular issue of human rights, but also some of the wider misgivings that have been expressed in recent communitarian writing.

Abstraction

The charge of abstraction is common in the rhetoric of political theory. It was made popular as a term of abuse by Hegel and Marx in their critiques of individualism, respectively, in Rousseauian moral theory and in liberal political economy.[33] Initially it is difficult to see the point of the accusation: *all* theoretical work involves some abstraction from the particularity of given experience, whether it is the abstraction of the idea of self in quest of spirit, or the abstractions of use-, exchange-and surplus-value. Often the charge amounts to little more than a reiteration of the claim that liberals have got hold of the wrong theory. But sometimes when the term is used, the charge is more comprehensive: it is an attack on theory in general and on the use or overuse of reason in some particular context. We shall examine this sort of attack on human rights theories in the section that follows.

The version of the abstraction charge that I want to discuss in this section concerns the *universalist* pretensions of a theory of human rights. Human rights represent entitlements and generate duties that are said apply to all men and women, at all times, and in all the circumstances and societies in which they live. They purport to reduce and distil into a few ringing principles all we know and all we need to know so far as the norms of social and political organization are concerned. They push aside all the detail of local custom, complex practice and ways of doing things that have evolved to suit particular environments, and replace them with norms of right that are supposed to apply uniformly and without exception across all the circumstances of human life. If people in a given society have accustomed themselves to monarchical rule and have not sought a hand in government, that counts for nothing: they have a *right* to democratic freedom which is inalienable, it is said, and they must be brought to recognize that fact. If a church has grown so long and deeply into a community that it permeates all customs and manners and it is unthinkable that anyone should question the common faith, that counts for nothing: they have a right to religious freedom which is imprescriptible, whether they want it or not. Though human rights may be mysterious or unintelligible to the people who are said to have them, they are said to have them just the same, and those claims of right are supposed to capture the moral truth about them in a way that their own customs, practices and shared understandings do not.

Described in this way, the abstract universalism of a theory of rights sounds unattractive. Opponents of rights suggest that it is also dangerous and misguided. Theoretically, they say, it is misguided because there is nothing to human life apart from the practices and ways of doing things that are constituted by shared understandings in a community. It does not make sense, they say, to appeal to a set of standards over and above those understandings in order to try and evaluate them. Such an idea is a fantasy of reason and can have no grip at all on social life. And practically, they say, the universalism of human rights is dangerous because it tempts us to do violence to local practices, tyrannically imposing values and ideals on other communities because they happen to appeal to the standards of *our* moral thinking. Often this is insulting as well as tyrannical. We interfere in the name of the 'human rights' of certain men and women using standards that make no sense to them, principles that violate their cherished frameworks, and bewildering conceptions that fly in the face of all they believe about themselves.[34]

Sometimes, paradoxically, the charge is that we have not been abstract enough in our thought about human society. We *say* we have got hold of universal rights, eternal moral truths that stand for all people and times. But in fact what we have is nothing but the local way of doing things in our own (capitalist, western, late-twentieth-century) society. This is what socialists have often alleged: liberals are in the habit of putting forward as laws of nature, categories and ideas that are in fact quite specific to capitalist political economy.[35] And it follows from the considerations in the preceding paragraph that this is all they can do. Full-blooded moral thinking can never escape the particular social circumstances that engender it. If we purport to do more than this, if we endeavour to raise ourselves in thought above the parochial preoccupations and understandings of our society, we produce *at best* a set of bloodless abstractions that have no grip on the colour, detail and reality of human life anywhere.

The moral relativism that lies behind these criticisms is not the crude (indeed barely coherent) view that whatever is thought right *in* a society *is* right *for* that society. It is rather a relativism that questions the whole business of making moral judgements (even the condescending anthropologist's super-tolerant ones) about social frameworks. The idea is that the business of moral judgement makes sense in relation to shared understandings and ways of doing things, but that there is no 'Archimedean point' for judging those understandings and ways of doing things from the outside. Another way of stating the position is to say that judgements made from such a spurious point of view can make no credible claim to acceptance or understanding by those to whom they are addressed. With no grip of their own in social consciousness, they can be only imposed, never recognized.

These are points that must be taken seriously by a theory with the sort of universalist pretensions that characterize human rights. It is true that there is a long tradition of universalist moralizing in the west: Aristotle's search for the final good for man, not just for the Athenian; Christ's ministry to the Gentiles; Kant's imperatives that purported to cut categorically across all contingent concerns and circumstances. But we must not assume in advance that it is a tradition that remains intelligible under scrutiny. Perhaps as long as there was confidence in the idea of moral reality – *objective* standards and values that would verify or falsify our claims – it made some sense to put forward judgements about human rights to and about people who barely understood let alone accepted them. But that confidence is now problematic, at best, and so we have to consider what the *point* is of saying to a person, quite unlike ourselves, who has lived and whose ancestors have lived quite happily with some practice or other for generations, 'This practice violates your human rights.'[36]

One response might be that we must at least do justice to our *own* moral traditions, and that we in the west have evolved *mores* that simply cannot be understood, even on their home ground, if an attempt is made to restrict their wider applicability. Around here we evaluate things using, say, Judaeo-Christian or Kantian standards: those standards help to constitute the shared understandings and practices of *our* culture. To use these standards in accordance with *our* shared understanding of them – for example to condemn a piece of political deceit in our society – is to hold ourselves disposed to apply them universally, to *anything* that can be recognized as deceit, whenever similar cases arise. To strike anything less than this universalist attitude towards deceit is to fall short of making the sort of evaluation we usually make around here. To put the point provocatively: our local mores are intrinsically imperialistic; to attempt to limit that imperialism is to commit what for the relativist is the cardinal sin of doing violence to local understandings (namely ours).

Now this is not a complete answer, for it shows only that it is unreasonable to expect us to refrain from universalistic evaluation. It does not provide an intellectual warrant for this practice. But it points us in the direction of a stronger argument.

One of the fallacies of the cruder forms of relativism is their assumption that there are a number of distinct 'societies' or 'cultures' in the world, each of which would exist happily and hermetically sealed off from the values of the others were it not for the misguided meddling of universalist liberals and other moral imperialists. But in fact, with almost no exceptions, every society or culture on the face of the earth is already open, willy-nilly, to the influence of others, and grows and thrives largely by filtering and feeding on extraneous materials, relating and connecting them with its own developed heritage. The triteness of phrases like 'global village' should not obscure the truth they connote: each culture and each society must come to terms with its neighbours and with the world; there is no question of any one effectively insulating itself from outside influences; and attempts to do so, far from being a desirable norm of intercultural relations, have been exceptional and, on the whole, tyrannical and disastrous for the people concerned. Quite apart from anything else, the geopolitical situation we face rules out the option of comfortable relativism. In a world where borders are disputed, peoples cross frontiers, local conflict is not containable and world war means global catastrophe, each society has an urgent concern with the existence of tension and conflict in other societies. Whether we like it or not, there is a legitimate *subject-matter* for moral evaluation that has to transcend local practices, narrowly understood.

Given this background, we need to look more closely at the relativists' contention that we do not have the moral tools to evaluate and criticize on a universal scale, and that anything beyond the frontiers of our locality must involve mere force and self-assertion, not intelligible judgement. That contention, I think, radically underestimates the resourcefulness of human evaluators. Even if it is true that moral judgement cannot take place in a vacuum but always in relation to some shared practice, our evaluations themselves – when we are confident that we are making them in the company of others – can constitute the background practice that gives them sense and substance. The process may go something like this. The members of a given society, S_1, find themselves holding views about the practices of a neighbouring society, S_2. These views are not just reflex applications of their own mores, for in S_1, as in any complex culture, the idea that circumstances may sometimes make a moral difference will be understood in a sufficiently sophisticated manner in local evaluations to justify its wider application in the case of differences between societies. Moreover, views like these may sometimes be not only held out but also reflected on, as members of S_1 ask each other whether their reaction to S_2 is appropriate, whether there is not some aspect of S_2 they are missing, and so on. And if they are aware, as again sophisticated people will be, that people in S_2 are having thoughts of a similar kind about S_1 (including the thought that people in S_1 are having thoughts of a similar kind about them . . .), it may occur to them to include in their reflections the question of whether there is anything in common between the external evaluations they are making and the external evaluations that they are aware are being made from S_2. And so it goes on. Where there is close and intimate contact between two societies, the line between the internal and external evaluations will blur (or at least the line between internal and external *reflective* evaluations will). For other societies more distant from one another, how much there is to evaluate will depend on what there is in the way of travellers' tales, for example, to go on. But even with a model this crude, it is possible to see how a practice of evaluation that transcends local circumstances will get underway, and provide conditions for the intelligibility of particular judgements that participate in that practice as it grows. And a moment's reflection is sufficient to convince us that such practices *have* gotten under way in the world. It may be saying too much to suggest that human rights theory is the epitome of this inter-societal evaluation. But there is no justification whatever for the view that we are all stuck in our local moral communities and that we make grave (socio)logical mistakes when we raise our sights to make the sort of far-ranging judgements that a theory of human rights commits us to.

There remain, however, grains of truth in the relativist position which should not be lost sight of too easily. Local mores *do* sometimes make a difference. Consider cases where a moral problem has the character of something like a co-ordination game. If a baby's mother dies in childbirth, who is to look after it – the father, one of its grandmothers, its aunts, its uncles? Often local custom will designate a particular solution, say the maternal grandmother. Now even if we come from a society where this responsibility falls 'naturally' on, say, the other parent, we should recognize that in a case like this the *right* solution is simply *whatever* the local customs stipulate (the solution around which local expectations have become established). That is, of course, provided it is a solution to the problem of looking after the child: a local practice of infanticide in these circumstances would raise quite different issues. And that should lead us to recognize that even this modest insistence on the autonomous authority of the local solution depends on a transcendent recognition of the problem it purports to solve. Indeed it turns out that the argument about such cases does nothing to establish any radical relativism in meta-ethics. It shows only that a plausible and attractive set of first-order moral principles will contain some indexical elements referring to variations in the social circumstances to which they are to be applied. A set of principles can have such an element and still be regarded as universal.

The relation of human rights to local morality is just one of the issues raised when the charge of abstraction is made. That issue can be seen as a particular instance of a more general complaint: that theories of human rights, in common with liberal theories of justice generally, do not pay sufficient attention to the concrete features of the human condition and of the moral and political predicaments real-life men and women actually face. We are not the abstract persona of liberal theory washed ashore on a desert island where we can design our society as we please; nor are we astronauts stumbling on a distant planet with the technology to implement whatever principles of justice and right we agree upon.[37] A plausible morality – and in particular a plausible *political* morality – must come to terms with the fact that we are embodied albeit thinking animals, vulnerable to each other and our environment, with conflicting needs, desires and commitments, living both in a natural world that offers limited opportunities for satisfaction and in a social world that is largely not of our making. A theory ignores or abstracts from these facts – what Hume called 'the circumstances of justice', and Hart 'the minimum content of natural law' – at severe cost to its credibility and practical usefulness.[38]

The issue of relativism arose out of the fact that we are not in a moral vacuum, where philosophic reason alone provides principles for us to live by; we find ourselves in a world already moralized by custom, precedent and practice, and an adequate moral theory has to come to terms with that fact. Equally an adequate theory of politics has to be based on the recognition that we live in a *particular* polity – with its rules, institutions and established forms of power and practice. A Declaration which affirms that 'every community in which a security of rights and a separation of powers is not provided for needs a constitution' must therefore face the problem of *transition*: how are we to move from our present polity to one constituted around principles of respect for individual rights?

This problem is one which radical writers have been notoriously reluctant to face. Rousseau's work, for example, pointed up both the corruption of contemporary society and the *possibility* of what he regarded as a genuinely free political order; but no attempt was made to show how we could move from one to the other. Indeed Rousseau's teachings on the effects of socialization – the idea that natural man might aspire to moral freedom through socialization in a free polity only if the corruption of inequality had not gotten to him first – encouraged a sort of 'Year Zero' thinking about the problem of transition. It was a type of thinking that came horrifyingly near to realization in the Terror that followed the French Revolution in the 1790s. In modern liberal theory philosophers like John Rawls, Robert Nozick and Bruce Ackerman have similarly failed to address this difficulty. A just order is specified, and it differs markedly from the society around us. But no account is given of what we might call 'justice-in-transition'; indeed Rawls makes a virtue of not interesting himself in the problem (which, from a practical point of view, necessarily interests *us* most) of how to act in unjust or only partially just societies.[39]

But maybe theories of rights are less vulnerable to these criticisms than some more comprehensive theories of radical social change. However it may have presented itself in Jacobin thought, a theory of rights is not a Utopia, but a series of discrete moral constraints on power and politics. Each principle of right can operate and be enforced independently of the others (though there is of course something in the view that a set of rights should form a *system* and is easier to uphold as such). We can work on the issue of free speech or on some particular welfare right without necessarily raising the issue of across-the-board renovation of the society. Moreover, rights characteristically set minimum goals to be achieved; unlike some theories of justice, a theory of rights does not provide a complete social programme. It says something like this: 'Whatever your social aims, whatever your traditions and ideals, you must act within *these* constraints, so far as the elementary freedom and well-being of individual citizens is concerned.' Of course, if a society is characterized by oppression and brutality, the criticisms made by even such a modest theory will be cumulative and wide-ranging. But that need not be the case, and will not be the case in at least a partially just society. Theorists of rights then can lower their sights to provide a basis for piecemeal reform rather than Utopian renovation of the societies they are concerned with. To this extent the problem of transition is less difficult for them to deal with.

We saw earlier that socialists sometimes criticize theories of rights for concentrating too much on issues at the 'consumption end' of the social process – who is to get what? – rather than on the deeper issue of control of the means of production in society. Indeed it is a theme common to both left- and right-wing critics that liberals fail to address the question of how the goods distributed under their principles are to be provided. At one level this is Maurice Cranston's point about 'ought implies can': 'If it is impossible for a thing to be done it is absurd to claim it as a right.'[40] At another level it is Robert Nozick's point that we should not treat the 'From each according to his ——' and the 'To each according to his ——' as separate issues: an answer to the one will, in the real world, place serious constraints on what we can say about the other.[41] At a still deeper level it is the Marxist point that humans are primarily producers of their own subsistence; hence the issues of how the goods called for by human rights are to be produced – in what conditions and under what modes of control – are issues whose importance for social theory is intrinsic not just instrumental.

Marxists are right to note that this last point is not adequately dealt with simply by including something like guaranteed employment as one of the rights on one's list. Their point is that if we insist on viewing social relations in adversarial terms – rights *against* the government, the claims that consumers can make *on* producers – then we should face the reality of the antagonism that will exist when these functions are divided among different classes. Needs will be satisfied only on a universal scale and in a way that people can count on when humanity as a whole takes control of its government and the production of the wherewithal to satisfy human needs.

We should not assume, however, that there is only one way in which that control might be exercised. The members of a society control the means of production first and foremost in the sovereignty that they have over the property arrangements of their society. There is not a simple choice between private or class ownership, on the one hand, and socialism, on the other; if private property exists in some form, that does not mean that people in general have lost control of the means of production. The members of a society can determine what form of private property to have, how much state enterprise and state regulation there should be in a mixed economy, what the forms and levels of taxation should be, and so on. In determining these matters and in tinkering with them from to time in accordance with the goals and constraints of social policy, they control the conditions of their life every bit as much as they would under a communist economic system.

Still, the underlying point remains valid: rights and property cannot be set apart from one another. All rights are costly, and if we take them seriously as the required minimum standards of life in society, we must be prepared to impose them as constraints on our choice of an acceptable property regime. We invoke rights to freedom and welfare because of the depth and urgency of our commitments to making the lives of men and women tolerable in these regards. Those commitments are not diminished when property rights are introduced into the picture: one does not become any less concerned that something should be done for the plight of the starving when one is told that all the food is privately owned by others. Even if it can be shown that the private property rights which stand as an obstacle here embody values and commitments as important as those at stake in the case of the starving, the introduction of those values only complicates the picture; it does not diminish or remove the original concern. At best it means we face a moral dilemma. What we cannot say, then, is what Robert Nozick urges us to say: that private property rights over resources 'fill up the space of rights, leaving no room for rights to be in a general material condition'.[42] That is not how our moral concerns work. On the contrary, it is likely to be our convictions about freedom and general well-being that enter the field first, placing considerable constraints on what we are able to say about property.

Rationalism

The charge of rationalism is connected with that of abstraction. The suggestion is that we go seriously wrong when we think of a society as something that can be comprehended, let alone designed or reno-vated, by the rational faculties of the individual mind. In Burke the charge involves a celebration of the role of 'prejudice', 'affection', 'untaught feeling' and 'awe' in political life, and a corresponding distrust of the 'private stock of reason' with which each thinking individual confronts the structures of his society. In modern conservative thought it is Oakeshott's image of politics as 'a boundless and bottomless sea' in which we sail with 'neither harbour for shelter nor floor for anchorage, neither starting place nor appointed destination'[43] – in short, none of the conditions that might provide an opening for rational thought as that is usually understood.

Theories of the rights of man seem to fly in the face of this wisdom by conceiving of politics and political practice in terms of the application of rational principles. Society is said to be in need of a *constitution* – that is an articulated and discursively comprehensible set of propositions to serve as the basis for all institutions and the actions that come under them. Rights theorists insist that society must have a rational design and be fully transparent and intelligible to those who are part of it. They say it must be built up rationally from first principles and exhibit its logic to anyone who cares to grasp it. But according to the criticism I want to consider in this section, that whole way of thinking involves a radical overestimation of what reason can achieve as the basis of institutions, tradition and political practice. Reasoning, particularly in the highly abstract formal mode favoured by philosophers, should not be thought of as the be-all and end-all of politics. It is an important enough faculty, to be sure – in its place. But, so the criticism goes, we should not assume that what fits the needs of metaphysics or geometry has anything in common with what is required for the wise ordering of public affairs. Those who make this criticism often invoke the spirit of Aristotle's injunction not to look for a greater precision than the subject-matter admits of:

> Man acts from adequate motives relative to his interest; and not on metaphysical speculations. Aristotle, the great master of reasoning, cautions us, and with great weight and propriety, against this species of delusive geometrical accuracy in moral arguments, as the most fallacious of all sophistry.[44]

Some of the points in this critique can be accommodated without abandoning all faith in reason as a basis for political evaluation. There are good *reasons* for saying that individuals do well 'to avail themselves of the general bank and capital of nations, and of ages' when they think about politics (p. 115). Reasoning about politics cannot be an entirely solipsistic enterprise, and in our culture it has always been the work of a *community* of thinkers and a *heritage* of thought. But, for all that, it is a community to which individual members contribute actively not passively, and in which the thought of the past is appropriated and built on critically rather than merely approached with veneration. Equally there are good *reasons* for assigning 'prejudice' (or, as it is sometimes called, 'intuition') an important role in practical life. Burke is right to note that 'prejudice is of ready application in the emergency . . . and does not leave the man hesitating in the moment of decision, sceptical, puzzled and un-resolved' (p. 116). This is the sort of thing that modern utilitarians have often stressed.[45] Even that most calculating of theories can make sense of the suggestion that sometimes more value may be lost than gained by persevering with calculations of value when a quick decision is called for. As reasoners we can work out in advance that we sometimes do better by acting from habit or prejudice and not trying to work out for ourselves what would be the best thing to do. But that is *not* a deep thesis about the limits of reason. On the contrary, it is itself the product of sophisticated second-order reasoning in politics (reasoning about reasoning), and it derives not from any inherent lack of faith in the usefulness of human thought but from a very considerable confidence in our ability as thinkers to set the agenda for the application of reason in political life. The political reason so employed, far from being meagre and inconsiderable, is sophisticated and multi-levelled. Indeed when Burke writes –

> The science of constructing a commonwealth, or renovating it, or reforming it, is, like every other experimental science, not to be taught *à priori*. Nor is it a short experience that can instruct us in that practical science; because the real effects of moral causes are not always immediate; but that which in the first instance is prejudicial may be excellent in its remoter operation; and its excellence may arise even from the ill effects it produces in the beginning. (p. 106)

and so on – that is best interpreted as a call for more reason, not less, in political thought. It is not an attack on political rationalism as such, but on a particularly unsophisticated, naive and over-enthusiastic form of political thinking. It is the *thinker* who recognizes that 'in states there are often some obscure and almost latent causes'; and 'the men of untaught feelings' are as often to be found in the incendiary mob as on the side of tradition, practice and caution.

Once we concede that in politics, as in all moral life, it is important for people to have habits, traditions and prejudices to fall back on, there is still the further question of what their content should be. Of course, as a practical matter, this is not entirely an open question for us: no drastic or immediately comprehensive reformation of our habits and traditions is possible, and any attempt to bring it about would disrupt and undermine the processes of socialization on which these very things depend. But it is not entirely closed either. There are decisions we can make – more or less important ones, occasionally central, mostly at and around the margins of our moral dispositions. For example we may see that, if left to itself (whatever that means), a certain practice will fall into desuetude: are we to intervene and shore it up? Perhaps new circumstances or new technology has arisen: what are their implications for the way we bring up our children? Should we go on exactly as before, persevering with traditions that had adapted themselves to the conditions of a different age? If so, how do we handle the tensions that inevitably result? It cannot always be the course of wisdom to shy away from these decisions and let things take their own course (whatever 'their own' can possibly mean in the context of social life). But if we are not to avoid them, we have to ask what thoughts, commitments and principles we should face them with? The anti-rationalist position seems to be that there is *nothing* original for thought to do here: 'We know that *we* have made no discoveries, and we think that no discoveries are to be made, in morality' (p. 114). Such modesty, though rhetorically becoming, obscures the fact that the business of thinking things through is not a game we indulge in but a duty we have to discharge. Working out how to cope with new circumstances and how to think about old ones when, through no desire of ours, familiar practices begin to seem distant from us, may be not a conceit of vain reason, but an inescapable responsibility. In other words a reasoned political theory – say a particular formulation of human rights – need not be paraded as a triumph of speculation; it may simply represent the best we have been able to manage in our sincerest efforts to think through and act on the problems that suddenly confront us.

In recent discussion it is often the *articulacy* of reasoned theory that attracts particular critical attention. Even if it is conceded that we have an inescapable duty to reason about politics, need we be committed to the view that our reasoning has to yield a set of statable principles and formulae such as those found in declarations of human rights – a clearly formulated set of verbal principles applicable almost algorithmically to yield conclusions about the conduct of our political life? Bernard Williams has argued that it is far from obvious that the upshot of moral thought should always be 'a principle, in the sense of a summary and discursively statable description that does not rely too much on a vague reference to degree ("too much", "balances out", "does not pay enough attention to . . .").'[46] There is a tradition in ethics that we can often learn more from a story or a parable than from any summary formulation of its 'moral'; and that acting well or becoming virtuous is somewhat more like learning to ride a bicycle than like working one's way through a textbook of geometry.

Though this sort of Aristotelianism has a certain appeal in personal ethics, one should be wary of generalizing too quickly into the political realm. There is a lot to be said for the view – *also* associated with Aristotle and more recently with Hannah Arendt – that politics is a realm of action in which people deal with one another and reveal themselves to one another, in their words, as speakers, discursively.[47] The idea that our values and commitments in politics should necessarily be implicit, never stated, never raised for consideration by the many to the level of verbal formulations, seems radically at odds with the idea that it is in our *speech*, in our readiness to be articulate with one another, that our politics is constituted as something set apart from the implicit enthusiasm of violence. There is both snobbery and dangerous irresponsibility in the idea that political morality is like the ethics of a gentleman – something that is necessarily destroyed in the attempt to articulate it.

Maybe it is important for there to be implicit commitments – as background or stage-setting conditions – *as well* as the articulated 'up-front' elements of our political morality. A theory of rights does not rule that out, for it does not purport to be a complete political morality: apart from anything else, a theory of rights needs to be complemented by ideas of virtue and decency which can be brought to bear on personal decisions about how to *exercise* our rights.[48] Equally, however, the celebrated implicitness or inarticulacy of an Aristotelian or Christ-like ethic cannot preclude the need for firm and explicit constraints and requirements *somewhere* in one's system of moral thought. To take an extreme example, the European Convention on Human Rights lays down categorically and without exceptions that 'no one shall be subjected to torture' (Article 3). Is it seriously supposed that a morality can do without principles of this bluntly articulated sort, on matters like these, somewhere at the level of practice? No doubt, Aristotelian gentlemen will not be disposed to pull each other's fingernails out or to use cattle-prods on each other's genitals, and raising the issue in the context of the *Nichomachean*

Ethics does seem like an exercise in bad taste. But that does not show that a morality has no need of such constraints; it shows only that it is sometimes possible to think about the nature of the good life on the quiet assumption that elementary questions of freedom, security and welfare have been taken care of. Our experience is (and Athenian experience certainly ought to have been) that that cannot always be taken for granted, and that a political morality has to reserve a corner for addressing the elementary issues as well.

Still, there is sense in the suggestion that we should think carefully about what is involved in the formulaic articulation of our moral principles. We should take care not to confuse the idea that there are human rights with the view that a certain set of verbal formulations – for example those contained in the Universal Declaration or the European Convention – can adequately express the depth and complexity of even our strongest and most elementary moral concerns. A human right is a moral position in relation to a particularly important type of individual interest. To point to that interest and capture its importance for us, we may use a form of English words like 'free speech' or 'a right to a nationality' or 'reasonable limitation of working hours and periodic holidays with pay'. But words – the language we use – are much more closely tied to a particular society, to a particular historical period, and to a particular (though indeterminate) set of cultural resonances than the moral ideas associated with human rights are supposed to be. Now the use of simple phrases, legislative forms, even political slogans is unavoidable in the politics of human rights: the point about the spoken-ness of a political culture applies once again. But it is in the theory and argument that lies behind the formula, not in the formula itself, that we find the sense and substance of the right as a *universal* aspiration. Though theories too are expressed in words, we have a greater opportunity to capture the subtlety of an abstract moral idea from a sustained passage of argument, in which a point is rehearsed in a number of different ways, and elaborated and qualified carefully and at length, sometimes in noble rhetoric, sometimes in awkward analytical prose, than from the simplistic slogan in which unavoidably the right will be publicly expressed. A phrase – in English or French or whatever – will inevitably sound local and relative to our particular ways of doing things. Only the *argument* with which we defend and elaborate the aspiration which the slogan expresses can make it clear how this formula relates to anything like a universal human concern.

Recently political theorists have taken to distinguishing between the *concept* and the *conception* of something. For example the concept of democracy is something more abstract than particular conceptions such as plenary democracy on the Athenian model, Westminster-style representative democracy, the democracy of revolutionary soviets, and so on.[49] Similarly we may want to say that a particular form of words used in a document like the Universal Declaration can inevitably capture only one particular *conception* of a right that is to be regarded as something important for all humans, in all places and all times. The theory of rights may get at the *concept* of whatever it is we are interested in – political liberty, a decent minimum standard of living – but the verbal formulation in the charter takes us only as far as a particular conception and points us in the general direction of the concept from there.

An example may help to illustrate the point. In his paper 'Human Rights – Real and Supposed', Maurice Cranston attacked Article 24 of the UDHR among other reasons because it included a right to 'periodic holidays with pay'. That is not a universal or human right, he argued, but one that pertains only to people in certain types of employment positions in certain forms of developed economy.[50] But Cranston is mistaking a conception for a concept here. There *is* a universal human interest – recognized in all societies – in having longish periods (days and weeks rather than hours) of sustained respite from the business of getting a living, whatever that happens to involve: holidays, holy days, fiestas (as opposed to siestas), times when the tribe will dance and feast rather than hunt, and so on. Now the language of a modern capitalist society may denote this interest with a form of words appropriate only to the highly structured and time-detailed character of its economic relations. But the use of that form of words should not blind us to the possibility that nevertheless some *universal* human interest, one that transcends wages and the forty-hour week, may be involved.

The simple formulations of our charters have the additional disadvantage that they present all rights as moral absolutes, apparently leaving no room for the possibility that they may conflict with, and therefore need to be balanced against, one another in a subtle and sensitive way. Rights are put forward as matters of principle, apparently without qualification, yet even the most cursory reflection indicates that they need to be adjusted to one another in the complex circumstances of modern life. I have remarked already that this has been acknowledged now much more in modern philosophical theories of rights.[51] But the language of our political declarations still veers alarmingly between two extremes – of insisting, on the one hand, that rights are sacred and may never be compromised and, on the other hand, of admitting a catch-all saving clause that allows the abrogation of any right at all whenever that is demanded by 'the just requirements of morality, public order, and the general welfare'.[52] Once again, we should recognize how difficult it is for a slogan to express the subtlety of the conviction that individual rights should prevail over some moral considerations but not others.

In the discussion so far, we have used the term 'reason' without much explanation of what its employment in politics is supposed to involve. Certainly it involves thought, abstract theory, maybe even theoretical speculation. But few have ever seriously believed, even those 'rationalists' whom Burke and Oakeshott take as their targets, that theorizing about politics can get under way on the basis of ratiocination alone. What about the values and commitments that *move* us in (and *to*) our political thought? There are problems enough with the idea of a 'value-free' political science; but the idea that *normative* political theory could be an entirely intellectual enterprise seems preposterous. The history of moral and political philosophy is littered with the remains of theories which sought to base practical commitment on the workings or even the form of reason alone. As Hume pointed out, reason without passion moves nothing.[53]

There is no reason why a theorist of rights should deny any of this. The concerns that drive our political thought are matters of feeling: we *find* ourselves with certain capacities for sympathy, distress, commitment and fulfilment and, when we start thinking, we first *notice* that we are moved (rather than decide to be moved) by the concerns expressed in our values and principles. But these motivations are by no means a matter of 'untaught feeling' as Burke sometimes seemed to suggest. Long before Burke wrote, David Hume had exploded the idea that '*natural*' sympathies by themselves could serve as a foundation for social life.[54] Though, as I have said, we find out that we are moved in certain ways as we begin thinking, those concerns may still be the products of our being brought up and socialized in a culture where people have mingled thought and affect in their reflection on politics for millennia. And anyway, we are far from at the mercy of our given concerns. Finding ourselves moved in various ways, we go to work on ourselves and on each other, plunging deep to find articulate principles to unify and account for our concerns, and breaking the surface of conduct to draw out their implications for our behaviour. Because our concerns are complex, we can change the way we feel. Reflecting on some concern or attraction which we discover we have, we may resolve perhaps not to be moved by it in the future, or to bring some other commitment to greater prominence in the scheme of our evaluations – leaving others intact in the mean time to serve as the driving basis for these resolutions. Thus as emotion continues to play a part in our practical life, it is as a product of the *interplay* of our capacity for thought and our capacity to be moved. It is not a matter of brute, unexamined feeling alone. (Quite apart from anything else, the image of 'untaught feeling' as the basis of conduct underestimates the affective allegiances that we have in respect of the integrity and operation of our own intellectual faculties!)

The suggestion is also present in Burke's writing that the rationalist republican spirit of the rights of man leaves no room for feelings of loyalty, awe, allegiance, chivalry and majesty as constituents of political life. Any response to this must be complex. A theorist of rights must pluck up his republican courage sooner or later and say outright that many of the feelings that Burke celebrates – reverence for priests, awe for kings, genuflection to nobility – have done vastly more harm than good to the human spirit and in human affairs. But still, Burke is right to point out the impoverishment of a political theory whose only affective components are fear of the gallows and hope of material advantage. Again, however, it is important to insist that feeling in politics is a complex matter; it is suffused with thought and belief and therefore cannot simply be dissociated from the reasoning processes that sustain thought and belief. Respect for authority, love of one's country, loyalty to its institutions and fidelity to its law are bound up with the judgement that these things are 'good' as well as 'mine'. As Tom Paine pointed out, 'No man is prejudiced in favour of a thing, knowing it to be wrong.'[55] And it is also bound up with beliefs about the way the authorities and institutions in question work, how and why they were set up, and what their tendency is. We *think* our allegiances as well as feel them; if we did not, we might view them simply as urges which afflict us rather than as motives we embrace.

This leads to a final point. Austere and rationalistic as it may seem, the philosophy of human rights is quite capable of generating an aura of feeling of its own when it is realized in the constitution and life of a nation. Besides the enthusiastic fervour of the revolutionary crowd, there are also the deeper, calmer feelings of profound respect for human dignity and for humanity itself that are embodied in the rejection of hierarchy and the assertion of equal rights for all. (In fact if Kant is right, the very universality of this commitment is capable of evoking the powerful affective response of reverence for the moral law.)[56] These attitudes towards one's fellow citizens and the way one treats them form the basis of the respect and loyalty owed to republican institutions; for these have been set up, sometimes under conditions of the greatest danger, as a social and political order that enables people to live together as equals. The fact that these institutions are explicitly human creations, whereas those they replaced had been viewed as naturally or divinely ordained, does not lead those under them to regard them with contempt. On the contrary, the realization that these institutions are truly *theirs*, made by and for people like them, coupled with an awareness of their human fragility, can evoke a sort of caring and cherishing at least as substantial as the feelings exhibited by people who regard their constitution as part of the natural order of the universe. And as Hannah Arendt has argued, the founding of these institutions, and the very idea of such a foundation, can serve as a powerful point of reference for tradition and legitimacy in a republican regime.[57]

Individualism

In one of its aspects the charge of individualism is closely related to the charge of political rationalism. Modern liberal theories take the view that the structures and institutions of a society must be capable of being justified to the individuals who comprise it, and that in this sense they must answer adequately at the tribunal of individual reason. According to this model human rights are an expression of the limits on what individuals are prepared to accept in the way of a justification of their society; they are the *minimum specifications* for such a justification, as it were. But opponents of liberalism may believe that this notion of justification-to-individuals is only one among several modes of social legitimacy, and that there are other modes like justification-to-a-community (what *we*, understood in some non-aggregative sense, can accept) or justification-to-a-people-throughout-its-history.

The issues that this raises are complicated ones. Certainly a model of justification in politics is inadequate if it focuses only on the individual interests of those immediately involved. The worth of many communal goods (like the good of a shared language) or the importance of intergenerational principles (like some principle of conservation) cannot be captured in such a model.[58] However, given that such goods and principles are thought important, the fact remains that it is possible for the individual evaluator to apprehend their importance (even when it is not importance *for* individuals as such), and indeed it is difficult to imagine any other way in which their importance *could* be apprehended. The point is that we function as *individual* evaluators and *individual* thinkers even in our altruism, even in our communitarianism, and even in our concern for posterity. No doubt it will be argued that this is not necessarily the case and that this aspect of individualism is a social construct. The truth of that (if it *is* true) does not make it any easier (for us) to avoid evaluation in this mode or to comprehend what another mode of evaluation would be like. *We* are constructed (naturally or socially) and we treat ourselves as independent centres of consciousness, thought and responsible agency. Each of us – even those with altruistic or communitarian concerns – assesses and evaluates social arrangements using his own individual critical faculties. Even when we do so in the company of others, learning from them, gaining fresh insights, and so on, it is still the meeting of individual minds, the interaction of individual critical intelligences that is going on. If this book is read by opponents of rights and individualism, it is read by them individually; even if people talk in groups about its arguments, they will be bringing together their several reactions and forging those into a public evaluation. As I have said, perhaps it was not always so. Perhaps it has something to do with our Cartesian heritage and with the emphasis on individual conscience and understanding that has dominated western thought since the seventeenth century at least. At any rate, it is hard for us to imagine it otherwise and it does not seem to be something any of us can do anything about. We can change how selfish and acquisitive we are, and how limited our perspective is on community and posterity; but we cannot alter the fact that it is to us, severally as individuals, that communitarian and conservative arguments must be addressed.

All the same, it is one thing to say that we evaluate as individuals, quite another to argue that our evaluations are necessarily individualistic in their content. Theories of rights appear to extol the importance of certain strictly individual interests – things like bodily security, personal liberty, privacy, material well-being, and so on – to the neglect of those goods or values that cannot be so easily rendered in individualist terms. Is this a valid objection?

It is easy for the objection to be exaggerated. Whilst some of the rights that we find in the various charters protect strictly individual interests, others, as Marx noted, are oriented towards participation in a common life with others. Free speech, for example, is not just liberty to talk to the bathroom mirror; freedom of association is not just the right to prefer one's own company; and it does not make sense to think of democratic rights being exercised in isolation from the mass of one's fellow citizens. The point here is not merely that these rights are universalizable but that, as Marx put it, they 'are only exercised in community with other men' (p. 144). To be sure, these rights protect *individual* interests in relation to communal activities. But that shows only that certain forms of individual security may be preconditions for communal engagement. *We* cannot participate in discussion if *I* am gagged and bound; *they* cannot live and thrive as a polity if *she* is under a banning order, and so on. Without wanting to be at all reductivist about communal life, one can insist that there are certain things *individuals* can suffer which may make communal life impossible and which therefore anyone with a concern for community will want to prevent. We shall return to this theme in the final section of the essay.

The objection can be exaggerated in another way by taking as one's target a theory that says, not only that human rights are *important*, but also that they are the be-all and end-all of political morality. It is easy to show that a theory of rights cannot possibly be a comprehensive moral theory.

By its very nature, a theory of rights is an individualistic theory. Rights purport to secure goods *for individuals*: that is an elementary consequence of their logical form. A right is always somebody's right, and we never attempt to secure things *as a matter of right* unless there is some individual or individuals whose rights are in question. Thus the language of rights differs crucially from moral locutions like 'It would be a good thing if . . .' and '. . . ought to be the case'. Rights express moral desirability to or for some individual whereas those other locutions are used to express moral desirability *sans phrases*. Indeed the most plausible recent analysis of the rights-idiom presents a right as the assertion of a justificatory relation between the interests of an individual and the imposition of social duties: ' "X has a right" if and only if . . . other things being equal, an aspect of X's well-being (his interest) is a sufficient reason for holding some other person(s) to be under a duty.'[59] The individual interest – in bodily security, say, or in being able to speak one's mind without fear of punishment – must be important enough from a moral point of view to warrant the imposition on others of the duties normally associated with the right. Even when we think of the interest as one that all people share, still with rights the link between interest and duty is individualistic. Though X, Y and Z all share an interest in bodily security, still the interest in X's case must be of sufficient importance to warrant imposing all the duties necessary to protect *his* (X's) bodily security, the interest in Y's case must be of sufficient importance to warrant imposing all the duties that are necessary to protect *his* (Y's) bodily security, and so on. Even when we apply rights through universalization rather than on the basis of attention to individual detail, we do so because we are convinced more or less a priori of the importance of the interest in the case of each individual who may fall under the scope of our universalization. (This is one of the crucial differences between rights-based and utilitarian justifications of rules and duties: a utilitarian will base the rule – for example – against attacking X on a calculus of the interests that X *and* Y *and* Z have in the matter.)

Now it is evident that there are some duties that cannot be justified in this manner, and certainly there are some goods and values whose desirability cannot be analysed on an individual-by-individual basis. Certain ecologists take the view that the survival of the earth as an environment for living things and of its main ecosystems might be worth protecting even at the expense of all individual human well-being. And one can imagine an aesthetic theory in which the existence of things of beauty was thought valuable and worth cherishing quite apart from human enjoyment of them. But even without leaving the realm of humanistic values, there are certain things which are plausibly said to be good for people but whose value cannot be broken down reductively on the sort of individual-by-individual basis suggested by the language of rights. Examples like these spring to mind: the good of a shared language and culture to the people that have traditionally enjoyed it; the conviviality of a dinner party; the intrinsic value of solidarity in a common endeavour; and the importance of fraternity in communal association. These are not goods whose value to the group is merely an additive function of their value to individuals. I am sure that people do get individual pay-offs from the values I have listed: conviviality feels good to each guest; fraternity leaves each comrade with a warm glow and so on. But the importance of the values in question would be radically distorted by expressing them as the cumulation of these individual pay-offs. The individual pay-offs seem to be derivative from the communal enjoyment rather than the other way round.

If there are any goods like this, it is a mistake to try and express their importance in the language of rights. Their desirability will be the basis of whatever duties we recognize to produce and sustain them, but that desirability cannot be pinned down to the discrete interests of individuals in the way that the form of rights requires. It is because the members of a group – X and Y and Z – may enjoy a good, like fraternity or conviviality *together*, and because the participation of all in that enjoyment is partially constitutive of the enjoyment of each, that the good is worth pursuing. So since no adequate account of its desirability can be pinned down to either X or Y or Z. there is simply no point in saying that it ought to be pursued as X's or Y's or Z's right.

Now the force of this point is dissipated a little by the possibility of talking about the rights of groups as well as those of individuals. Can we not say that the Welsh have a right to retain their language and culture, meaning Wales as a people or nation, not the agglomeration of individual Welshmen? Maybe; but talk of group rights does not provide a complete answer to the individualism objection. The idea of group rights makes sense only in circumstances where the group exists as an 'individual' in relation to some wider entity (Wales versus the United Kingdom, for example) or some co-ordinate 'individual' (Cambodia versus Vietnam). It does not make sense when the duties correlative to the rights of the group are conceived to fall primarily on the members who compose it.[60] And anyway, the shift to group rights does not blunt but at most only re-expresses the criticism that individualism is inadequate as a complete political theory. The force of that criticism is that not everything of importance in politics can be pinned down to the freedom, security and well-being of individual men and women in the way that theorists of rights have sometimes suggested.

So – certainly a theory which asserts that all political values can be expressed as individual rights or that political morality is ultimately right-based will be embarrassed by this criticism. But theories of human rights need not make such a bold claim. Even if some of the important things in this life are communal in the sense I have outlined, still there may be important – perhaps even overwhelmingly important – individual goods *as well* that a political theory neglects at its peril. The modest function of a theory of rights is not to claim completeness but to draw attention to these important individual interests. One is not guilty of any crass or misguided individualism simply for expressing moral concern about certain of the ills that may befall individual men and women, or the harm and neglect that individuals may inflict on one another. It is *awful* to be locked up or silenced, *terrifying* to be beaten and tortured, and *appalling* to be left to starve or vegetate when resources are available for food and education; and one may think these ills so bad that their avoidance should be an overriding aim of any decent society. To hold such a view and base it on the moral significance of what it is like, as an individual, to suffer these evils, is to embrace a theory of rights. But except on very pessimistic assumptions, the business of avoiding these extreme individual evils is unlikely to occupy *all* our energies or consume *all* our resources. That leaves the possibility for other goods to be pursued. And certainly one who accords priority to the protection of these basic individual interests is not committed to the view that, once this basic task is taken care of, all the *other* goods to be pursued in society have to be individual in character.

The communitarian objection may be recast in the following form. It is no good saying that rights can coexist in a moral theory with communal goods. The trouble is that, if rights are admitted at all, they can too easily overwhelm communal goods. To see this, we need only consider how relationships like families, or other intimate relations, can be destroyed or undermined if people become preoccupied with their individual entitlements and with what they can claim as a matter of right against the other people involved. Hegel attacked Kant's contractarian account of marriage for precisely this reason. Marriage, he said, is not a contract between 'individual self-subsistent units', and as a moral institution it will be wrecked if men and women come to regard it like that. Even though it is based on an agreement, it is, Hegel said, 'precisely a contract to transcend the standpoint of contract', that is to transcend the standpoint of an individual making claims about his or her rights.[61] If we do come across a marriage characterized by querulous claims of right, we will be apt to conclude that something has already gone wrong. Similar points have been made by communitarian writers about justice:

> Consider for example a more or less ideal family situation, where relations are governed in large part by spontaneous affection. . . . Individual rights and fair decision procedures are seldom invoked, not because injustice is rampant but because their appeal is preempted by a spirit of generosity in which I am rarely inclined to claim my fair share. Nor does this generosity necessarily imply that I receive out of kindness a share that is equal to or greater than the share I would be entitled to under fair principles of justice. I may get less. The point is not that I get what I would otherwise get, only more spontaneously, but simply that the questions of what I get and what I am due do not loom large in the overall context of this way of life.[62]

If, by some misfortune, people started to become obsessed with their entitlements in this sort of society, we might want to say that the situation had deteriorated from a moral point of view, and we might, as Sandel points out, still want to say that even in the face of a reassurance that all legitimate claims of justice were being met.

To answer this concern, the theorist of rights can and should concede that there are many types of human relation where standing on one's rights *would* be inappropriate or undesirable. But he can argue that, even in regard to those cases, it is important for there to be rights available, at least in the background, for individuals to fall back on if they need to. The point is that intimate communal relationships, no matter how cuddly, cannot be guaranteed always to hold together. Marriages split, families fall apart, small-scale communities become riven with dissension. What happens under these unfortunate circumstances? The constituents of these relationships are suddenly thrown back on their own resources and it will be important for them to have some knowledge of where they stand and how they can start picking up the pieces. If there is to be an institution of marriage, for example, there must also be rules and rights pertaining to divorce (or something like it), for we cannot give anyone a guarantee that the affections which make rights superfluous will always last. Moreover, since people know this is the case, since they know about the fragility as well as the desirability of affective non-rights-based relationships, one suspects they will not always wait until a relationship falls apart before enquiring what their rights would be. Likewise, a person entering a commune may want to know at the time he goes in, what he can count on in the unhappy event that the thing falls apart; that is not just mean-minded selfishness, but a quite understandable awareness of the fragility of these set-ups in the real world. One of the other themes of the communitarian critique has been the insistence that moral and political thinking should address the concrete reality of moral experience as it actually is, not the abstractions of liberal speculation. In this case the concern works in the other direction, for it is our concrete experience of human affairs that makes us most sensitive to the apprehensions people may realistically have about the breakdown of communal relations. Indeed it is possible to argue that, in any real world we are ever likely to encounter (as opposed to the fictional golden age for which communitarians often evince a yearning), these apprehensions will be so comprehensively grounded that most people will not think themselves able to enter whole-heartedly into affective non-rights-based relationships without some guarantee that there is a just and adequate set of rights in the background that they can fall back upon if necessary.

It is no good saying that the individual who claims to need these rights is, from a communitarian point of view, an incomplete and abstract being when considered apart from his social relationships. That ontological point (even if it is conceded) is of little comfort to someone who finds that his commune has left him out in the cold. Even if the individual *is* a creation of the social rather than the other way round,[63] still it is the case that, for any given social relationship, there is always a possibility that it may disintegrate as a tolerable basis for living, leaving a naked individual bereft of any substantial bond to others wanting to know where he stands. To grasp the necessity for rights in this context, all one needs to accept is that, as it were, *individual fall-out* from social relations is possible. And indeed, if it is the case that the precipitated individual is going to be an incomplete and alienated being – truncated, distorted, necessarily confused about his identity – then the case for his protection and security in these circumstances is more, not less, substantial.

In all of this, I have been defending a version of rights theory which is somewhat more modest than many. Some theories of rights do unashamedly embrace many of the individualistic postures that I have been cautious about. They believe in ontological individualism, and they claim to be able to make no sense of the idea that there might be irreducibly communal values. There is always a danger that in defending a modest version of a well-known type of theory against criticism, one will be seen as attempting to give comfort and respectability to those who propose more extreme versions and against whom the criticisms in question are more properly directed. I want to insist that it is possible that a theory of rights can be defended, with appropriate concessions and elaborations, against communitarian objections. But not all theories of rights can be. The objections are powerful and important ones, and they should prompt very careful consideration by all who claim to be interested in rights.

Egoism

The final charge I want to consider is that of egoism: the suggestion that when we take rights seriously we introduce an unwarranted element of self-concern or selfishness into social life and moral discussion. This was one of the themes that emerged in all three of our writers. Bentham and Burke commented that the object of the Declaration of Rights seemed to be to reinforce the selfish and dissocial passions whereas, they argued, the prime need of any society was their restraint and discipline (pp. 48 and 105). And Marx asserted that the rights of man were 'nothing but the rights of . . . egoistic man, man separated from other men and the community . . . the right of selfishness' (p. 145). A philosophy dedicated to the importance of individual life, liberty and the pursuit of happiness, and which sees these as rights that can be claimed by the individual *against* his community, seems the expression of egoism *par excellence*. It seems a philosophy singularly unsuited to the exigencies of a world in which individual claims must be moderated by sensitivity to the needs of others and of the community at large.

The claim that rights-theories are egoistic is a complex one, and I want to consider three separate charges in this part of the indictment. The first charge is that to say a person has a right to something is to encourage her to exercise that right selfishly without regard to others. The second charge is that rights are characteristically claimed and enforced in an unpleasantly adversarial and self-centred manner. And the third is the charge that, behind these issues of exercise and enforcement, lies a deep and pervasive exaggeration in rights-theories about the ineliminability of self-interest from social life. I want to reply to each of these charges in turn, arguing that the first is downright false, the second not necessarily true, and the third fair in the sense that rights-theorists do emphasize the importance of self-interest but false inasmuch as such an emphasis is not necessarily an exaggeration of the role that it plays in social and moral activity.

The first charge is that to be told one has a right is to be encouraged to act selfishly, inconsiderately or insensitively in the exercise of that right. There may be something in this as a matter of empirical fact: it is difficult to deny that on occasion bringing to people's notice the fact that they have rights has been followed by selfish action in the exercise of those rights, action which might not have occurred if the right had not been publicized. So maybe rights sometimes do encourage selfishness in the brute sense of being correlated with its occurrence. But if they do, it is either because people misunderstand rights or because the background inclination to selfishness is anyway so strong that *any* indication that one will not be restrained is sufficient to trigger such action. Since the strongest charge on the indictment in Bentham's claim that the encouragement of the selfish passions is 'the perpetual and palpable *object*' of a Declaration of Right (p. 48), I shall discuss the former suggestion first.

Is there anything in the content of a claim that 'X has a right to do A' which justifies Bentham's allegation?[64] The first thing we need to remember is that we are unlikely to find in a Declaration of Rights (or anywhere else) a claim of right that is made solely and exclusively in relation to a selfish action. Where rights to action are involved, we are almost always talking about X's right to perform an action *of a certain type* or an action *from a certain range of choices*; and that range will include acts that are noble, benevolent, community-minded, decent and good-hearted, as well as ones more selfishly oriented to X's own personal advantage. X's right to free speech, for example, is as much his right to warn others of some social danger, or to urge them to greater efforts in the pursuit of some common endeavour, as his right to persuade them to fall in with his own selfish interests. Or take the right of property: Marx is quite wrong to suggest in his critique that this is nothing but the right to take decisions about resources without consulting society. A proprietor can consult social interests if he wishes: he can keep his business running at a loss for the sake of full employment or he can give his money away to fight world hunger. He can exercise his property rights philanthropically as well as meanly, with conservation instead of acquisition in mind, or in the interests of others rather than his own. In other words there is seldom anything in the content of particular rights (or in concepts like property) to require people to act as egoists. The nature of a human right is always such as to present other options as well.

Still, suppose that among the range of choices, *some* of them are selfish. Is it the gist of a claim of right to encourage the right-bearer to choose these ones? The answer is clearly 'No'. To say that X has a right to do A (where A is perhaps a selfish action) is quite different from telling him that A is the right thing to do. It is even different from telling him that A is *all right* from a moral point of view or that he does no wrong in doing it (though there is a use of the word 'right' – Hohfeld's concept of a privilege – in which this is roughly all that is indicated). A claim of right – in the strong sense of a claim-right – to perform some particular action simply leaves these issues open: its content gives no information whatever about the moral value of the action in question. All it does is to indicate the wrongness of interfering with it. It is an elementary fallacy of illiberal thought to infer from this any seal of moral approval.

I believe that the opposite view – that a claim of right asserts the moral indifference of the action in question – leads to incoherence. The function of rights is presumably to protect significant choices for a person's life, not just trivial ones like the choice of which side of my face to shave first in the morning or of which route to take to work. Human rights protect things like democratic voting, free speech in a political context, free choice of lifestyle, free choice of sexual partner and sexual mores, freedom of conscience, religion, and so on. These are important areas from the moral point of view and from the point of view of moral personality, and that is why we consider it important that they be protected by rights against outside interference. But then if they *are* important choices, it is inconceivable that the rest of morality (which is, at bottom, the enterprise of guiding, assessing, evaluating and criticizing important choices) should have nothing to say on the matter; it is inconceivable that the morality of duty or virtue or decency should be silent on the way these choices are exercised. To exclude the rest of morality from the evaluation of these choices and yet insist that the choices are still so important, is to come perilously close to self-contradiction. If, on the other hand, the standards of the rest of morality *can* be deployed to guide and evaluate the way in which a person exercises his rights, we simply cannot lay it down glibly as an a priori rule that no action capable of being a right can ever be adjudged to be, on balance, the wrong thing to do.

(No doubt moralists vary in their uses of the term 'wrong': some may reserve it for breaches of rules that affect the rights of others. But if so, my point can easily be restated. The choices which a right leaves open for a person, even if they do not include choices of *wrong* actions (in this narrow sense), will nevertheless certainly include actions on which a negative moral judgement may be made. That judgement may concern the character of the action itself (as indecent, ignoble, inconsiderate, and so on), or it may be a judgement about the merits of that choice compared to the other choices that were available (could have done more good elsewhere, for example). This follows simply from the fact that some evaluative standards are bound to be deployed to guide choices deemed important enough to be protected by moral rights. Therefore it cannot be inferred from the fact that one has a right to do A (that is from the fact that A is among the options one has a right to choose between) that A can never be subject to moral criticism by standards appropriately deployed in that context.

It is important that this claim should not be watered down. I am not saying merely that acts which are prima-facie wrong (or ignoble, inconsiderate, badly chosen or whatever) may be the subject of a right, or even that we may have a prima-facie right to perform acts that are wrong (etc.) *tout court*. That particular apparatus of moral qualification is unnecessary. The idea of a right to do wrong sounds verbally paradoxical, but on analysis reveals no hint of contradiction, and no special apparatus like a 'prima-facie' qualifier is necessary to handle it. To say to X that A is wrong is, among other things, to urge him not to do it, or to draw his attention to the reasons there may be for refraining from the performance of A. To say that nevertheless he has a right to do A is not to detract *in any way* from these reasons or prescriptions. (This is important because it follows that the principles which establish A as the subject-matter of a right and the principles which condemn A may co-exist perfectly well in the same moral theory.)

Another way of putting this is to insist that it is not the function of rights to prescribe or give reasons, at least not to the people who have them. Saying that X has a right to do A is not to provide reasons or encouragement for X. It is rather to indicate reasons for *people other than* X to refrain from some action (interfering with A) which they might otherwise be tempted to perform.

Returning then to the accusation of egoism: we can say that it is not part of the meaning of a rights-claim to encourage selfish actions (or for that matter altruistic ones); it is part of their meaning, though, to discourage interference with the egoistic (or altruistic) actions that form the subject-matter of the right.

If all this is correct, two points follow. To have a right is not to be insulated or protected from moral criticism about the exercise of one's rights. One may use a claim of right to resist interference by other people, but not to rebuff their criticism or their demands for justification. An example from recent politics will illustrate. Acknowledging that a public official has a right, in terms of the Fifth Amendment to the American Constitution, to withhold information from a public inquiry into matters of grave political importance, does not preclude criticism of him for exercising that right. The Fifth Amendment gives one an option, and protects one from coercion and sanctions in the exercise of that option. But it does not in itself offer any moral guidance, and hence no seal of moral approval, on the matter of how (or even whether) that option is exercised. For that, the theory of constitutional rights would need to be supplemented by a theory of civic virtue.

This leads to a point I have stressed a number of times in this essay. A theory of rights – particularly a theory of rights to liberty – is not capable of standing on its own. It needs to be complemented by a general theory of virtue or moral action to guide the conduct of the right-bearers in the exercise of their rights. In a recent paper called 'Atomism', Charles Taylor argued: 'If I have a right to do what I want with my property, then any disposition is equally justifiable from the point of view of this principle.'[65] But that is a silly way of putting it, since it is not the function of a principle of right to justify (or condemn) *anything at all* so far as the right-bearer is concerned. Taylor goes on:

I may be judged uncharitable if I hoard my property to myself and won't help those in need, or uncreative if I bury it in the ground and don't engage in interesting enterprises with it. But these latter criticisms arise from our accepting other moral standards, quite independent from the view that we have a right to do what we want with our own.

Precisely! Our morality is a complex and articulated one, and we are not trying to do everything *at once* (banning interference with A *and* evaluating A) when we say things like 'A is X's right'. There are other standards to be brought in, other sorts of moral judgements to be made, before all the tasks of morality have been discharged in that regard. A theory of rights leaves agents needing more in the way of moral guidance, *not* because rights are egoistic and because that egoism needs to be outweighed by other considerations, but because rights offer no guidance at all – egoistic or otherwise – to those who have them, and there is a need for that function of guiding action still to be performed.

I said earlier that rights may nevertheless encourage selfishness in the crude sense of being correlated with its occurrence. If we believe that human action is normally or naturally selfish, we may think that any intimation that social restraints are to be lifted – and a claim of right certainly contains such an intimation – will open the floodgates to egoism. I think Bentham actually believed something along these lines. But it is perfectly open for a philosopher of rights to dispute that background theory of human nature. Some of the actions people may be expected to perform in the absence of restraint may be selfish, others will not be. Generalizations about human nature are perilous, but it seems crazy to suggest that the *only* motives we *ever* have for altruistic or socially responsible action are the sort of restraints with which a theory of rights is concerned. Certainly rights do aim to weaken some of the *bonds* of social life, but that is to be construed as the promotion of egoism only by those who consider community as essentially *bondage*. Others may want to regard rights as a way of clearing space for the individual to take upon himself the responsibility for moulding and constructing a life with others and of providing the social and spiritual conditions that make that responsibility possible.

The second count in the egoism indictment focuses on a different sense of the exercise of rights. If I have a liberty-right and someone interferes with my choice, or if I have a welfare-right and some official withholds the benefit to which I am entitled, it is often said that it is then *for me* to make the complaint, *for me* to insist on enforcement and sanctions, or *for me* to waive the claim that I have if I am feeling for some reason magnanimous. The objection is that this leads to a rather unpleasant and morally unhealthy situation of a lot of self-centred individuals going around querulously making claims against one another all the time, and demanding benefits, protection and remedies from their society in an adversarial and contentious spirit.

Certainly there are some theories of rights which do give this priority to self-centred claiming. The so-called 'Choice Theory', associated for a long time with the work of H.L.A. Hart, made it essential to the idea of a right that the individual right-holder be in a position to demand, insist on, claim, or – if he wanted to – waive someone else's duty.[66] Indeed Hart used to argue (he does so no longer)[67] that having the power to demand that someone else perform his duty or to waive it was more important to being a right-holder than having the interest which the right was protecting or promoting. In American political philosophy the connection between having a right and making a claim has been quite strong. Joel Feinberg has maintained that a world without rights would be a world which put no individual ever in a position to make a claim against anybody else. Feinberg goes on to argue that this business of *making claims against* other people, or being in a position to do that, is an important part of self-respect and 'gives a sense to the notion of personal dignity'.[68]

When the point is put like that, it is easy to see what the opponents of rights are uneasy about. Does self-respect and human dignity really depend upon being in a position to make strident, querulous, adversarial claims *against* other people? Is that what it really boils down to? This indeed would be a theory which not only (as Marx put it) leads me to see in others the limitation of my freedom; it would be a theory that leads me to see that my fulfilment, my freedom and my self-realization depend on my muscular and self-assertive capacity to place limits on yours. This image of a society of *claimers*, each preoccupied with his own grievances, with the wrongs that may or may not be done *to him*, is not an attractive conception of the Kantian kingdom of ends.

Fortunately things are not so bad in relation to all theories of rights. If we look at the way in which moral claims of right are put forward in the real world (as opposed to what philosophers say about them), in cases where rights really matter, what is striking is that, on the whole, claims are put forward by people *on other individuals' behalf*. The demand for human rights in the USSR, Eastern Europe, South Africa, Chile and elsewhere is often a demand by western governments or by pressure groups (like Amnesty International) based in the west, put forward not on behalf of their own constituents, but on the basis of a concern for the well-being and freedom of people they have never met and from whom they are not expecting to receive any benefit in return.

Of course, it would be insulting to underestimate the importance of the local campaign for human rights, both open and illicit, in these countries. Those who demand their rights in, say, Chile or the USSR, do so heroically and at considerable risk to themselves. But even there it is wrong to say (though it is something that, for example, the Soviet authorities are fond of saying) that the agitation is egoistic in character. Dissidents in the USSR clamour for the individual rights of *all* their fellow citizens, and their claims are rarely put forward in the self-centred idiom of the *personal* claim that Feinberg regarded as so crucial for self-respect. If we look at what these people say when they come into exile in the west, the concern they express about human rights is rarely a personal complaint – except to the extent that their story may help to galvanize action in the west to save their comrades and fellow-dissidents from continuing to suffer similar violations.

There are some important general points here. Theories of human rights are universalistic and universalizable: that is they proclaim the rights of all persons, so that everyone who makes a personal claim on his own behalf is immediately aware that exactly the same claim can be made on behalf of anyone who is like him in the relevant respect. This is not just a formal matter; it relates to what counts as *moral* concern for one's rights. An attack on anyone's rights is a matter of legitimate and indeed necessary concern for all. This is not just on the grounds of long-term enlightened self-interest: the chance that what threatens your rights today may if left unabated attack mine tomorrow. It is because concern about the violation of one's own rights cannot possibly count as a *moral* attitude unless one is prepared to apply and act on that concern in the case of all relevantly similar violations on others.

This is one of the reasons I found it necessary to deal separately with the issues of egoism and individualism. A theory of rights, as we have seen, is a theory that accords special moral protection to certain *individual* interests (or rather to all individual interests that fall under certain types). It is a theory that provides a basis for moral concern whenever individual interests of those kinds come under attack or whenever they are left inadequately protected. But that concern need not be *egoistic* concern. The moral importance of each individual interest to the individual who has it is capable of being apprehended by other individuals. Individualism as such is not incompatible with altruism. Indeed people, whether as individuals or as groups, ought to be concerned when any person is tortured or is starving, or is taken away from his loved ones or prevented from speaking his mind. The fact that that concern is focused on the interests of the individual person, and what it is *for him* to suffer those wrongs, does not mean that only the individual being attacked is entitled to express it.

Rights connect individual interests with the justified imposition of *duties*; a duty is something more than the reflex of an individual's own expectations and desires. To say that someone has a duty is to imply the legitimacy of widespread moral concern about the performance or non-performance of some action. It is not just that the right-holder wants or expects it; it is that, on the basis of the importance of the right-holder's interest, this is something that ought to be done. Even when the duty associated with a right is strictly *in persona* – like the duty to repay a debt or carry out a promise – moral concern by others is by no means excluded. We make legitimate judgements about someone who 'welshes' on such obligations – 'he breaks his promises' or 'he doesn't keep his word' – and we may bring pressure to bear on him, even though the obligations in question are not specifically owed *to us*. Nor is this merely a result of the fear that we may fall victim to his welshing in the future. We do it because the obligations, though owed *to* someone in particular, are also *moral* obligations and not just the personal expectations of the person to whom they are owed. It remains the case that it is not for us to forgive his debts or waive the promises made to him. But concern about the violation of rights is certainly not peculiar to those whose rights have been violated.

In his book *Rights and Persons* A.I. Melden defends the opposite view. He cites a comment by Frederick Douglass, a black leader in the Abolitionist movement last century, attacking what he thought was the passive role assigned to the slaves themselves in that mobilization of what was very much an expression of white concern.

> The man who has *suffered the wrong* is the man to demand redress
> . . . , the man STRUCK is the man to CRY OUT – and . . . he who
> has *endured the cruel pangs of slavery* is the man to advocate liberty.
> It is evident that we must be our own representatives and
> advocates, not exclusively but peculiarly – not distinct from but in
> connection with our white friends.[69]

A declaration like that is terribly impressive and moving. Am I saying there is nothing at all in that position?

I do not want to say that (though it is true that such claims are often quoted in bad faith by whites or onlookers generally, to rationalize their culpable failure to aid those whose rights are under attack). The Douglass/Melden position does express a number of important ideas.

It may, first of all, be an epistemological claim – the idea that only the person who has suffered injustice is capable of knowing its extent for only he knows how badly his interests have been affected. It is therefore presumptuous of others to make claims on his behalf unless, exceptionally, they have the imaginative capacity to put themselves subjectively in his shoes. Connected with that, it may be a way of resisting paternalistic or patronizing theories of rights which attribute false consciousness to the victims of oppression. It may be a way of resisting that in the name of the subjective authenticity of experiences of the people concerned. A right-based concern, after all, is a moral concern about what it is like to suffer some violation or setback. Though of course it is disingenuous to say we have no idea when someone else is suffering, it is nevertheless *their* account of the suffering which should have primacy in the mobilization of any concern.

A little more controversially, the Douglass/Melden position may express a sort of moral relativism. It may be a basis for resisting the claims to universalism in international declarations of rights in the name of the entitlement of each group or community to define for itself what are to count as important rights. This raises some of the important issues about relativism and universalism which we have discussed already in this essay under the heading of *abstraction*.

It may be meant to express a substantive ethical concern about the undesirability of servility as a personal trait. One of the awful things about oppression is the stoic passivity which it often induces in its victims as a standard and quite understandable response. It may be thought that such a state of mind, though understandable, becomes almost *wrong* once it is known that a campaign for liberation is underway; or that it is quite wrong for the campaigners to neglect the task of awakening those they are campaigning for.[70] In an extreme form, this is what Jean-Paul Sartre and Frantz Fanon were arguing when they urged the use of violence by the Algerians, rather than politics by French liberals, in their struggle against their colonial oppressors.[71]

And there are also other points of a less substantial kind. The Douglass/Melden position may express a valid hunch about efficiency: in some sort of 'invisible hand' way, perhaps rights will be better enforced on the whole if everyone is preoccupied with his own. Or it may be a valid point about compensation. Though everyone ought to be concerned to uphold others' rights, still compensation for the violation is due peculiarly to the right-holder. Thus, for example, though in John Locke's theory everyone in a state of nature has a right and indeed a duty to punish transgressions when she comes across them, Locke insists that 'he who hath received any damage, has besides the right of punishment common to him with other Men, a particular right to seek reparation from him that has done it'.[72]

All these points may be important, but none involves the suspect view that people should limit their concern to the vindication of their own rights. The points counsel caution, humility and sensitivity when acting to uphold the rights of others, and they indicate that there may be additional reasons for people undertaking action on their own behalf. But they do not necessarily evoke the sort of picture I want to reject – that of a society of self-absorbed claimers, each preoccupied querulously with her own interests and concerns. Rights are individualistic, as we have conceded. But people are capable of showing concern about the integrity of one another's individual interests.

The third objection takes us away from questions about the exercise and enforcement of rights and confronts the role of egoism in the rationale of the rights themselves. Even if we are all altruisticaly standing up for one another's rights, nevertheless isn't the whole point of the exercise the idea that it is all right for individuals to hold certain things back from their society, to refuse to submit certain interests to the calculus of social utility, and to withhold certain sacrifices when those sacrifices are necessary for the good of all? Isn't *that* the unacceptable egoism of a theory of rights?

The issue has often been discussed in the context of a long-running debate between rights and utilitarianism. This is partly due to Bentham, and partly to the hegemony of utilitarian moral theory at the time when theories of rights underwent their most recent revival. I do not want to spend much time on that debate, for I think it can be shown quite easily first, that rights-theorists must offer a number of concessions to the utilitarian, and second, that the concessions they cannot make are concessions which it is quite unreasonable to demand.

Utilitarians like all consequentialists believe that when our moral aims conflict we should weigh up *all* the consequences of acting in one way or the other, and that, since conflict is endemic to moral life, there can be no *absolute* principles of duty and conduct. Theorists of rights should concede this. After all, rights themselves express important moral aims and *they* are liable to conflict with one another. One person needs our help on the basis of her right not to be tortured; but perhaps the only way we can help her is by torturing those who have influence over her assailants, or by diverting our efforts from rescuing somebody else from a similar predicament. What are we to do? One person has a right to certain procedural safeguards in the trial that takes place when he is accused of violating rights, but these safeguards allow a certain number of guilty people to escape conviction and to continue violating the (equally important) rights of others. What are we to do? Everyone in Ethiopia has the right to be saved from starvation, but there is only so much food. What are we to do?

It is idle to suggest that people don't have the rights in question until it is established whether we have the wherewithal to carry out the corresponding duties. That disingenuous use of 'ought implies can' suggests, first, that rights cannot guide us in our decision about what resources to make available, and second, that our moral concerns are entirely subordinate to our beliefs about what can be done.

Equally it is a mistake to say that all that rights demand of us in these complex situations is that *we* should not actively violate any rights, no matter what others are doing. This is the view that rights are agent-relative side constraints, associated most recently with Robert Nozick.[73] The trouble with this is that it makes rights sound as though they were concerned more with the integrity of agents' behaviour than with the interests and well-being of potential victims. Such a concern is by no means disreputable (it forms the basis, for example, of Kant's theory of ethics); but it is not what is usually involved in a concern about human rights. Anyone who feels for (all) the victims in these situations and is concerned for the basic interests they all have at stake must, so to speak, try and do the best he can for all concerned. The various conceptions of consequentialist decision-making (of which utilitarian-style aggregation is the best known) are attempts to elaborate that idea. It is simply not open to a rights-theorist who professes a greater concern for the interests of victims than for himself to repudiate these conceptions in advance. By the same token, it must be understood by everyone who has rights that his rights can for this reason never be absolute, for sometimes they must yield at least to the rights of others in cases where, crudely speaking, more can be done for them than for him. To acknowledge this is to place limits on what critics call the egoism of rights, and to indicate that even rights may be sacrificed when others' rights demand it.

Utilitarians, however, have usually wanted more than this. They claim that *all* moral aims, indeed *all* values, must be weighed against one another in this way. Suppose that a large number of people (perhaps millions) would feel more comfortable if some dissident were done away with. A utilitarian is committed in advance to weighing the discomfort caused by the dissident's existence against the loss to the dissident of his life or liberty. Leave aside the technical difficulty of making this comparison – the problem of the commensurability of values of different types. Utilitarians believe that such comparisons can be made and that if only there is *enough* discomfort on the one side of the scales, the dissident's interest in life or liberty is outweighed and he must be killed or left to die. Maybe (as a matter of fact) the scales would never be tipped to that extent; perhaps there are good utilitarian reasons for prohibiting us from examining this question too closely. Nevertheless the very idea of such a calculation would strike most rights-theorists as outrageous. The dissident's interest in life and liberty, they will say, is so much more important from a moral point of view that it should not be weighed in the balance *at all* against run-of-the-mill interests such as other people's comfort. Of course, if others' lives are at stake, that is a different matter: the arguments from the previous paragraph come into play. But one of the purposes of having a theory of rights is to give certain specified types of individual interests absolute priority as against the run of interests generally. We think that ordinary interests in comfort and convenience can be dealt with quite nicely in utilitarian terms; people are quite rightly expected to submit their interests in these things to the calculus of social utility. No one is entitled to be egoistic about his comfort, when the convenience of large numbers of other people is at stake. But there are certain interests which are not to be dealt with in this way. They are so important for the lives, the well-being and the freedom of individuals that morality demands they be dealt with separately. Though we can offer no absolute guarantees that all of them will be taken care of (for, as we have seen, they can sometimes conflict *inter se*) it would be insulting and lacking respect for individual humans to deal with them as though they were on a par with, and simply reducible to a finite aggregation of, lesser interests like comfort and convenience. The aim, then, is to give *priority* to looking after these interests and working out conflicts between them. Only then, the rights theorist argues, are we in a moral position to go on to the utilitarian calculus of all other interests in society.

Similar points can be made about the relation between rights and the political principles of majoritarian democracy. In constitutional theory rights are quite properly presented as constraints on democratic decision-making. It is not that theorists of rights are opposed to democracy; they acknowledge that the democratic procedure is a fair way to resolve conflicts of preferences in a large number of cases. But all such decisions involve winners and losers – those whose preferences prevail and those whose preferences do not. A theory of rights can be represented as the view that there are certain losses whose infliction on individuals in the resolution of political conflict is morally unacceptable. That is, there are certain losses that people should not have to run the risk of suffering when they agree to be bound by the democratic process. This may be because they are losses that, as a matter of fact, no one can reasonably be expected to put up with, and which are therefore losses whose infliction is likely to undermine stability and support for the political system. People will rebel or attempt to secede rather than sustain losses of this kind; at the very best one will secure little more than their sullen acquiescence in the outcome.[74] Or it may be because they are losses whose infliction will undermine other social aims, like the capacity of the individuals in question to continue in the pursuit of the general good. (A theory along these lines will be sketched out in a moment.) Or the losses themselves may be related internally to the democratic process, so that it would be, in a sense, self-defeating for them to be inflicted democratically. For example, one cannot have a democratic system if (even as a result of a majority vote) a portion of the population is silenced or disenfranchised.[75] Whatever the argument is, the point of a theory of rights in a democratic context is to give a priority to certain interests which all individuals have which in effect insulates them from the vicissitudes of normal political decision-making. By contrast, the *pure* democrat would be willing to take the view that, in principle, there is no loss to an individual so severe that its infliction could not be warranted by a sufficiently extensive popular enthusiasm for its infliction. Like the pure utilitarian, the pure democrat believes that in principle any loss to an individual can be outweighed in the scales of political morality by a sufficient accumulation of lesser benefits to others.

It may be worth adding a little more on the way in which the priority given to rights is to be understood. The charge we are responding to is that of egoism and it is certainly the case that the way rights are sometimes modelled in political theory lends them an egoistic flavour or appearance. After a century or two of academic disrepute, the idea of the *social contract* is now increasingly being used by philosophers as a device for modelling and, as it were, packaging their theories of justice and rights. The best known example is the work of John Rawls in which basic rights to freedom and equality are modelled as the terms of the bargain that might be expected to emerge if a group of rational individuals, each concerned to promote his own good in his own way, came together to settle the terms on which they were prepared to co-operate in society. Nothing like the 'original position' of the Rawlsian contract is ever supposed to have taken place. But we are told that it is *helpful* to think of these rights as the concessions self-interested contractors would insist on. Rights are conceived as the terms they would hold out for, as the interests they would say they were not prepared to sacrifice to the interest of society at large even to obtain the benefits of co-operation and community.[76]

The model has been criticized by communitarians for the way it represents a person's social allegiance as in some sense detachable from his self. It parades his social connections as something he can distance himself from, reflect on and therefore bargain for, and it presents the rules and practices constitutive of his community as something to be toyed with and haggled over in the interests of a self that is somehow mysteriously detached from them. This, the communitarians argue, is the unattractive and perhaps unintelligible face of modern liberalism.[77] Partly the force of this criticism depends on an association between what one might term *detachability* and *superficiality*. The suggestion seems to be that a person whose ideals are self-chosen (and whose commitment to them therefore pre-supposes a self that is in some sense antecedent to that commitment) is incapable of the depth of commitment that can be attained by someone who cannot conceive of himself apart from his communal or ethical ideals. I am inclined to think though that this is a mistake. To retain the capacity to review or distance ourselves in thought from our commitments, we do not, as it were, have to be always *holding something back* from them. Having the capacity to reconsider one's commitments is a matter of being able to make an effort when one needs to (in a crisis or in a period of personal review), to wrench away and construct, for the moment, the necessary psychological distance. It does not necessarily require a continuous reserve of commitment and energy which *could* have been associated with the commitment but which is held back by the liberal individual. Communitarians are often too glib about the phenomenology of commitment. In modern experience, intensity, wholeheartedness and the sense of having identified comprehensively with some community are as much features of the commitments which people choose and which they know they could give up if they decided to, as of the commitments they discover they have and find they cannot question.

However, I am sure that only partially answers the communitarian concern. For there are all sorts of ways of reflecting on one's commitment to a community, and a lot is going to depend on how the process of reflection is presented in liberal theory. If it is presented, for example, in terms of a contractual model, then we will want to look a little closer at the way in which this business of contractors' holding out for certain terms is understood. In some accounts that holding out may be understood in a way that makes it intrinsically antipathetic to the demands of community; in other accounts the two concerns may be much more intimately related.

The crudest and least attractive model is that of pure market self-interest: 'This is the lowest price for which I am prepared to sell my co-operation.' One of the (many) problems with this is the implication that, like the purchaser of a commodity, I am in a position to forgo the deal if my terms are not met. Critics of contractarianism rightly point out that non-co-operation is not an option for us. We *find* ourselves in a scheme of co-operation (and compliance and obligation) and the question is how that is to be understood, not what price we arbitrarily charge for the privilege of our involvement.

Other models, however, are more interesting. For Thomas Hobbes in *Leviathan* our holding out for certain guarantees is conceived as something that is *unavoidable* for beings like ourselves. Though the formation of political society involves the reciprocal surrender of most aspects of our natural right, there is one right which it is psychologically impossible for individuals to renounce: the privilege of defending oneself against an immediate violent attack. Given his initial premises about human nature, Hobbes argues that there could not possibly be any point to anyone's renunciation of this right. The aim or end of rights-renouncing is always some increase in security and diminution of the fear of violent death:

> And therefore if a man by words, or other signes, seem to despoyle himselfe of the End, for which those signes were intended; he is not to be understood as if he meant it, or that it was his will; but as if he was ignorant of how such words and actions were to be interpreted.[78]

We find a similar line in *De Cive*. As no one can be obliged to perform the impossible, and since people shun death and fight off attack by a sort of natural necessity, no contract can be binding if it purports to oblige someone to refrain from doing that.[79] So what we hold back from our society – our rights *against* society – are beyond the limits of what we were capable of offering anyway. Rawls adopts the same position in *A Theory of Justice*: parties in his 'original position' are thought of as rejecting utilitarian principles of justice, since those principles may turn out to demand sacrifices of them for the sake of the general interest which they know they could not bring themselves to make.[80] Now these arguments are still egocentric in reference: there are certain interests of *mine* which I am incapable of surrendering. But if the background assumptions about human nature are correct (of course, a big 'if'), it is a form of egoism that any credible social theory just has to live with.

Moreover, the Hobbes/Rawls approach does not involve any radical split of the self away from its social connections. All it requires is that human beings are capable of *reflecting* on what they can offer their community, and abstracting in thought to the extent necessary to entertain the idea that 'I might not be able to offer this' or 'I might not be able to offer that'. Liberalism does not require them to *live with* the 'I' so abstracted, but it insists that our powers of reflection and our conception of ourselves are sufficiently complicated to make such abstraction occasionally possible. The idea of a community in which we are immersed to an extent that prevents us from reflecting on the extent of the contribution we can make to it is a nightmare and not a Utopia.

There is one further line that a contract theorist might want to run, to present this business of holding things back from one's society in a more attractive light.

Suppose we agree that it is important for community and social co-operation that individuals be prepared to act morally, to respond to considerations of civic virtue, to exhibit altruism and concern for others, even those to whom they are not tied with bonds of blood or affection and to submit their own convenience to the calculus of social utility. Suppose we concede all that. It may be thought, nevertheless, that this is quite a tall order, and not something which can simply be *expected* of individuals or *taken for granted* under any conditions you like. Maybe on the whole this sort of moral sensitivity and moral action is to be expected from the general run of people only on condition that the integrity of one or two basic interests of theirs is guaranteed. A few exceptional or heroic individuals may be capable of rising to the social challenge under any conditions. But as a general rule maybe people need to have such things as the assurance of a freedom from Hobbesian terror, an assurance of bodily security, a modicum of personal privacy and the intellectual and political space to start thinking things through for themselves, before they are capable of rising to the demands of social morality.

If anything like this is true, then we must not expect ordinary people to be moral or community-minded except under the conditions secured by some of the traditional human rights. If we think it morally important for people to act socially, altruistically and sensitively to the needs of others and of the community, we will be morally concerned that they should live and thrive in the conditions of freedom, security and well-being that make that sensitivity and action a real option for them. Precisely because it is important for individuals to be able to raise their sights above self-interest, we will want to ensure that the most desperate and fundamental aspects of their interests are catered for.

This is not simply the point that each individual needs to have his own interests taken care of before he can help with those of others. On an aircraft when the stewards talk about safety procedures, they instruct people travelling with young children to fasten their own oxygen masks first before attempting to assist those who are dependent on them. Similarly someone might say that you cannot work for freedom unless you yourself are free, or that you cannot feed the hungry if you yourself are starving. But the point goes deeper than that. The needs we are talking of here are ones which not only are instrumentally necessary for action in the interest of others, but also are perhaps partially constitutive of moral agency. I cannot be a moral agent without space and security to think and reflect on what I ought to do. For most people that requires freedom from things like terror and starvation – in other words, a guarantee of the substance of certain basic human rights. Respect for these rights, then, is bound up with the very meaning of the demand that people act morally in the interests of others. If our social contract model has this complexion, then the unpleasant aspect of its egoism begins to fade. It need not involve the idea of people holding out on social co-operation in order to achieve the best deal possible for themselves. It may be instead the idea that the common commitment to life in a society that a social contract attempts to articulate cannot be carried through unless the individuals who are to assume that moral burden are granted the wherewithal to enable them to bear it.

But perhaps it is a mistake to think of it as a *burden*. The demand for communal responsibility and therefore for the conditions that make it possible is not made exclusively on the basis of a concern for the 'others' involved. The communitarians are right to insist that we have an interest in our moral agency, in being the sort of person who can respond to this sort of demand. Such an interest lies close to the basis of self-respect, given the social nature of humans. Any concern, then, that modern individuals are being alienated from involvement in their community must, to be credible, be a concern that the conditions be provided that make that involvement possible. Concern for the *moral* self can be the basis of a concern for individual rights.

An argument along these lines (and, of course, this is nothing but a sketch) has a number of attractions.

First, it indicates a way of understanding the *priority* of rights in moral argument that is more subtle than the way that is usually understood. Usually when it is said that rights are to prevail over other things like utility – when it is said, for example, that rights are 'trumps' over utility – the assertion is understood to mean that rights protect values that are more important, things that are more valuable, than those protected by the considerations over which they are to prevail.

But on the present account that is a misleading picture. One reason human rights are given priority over communal or utilitarian requirements is that attention to the former is a necessary pre-condition of any credible commitment to the latter. But while the moral commitments *presuppose* human rights they are not *subordinated* to them in the scheme of values. One value or principle may rank lower than another in its intrinsic importance and still be given priority if its fulfilment is a necessary condition of any attempt to pursue or act on the intrinsically more important one.

Secondly, it indicates one possible line of compromise in the modern debate between communitarians and those who persist with traditional liberal concerns. It is easy to accuse modern communitarians of moral totalitarianism, of fostering and advocating potentially oppressive and claustrophobic forms of social life. The answer is too often a glib 'Don't panic – of course a genuine community will take care of human rights', without giving any very serious indication of how they propose to do that. Now, if there is anything in the argument I have outlined, maybe it is possible to articulate an internal connection between communal and liberal concerns that shows exactly where the demand for rights fits into the moral ideal of community. The moral agent, whose unselfishness and social identity the communitarian wants to foster, is himself partly constituted by the atmosphere of respect for human rights that the liberal demands.

That way of uniting these concerns depends, of course, on a particular sort of conception of community. If the life of a community is conceived as a simple mechanical solidarity – following orders of elders, or the mindless and uncritical pursuit of traditional ways of doing things – there is no room for my argument. Slaves and those who move in pre-ploughed furrows need no space or security in which to deliberate, for no reflective deliberation on communal responsibility is ever called for. It is only if we are looking for community in a complex changing world, populated and sustained by sensitive and reflective individuals, responding intelligently and at times creatively to complex moral problems, that we have to give priority to human rights as a presupposition of community.

Thirdly, the argument acknowledges in an attractive way the *importance* of self-interest in moral life. Often when it is said that rights protect self-interest, that is seen only as an accusation. But a concern for one's own interest is not always discreditable. We have moral responsibilities in respect of ourselves, under most circumstances, to develop our abilities, take care of our needs, and keep our fragile psyches in some sort of order. The capacity for moral action cannot be taken for granted, and each person has a legitimate and indeed morally imperative interest in the conditions that make it possible for him. We have seen that respect for rights need not encourage selfishness and that it is natural for people to be interested in the rights of other people. But to the extent that rights do focus our attention on our selves, it may be seen as self-absorption in a good cause. Self-interest and concern for others need not pull in opposite directions; in a complex world, one may be the precondition of the other.

Notes

Introduction

1   See for example Robert Nozick, *Anarchy, State and Utopia* (Oxford, Basil Blackwell, 1974), and Ronald Dworkin, *Taking Rights Seriously* (London, Duckworth, 1978), pp. 169ff.

2   For samples of these misgivings see the essays in Michael Sandel (ed.) *Liberalism and its Critics* (Oxford, Basil Blackwell, 1984), and R.G. Frey (ed.) *Utility and Rights* (Oxford, Basil Blackwell, 1985).

3   Richard Tuck, *Natural Rights Theories: Their Origins and Development* (Cambridge, Cambridge University Press, 1979).

4   Such criticisms might be based on the hermeneutical writings of Quentin Skinner, for example 'Meaning and Understanding in the History of Ideas', *History and Theory*, 8 (1969). See 'Political Thought and Political Action: A Symposium on Quentin Skinner', *Political Theory*, 2 (1974), for a useful discussion.

5   These sentiments owe a lot to Ronald Dworkin's account of interpretation in *Law's Empire* (London, Fontana, 1986), espcially ch. 2.

1
Natural rights in the seventeenth and eighteenth centuries

1   John Locke, *Two Treatises of Government* (1689), edited by Peter Laslett (Cambridge, Cambridge University Press, 1960).

2   See Peter Laslett, *Patriarcha and Other Political Works of Sir Robert Filmer* (Oxford, Basil Blackwell, 1949). Filmer's theory is discussed in Gordon Schochet, *Patriarchalism in Political Thought* (Oxford, Basil Blackwell, 1975).

3   Locke, op. cit., II, sect. 4, p. 287.

4   ibid., II, sect. 1, p. 285. The whole of Locke's *First Treatise* (or of the fragment that remains) is devoted to a comprehensive refutation of the theological basis of Filmer's position.

5   Thomas Hobbes, *Leviathan* (1651), edited by C.B. Macpherson (Harmondsworth, Penguin, 1981), ch. 13, p. 183.

6   Locke, op. cit., II, sect. 54, p. 322.

7   ibid., II, sect. 61, p. 326.

8   Jeremy Bentham, *Anarchical Fallacies*, see above, p. 50.

9   Locke, op. cit., II, sect. 87, p. 341.

10 ibid., II, sect. 95, p. 348.

11 Hugo Grotius, *The Rights of War and Peace* (1625), quoted in Richard Tuck, *Natural Rights Theories: Their Origins and Development* (Cambridge, Cambridge University Press, 1979), p. 78.

12 James Tyrrell, *Patriarcha non Monarcha* (1681), quoted in Tuck, op. cit., p. 155.

13 Thomas Hobbes, *De Cive: The English Version* (1651), edited by Howard Warrender (Oxford, Clarendon, 1983), ch. 2, sect. 18, pp. 58–9.

14 Locke, op. cit., II, sect. 135, p. 375.

15 ibid., II, sect. 6, p. 289.

16 Richard Overton, *An Appeal from the Degenerate Representative Body* (1647), and Henry Parker, *Observations upon some of His Majesties Late Answers and Expresses* (1642), quoted in Tuck, op. cit., pp. 149 and 146.

17 David Hume, *A Treatise of Human Nature* (1739), edited by L.A. Selby-Bigge (Oxford, Clarendon, 1888), bk II, pt I, sect. II, p. 469.

18 See John Dunn, *Locke* (Oxford, Oxford University Press, 1984) pp. 65ff.

19 Immanuel Kant, *The Groundwork to the Metaphysics of Morals* (1785), edited by H.J. Paton, s.n. *The Moral Law* (London, Hutchinson, 1961).

20 Jeremy Bentham, 'Supply Without Burthern', see above, p. 74.

21 Denis Diderot, 'Natural Right', in the *Encyclopédie* (1752–72), quoted in L.G. Crocker (ed.) *The Age of Enlightenment* (London, Macmillan, 1969), p. 153.

22 Peter Gay, *The Enlightenment: An Interpretation*, vol. II: *The Science of Freedom* (New York, Alfred Knopf, 1969), p. 458.

23 John Locke, *An Essay Concerning Human Understanding* (1689), edited by J.W. Yolton (London, Everyman, 1965), bk I, ch. 3, sect. 10, pp. 31–2.

24 See Mark Hulliung, *Montesquieu and the Old Regime* (Belmont, Calif., University of California Press, 1977).

25 ibid., pp. 108ff.

26 Quoted in J.A. Joyce, *The New Politics of Human Rights* (London, Macmillan, 1978), p. 7.

27 David Hume, 'Of the Original Contract' (1748), in *Social Contract: Locke, Hume and Rousseau*, edited by E. Barker (Oxford, Oxford University Press, 1960), pp. 151–2.

28 Locke, op. cit., II, sect. 119, pp. 365–6.

29 Jean-Jacques Rousseau, *The Social Contract* (1743), edited by Maurice Cranston (Harmonsworth, Penguin, 1968), bk I, ch. 1, p. 49.

30 idem.

31 Locke, op. cit., II, sect. 243, p. 446.

32 Rousseau, op. cit., bks II and III.

33 There is a useful discussion in Joan MacDonald, *Rousseau and the French Revolution 1769–91* (London, Athlone, 1965).

2
The 'Declaration of the Rights of Man and the Citizen' 1789

1   Louis Gottschalk and Margaret Maddox, *Lafayette in the French Revolution: Through the October Days* (Chicago, Ill., University of Chicago Press, 1969), p. 8.
2   ibid, pp. 88ff.
3   Gouvernour Morris in a comment to Jefferson, quoted ibid., pp. 15–16.
4   Thomas Paine, *Rights of Man, Being an Answer to Mr. Burke's Attack on the French Revolution* (1791–2), edited by H. Collins (Harmondsworth, Penguin, 1969), p. 76.
5   Gottschalk and Maddox, op. cit., pp. 93–4.
6   S.E. Finer, *Five Constitutions* (Harmondsworth, Penguin, 1973), p. 173.

3
Jeremy Bentham's *Anarchical Fallacies*

1   Jeremy Bentham *An Introduction to the Principles of Morals and Legislation* (1789) edited by J.H. Burns and H.L.A. Hart (London, Methuen, 1982), ch. 1, sect. 1, p. ll.
2   ibid., ch. 1, sect. 2, p. 12.
3   ibid., ch. 1, sect. 5, p. 12.
4   ibid., ch. 4, sects 2–4, pp. 38–9.
5   ibid., ch. 4, sect. 6, p. 40.
6   Jeremy Bentham, *The Philosophy of Economic Science*, in *Jeremy Bentham's Economic Writings*, edited by W. Stark, vol. 1 (London, Allen & Unwin, 1952), p. 103.
7   Bentham, *An Introduction*, op. cit., ch. 4, sect. 6, p. 40.
8   There is an intriguing discussion of Bentham's 'panopticism' in Michel Foucault's *Discipline and Punish: The Birth of the Prison*, edited by A. Sheridan (Harmondsworth, Penguin, 1979), pt III, ch. 3.
9   For a discussion see David Lieberman, 'From Bentham to Benthamism', *Historical Journal*, 28 (1985).
10 The Bentham Committee, initially under the directorship of J.H. Burns, is producing what one hopes will be a definitive edition of Bentham's writings. Several volumes have already appeared.
11 Letter to John Lind, September 1776, in *The Correspondence of Jeremy Bentham*, vol. 1: 1752–76, edited by T.L.S. Sprigge (London, Athlone, 1968), pp. 341–4. See also H.L.A. Hart, *Essays on Bentham* (Oxford, Clarendon, 1983), ch. 3.
12 Bentham, *An Introduction*, op.cit., 'Concluding Note', sect. 17, p. 311n.
13 There is a good account in Mary P. Mack, *Jeremy Bentham – An Odyssey of Ideas 1748–92* (London, Heinemann, 1962), ch. 9.
14 See Douglas Long, *Jeremy Bentham's Idea of Liberty in Relation to his Utilitarianism* (Toronto, University of Toronto Press, 1977), pp. 182ff. See also Bentham's response to his honorary citizenship in a letter to

Jean Marie Roland de Platière, 16 October 1792, in *The Correspondence of Jeremy Bentham*, vol. 4: October 1788 – December 1793, edited by A.T. Milne (London, Athlone, 1981), p. 401–2. See also Bentham to William Wilberforce, 1 September 1796, in *The Correspondence of Jeremy Bentham*, vol. 5: January 1794 – December 1797, edited by A.T. Milne (London, Athlone, 1981), pp. 252–8.

15 Samuel Bentham to Jeremy Bentham, 12–23 January 1791, in *The Correspondence*, vol. 4, op. cit., p. 222.

16 See Long, op. cit., p. 255, n. 48.

17 Bhiku Parekh, *Bentham's Political Thought* (New York, Barnes & Noble, 1973).

18 Jeremy Bentham, *Principles of the Civil Code*, in *Bentham's Theory of Legislation*, edited by C.K. Ogden (London, Routledge & Kegan Paul, 1931), p. 120.

19 W. Stark, 'Introduction' to *Bentham's Economic Writings*, op.cit., p. 67.

20 Page numbers in parentheses in the text refer to the pages of the present collection.

21 Jeremy Bentham, *A Comment on the Commentaries* and *A Fragment on Government*, edited by J.H. Burns and H.L.A. Hart (London, Athlone, 1977), P. 347. Compare Thomas Hobbes, *Leviathan* (1651), edited by C.B. Macpherson (Harmondsworth, Penguin, 1981), ch. 4.

22 There is an excellent discussion in Ross Harrison, *Bentham* (London, Routledge & Kegan Paul, 1983), chs 2–3.

23 Bentham, *A Comment*, op. cit., p. 495n. For a useful discussion see H.L.A. Hart, 'Definition and Theory in Jurisprudence', in his *Essays in Jurisprudence and Philosophy* (Oxford, Clarendon, 1983).

24 Jeremy Bentham, *Anarchical Fallacies*, in *The Works of Jeremy Bentham*, edited by John Bowring (Edinburgh, William Tait, 1843), vol. II, p. 495.

25 ibid., p. 494.

26 See also Hart, *Essays on Bentham*, op cit., pp. 85ff.

27 Bentham, *Anarchical Fallacies*, op. cit., p. 495.

28 ibid., p. 502.

29 ibid., p. 493.

30 See n. 12 above.

31 Bentham, *A Comment*, op. cit., p. 399.

32 Bentham, *Anarchical Fallacies*, op. cit., p. 528.

33 ibid., p. 506.

34 ibid., pp. 493–4.

35 ibid., p. 497.

4
Edmund Burke's *Reflections on the Revolution in France*

1 See F.P. Lock, *Burke's Reflections on the Revolution in France* (London, Allen & Unwin, 1985), p. 4.

2 See Conor Cruise O'Brien, 'Introduction' to his edition of Edmund

Burke, *Reflections on the Revolution in France* (Harmondsworth, Penguin, 1969), pp. 19–20n.

3   ibid., pp. 31–2.
4   There is an excellent discussion in Gerald W. Chapman, *Edmund Burke: The Practical Imagination* (Cambridge, Mass., Harvard University Press, 1967), ch. 3.
5   'A Letter to Sir Henry Langrische on the Subject of the Roman Catholics of Ireland', in *The Works of the Right Honourable Edmund Burke* (London, Bohuns British Classics, 1854), vol. III, p. 301.
6   Edmund Burke, 'Speech to the Electors of Bristol, on his being declared duly elected . . .', in *Works*, op. cit., vol. I, p. 447.
7   Lock, op. cit., p. 8.
8   For Burke on India, see Chapman, op. cit., ch. 6. For a helpful discussion of Burke's use of natural rights terminology in this and other contexts, see Michael Freeman, *Edmund Burke and the Critique of Political Radicalism* (Oxford, Basil Blackwell, 1980), ch. 5.
9   Thomas Paine, *Rights of Man, Being an Answer to Mr. Burke's Attack on the French Revolution*, (1791–2), edited by H. Collins (Harmondsworth, Penguin, 1969), Paine's Preface, p. 59; Karl Marx, *Capital* vol. I (1867), edited by E. Mandel (Harmondsworth, Penguin, 1976), pp. 925–6, n. 13; the claim is denied by O'Brien, op. cit., pp. 20ff.
10   Edmund Burke, *Thoughts and Details on Scarcity* (1795), in *Works*, op. cit., vol. V, p. 89.
11   Edmund Burke, 'Speech on American Taxation' (1774), in *Works*, op. cit., vol. I, p. 433.
12   See Lock, op. cit., pp. 6–7.
13   See O'Brien, op. cit., pp. 14–15.
14   Edmund Burke to his son, 10 October 1789, in *Burke's Correspondence*, vol. VI (July 1789–91), edited by A. Collins and R. Smith (Cambridge, Cambridge University Press, 1968), p. 29.
15   Chapman, op. cit., p. 182.
16   Burke, *Reflections*, op. cit., p. 121.
17   Paine, op. cit., pp. 62ff.
18   Edmund Burke, 'Speech on the Army Estimates' (1790), in *Works*, op. cit., vol. III, p. 281.
19   For the contemporary reception of the *Reflections*, see Lock, op. cit., ch. 5. The Burke/Paine controversy is exhaustively presented in Marilyn Butler (ed.) *Burke, Paine, and Godwin: The Revolution Controversy* (Cambridge, Cambridge University Press, 1984).
20   See for example Peter J. Stanlis, *Edmund Burke and the Natural Law* (Ann Arbor, Mich., University of Michigan Press, 1958).
21   Burke, *Reflections*, op. cit., p. 116.
22   idem.
23   ibid., p. 115.
24   ibid., p. 124.
25   ibid., p. 176.

26   R.M. Hare, *Moral Thinking: Its Levels, Method, and Point* (Oxford, Clarendon, 1981) provides the best example of this sort of theory.
27   Burke, *Reflections*, op. cit., pp. 131–4.
28   ibid., p. 191.
29   ibid., p. 229. Compare J.S. Mill, *On Liberty* (1859), edited by C.V. Shields (Indianapolis, Ind., Bobbs Merrill, 1956), ch. 1.
30   Edmund Burke, 'Speech on the Second Reading of a Bill for the Repeal of the Marriage Act', in *Works*, op. cit., vol. VI, pp. 170–1.
31   Burke, 'Letter to Langrische', op. cit., p. 326.
32   Burke, *Reflections*, op. cit., p. 281.
33   See especially ibid., pp. 284ff.
34   Edmund Burke, 'Speech on Moving his Resolutions for Conciliation with the Colonies' (1775), in *Works*, op. cit., vol. I, p. 482.
35   Burke, *Reflections*, op. cit., p. 175.
36   ibid., p. 181.
37   ibid., p. 175.
38   Jean-Jacques Rousseau, *The Social Contract* (1743), edited by Maurice Cranston (Harmondsworth, Penguin, 1968), bk I, ch. 8, pp. 64–5.
39   Burke, *Reflections*, p. 299.
40   Anthony Quinton, *The Politics of Imperfection* (London, Faber, 1978), p. 61.
41   'You might, if you pleased, have profited of our example' – Burke, *Reflections*, op. cit., p. 121.
42   ibid., p. 282.
43   ibid., p. 111.
44   ibid., p. 196.
45   It may be worth recording that Bentham regarded Burke as 'the agent and spokesman of the ruling few' and his appeals for caution and wisdom in public affairs as 'a fine-spun web with purity at the top and corruption at the bottom'; see Chapman, op. cit., p. 314, n. 19. I am not aware of Burke's opinion of Bentham.

5
Karl Marx's 'On the Jewish Question'

1   Karl Marx, 'On the Jewish Question' (1844), pt II, in David McLellan (ed.) *Karl Marx: Selected Writings* (Oxford, Oxford University Press, 1977), p. 58.
2   See David McLellan, *Karl Marx: His Life and Thought* (London, Paladin, 1976), pp. 5ff.
3   There is an excellent collection of writings in L.S. Stepelevich (ed.) *The Young Hegelians: An Anthology* (Cambridge, Cambridge University Press, 1983).
4   See for example Bruno Bauer, 'The Trumpet of the Last Judgement over Hegel' (1841), excerpted in Stepelevich, op. cit., pp. 177–86. McLellan, op. cit., p. 42, suggests that Marx may have been involved with the

drafting of this.

5   Marx in a letter to A. Ruge, 30 November 1842, in David McLellan (ed.) *Karl Marx: Early Texts* (Oxford, Basil Blackwell, 1972), p. 53.

6   Marx in a letter to D. Oppenheim, August 1842, quoted in McLellan, *Karl Marx: His Life*, op. cit., p. 52.

7   Karl Marx, 'Preface to *A Critique of Political Economy*' (1859), in *Karl Marx: Selected Writings*, op. cit., p. 389. McLellan in *Karl Marx: His Life* cites Engels's comment that Marx had always told him that it was these mundane issues in the Rhineland in the early 1840s that led him 'from pure politics to economic relationships and so to socialism' (op. cit., p. 57).

8   Bruno Bauer, 'The Jewish Problem' (1843), in Stepelevich, op. cit., p. 195.

9   G.W.F. Hegel, *Philosophy of Right* (1821), edited by T.M. Knox (Oxford, Oxford University Press, 1967), sect. 258, p. 157.

10 Karl Marx, 'Towards a Critique of Hegel's *Philosophy of Right*: An Introduction' (1844), in *Karl Marx: Selected Writings*, op. cit., p. 72.

11 ibid., p. 159.

12 Karl Marx and Frederick Engels, *The Communist Manifesto* (1848), ibid., p. 221.

13 Karl Marx, *The Eighteenth Brumaire of Louis Napoleon* (1851), ibid., p. 301).

14 Karl Marx, *The Holy Family* (1845), ibid., pp. 140–1.

15 Marx to Ludwig Kugelman, 12 April 1871, ibid., p. 592.

16 Notably Louis Althusser, *For Marx* (London, Allen Lane, 1969).

17 Cf. Karl Marx, *Capital*, vol. I (1867), edited by E. Mandel (Harmondsworth, Penguin, 1976), preface to first edn, p. 92.

18 See *Karl Marx: Selected Writings*, op. cit., pp. 541ff. and 555–6. Cf. Shlomo Avineri, *The Social and Political Thought of Karl Marx* (Cambridge, Cambridge University Press, 1968), pp. 239ff.

19 Marx, *Capital*, op. cit., 'Postface to the Second Edition' (1873), p. 99.

20 Frederick Engels, *Anti-Duhring* (Moscow, Progress, 1947), pt III, ch. 2, p. 333.

21 Marx to Joseph Weydemeyer, 5 March 1852, in *Karl Marx: Selected Writings*, op. cit., p. 341.

22 Karl Marx, *Critique of the Gotha Programme* (1875), in *Karl Marx: Selected Writings*, op. cit., p. 569. For an excellent critique see L. Kolakowski, 'The Myth of Human Self Identity: the Unity of Civil and Political Society in Socialist Thought', in L. Kolakowski and S. Hampshire (eds) *The Socialist Idea: A Reappraisal* (London, Quartet, 1977).

23 See for example Tom Campbell, *The Left and Rights* (London, Routledge & Kegan Paul, 1983), and Alice Ehr-Soon Tay, 'Marxism, Socialism and Human Rights', in E. Kamenka and A. Tay (eds) *Human Rights* (London, Edward Arnold, 1978).

24 Allen Buchanan, *Marx and Justice: The Radical Critique of Liberalism* (London, Methuen, 1982), p. 62.

25 Ernst Bloch, 'Man and Citizen According to Marx', in E. Fromm (ed.) *Socialist Humanism* (London, Allen Lane, 1967), p. 203.

26 Karl Marx, *The Holy Family* (1845), in *Karl Marx: Selected Writings*, op. cit., p. 148.

27 Karl Marx, *Grundrisse*, ibid., p. 346.

28 See especially Karl Marx, *Economic and Philosophical Manuscripts of 1844*, ibid., pp. 81ff.

29 For example Steven Lukes, *Marxism and Morality* (Oxford, Clarendon, 1985), pp. 61ff.

30 Buchanan, op. cit., p. 64.

31 Karl Marx, 'Critical Remarks on the Article "The King of Prussia and Social Reform" ' (1844), in *Karl Marx: Selected Writings*, op. cit., pp. 124–5.

32 Buchanan, op. cit., p. 65.

33 The sense used for example in Bernard Crick, *In Defence of Politics* (Harmondsworth, Penguin, 1964), or in Hannah Arendt, *The Human Condition* (Chicago, Ill., University of Chicago Press, 1958).

34 See n. 18 above.

35 Buchanan, op. cit., pp. 81ff.

36 This is also the view of a number of communitarian writers, prominently Michael Sandel, *Liberalism and the Limits of Justice* (Cambridge, Cambridge University Press, 1982), p. 33.

37 See D.N. MacCormick, 'Rights in Legislation', in P.M.S. Hacker and J. Raz (eds) *Law, Morality and Society: Essays in Honour of H.L.A. Hart* (Oxford, Clarendon, 1977), p. 205; Joseph Raz, *The Morality of Freedom* (Oxford, Clarendon, 1986), ch. 8.

38 Marx, 'Critique of Hegel's *Philosophy of Right*', in *Karl Marx: Selected Writings*, op. cit., p. 33.

39 Marx, *Critique of Gotha Programme*, ibid., p. 569.

40 Buchanan, op. cit., p. 68.

41 Marx, *Critique of Gotha Programme*, in *Karl Marx: Selected Writings*, op. cit., p. 569.

42 idem.

43 idem.

44 Marx, 'The King of Prussia', ibid., p. 125.

6
Nonsense upon stilts? – a reply

1 The literature of the 'new communitarianism' includes: Roberto Unger, *Law in Modern Society* (New York, Free Press, 1976); Charles Taylor, 'Atomism', in A. Kontos (ed.) *Powers, Possessions and Freedom: Essays in Honour of C.B. Macpherson* (Toronto, University of Toronto Press, 1979); Alasdair Macintyre, *After Virtue* (London, Duckworth, 1981); Michael Sandel, *Liberalism and the Limits of Justice* (Cambridge, Cambridge University Press, 1982); and Michael Sandel (ed.) *Liberalism*

and its Critics (Oxford, Basil Blackwell, 1984).

2   There is a helpful account in Cheryl Welch, Liberty and Utility: the French Ideologues and the Transformation of Liberalism (New York, Columbia University Press, 1984), especially ch. 1.

3   For example Adam Smith claimed that laws in restraint of trade were 'evident violations of natural liberty, and therefore unjust; and they were both too as impolitic as they were unjust. It is in the interest of every society that things of this kind should never either be forced or obstructed'. See Adam Smith, An Inquiry into the Nature and Causes of the Wealth of Nations (1776), edited by E. Cannan (Chicago, Ill., University of Chicago Press, 1976), bk IV, ch. 5 (vol. II, pp. 37–8). See generally the discussion in Istvan Hont and Michael Ignatieff (eds) Wealth and Virtue (Cambridge, Cambridge University Press, 1983).

4   Alexis de Tocqueville, Democracy in America, pt II (1840), edited by Richard D. Heffner (New York, Mentor, 1956), bks II–IV; J.S. Mill On Liberty (1859), edited by C.V. Shields (Indianapolis., Ind., Bobbs Merrill, 1956).

5   See for example Roscoe Pound, 'Liberty of Contract', Yale Law Journal, 18 (1909).

6   Covenant of the League of Nations, Article 23(b), quoted in George Scott, The Rise and Fall of the League of Nations (London, Hutchinson, 1973), p. 417.

7   Hannah Arendt, The Origins of Totalitarianism (New York, Meridian, 1958), p. 292.

8   Quoted in Richard Wild, 'Human Rights in Retrospect', in K.J. Keith (ed.) Essays on Human Rights (Wellington, Sweet & Maxwell, 1968), p. 4.

9   ibid., p. 5.

10 See Peter Laslett, 'Introduction' to his Philosophy, Politics and Society, first series (Oxford, Basil Blackwell, 1956), p. vii.

11 Robert Nozick, Anarchy, State and Utopia (Oxford, Basil Blackwell, 1974), p. 5.

12 Ronald Dworkin, Taking Rights Seriously (London, Duckworth, 1977); M.P. Golding, 'The Primacy of Welfare Rights', Social Philosophy and Policy, 1 (1984). Though he talks less explicitly about rights, John Rawls's A Theory of Justice (Oxford, Oxford University Press, 1971) falls into this category too.

13 Maurice Cranston, 'Human Rights, Real and Supposed', in D.D. Raphael (ed.) Political Theory and the Rights of Man (London, Macmillan, 1967), p. 50.

14 T.H. Green, 'Liberal Legislation and Freedom of Contract' (1881), in The Works of T.H. Green, edited by R.L. Nettleship (London, Hutchinson, 1889), vol. III, p. 370; J.A. Hobson, The Crisis of Liberalism: New Issues of Democracy (London, P.S. King & Sons, 1909); L.T. Hobhouse, Liberalism (New York, Henry Holt, 1911).

15 See especially Rawls, op. cit., pp. 7ff., 65ff and 258ff.

16 Nozick, op. cit., p. 238.

17 For example F.A. Hayek, *Law, Legislation and Liberty*, vol. II: *The Mirage of Social Justice* (London, Routledge & Kegan Paul, 1973), ch. 7.

18 There is an excellent evaluation in Tom Campbell, *The Left and Rights* (London, Routledge & Kegan Paul, 1983).

19 See for example A. Dworkin, *Pornography: Men Possessing Women* (London, Women's Press, 1981).

20 For the tip of this iceberg see for example John Hart Ely, *Democracy and Distrust: A Theory of Judicial Review* (Cambridge, Mass., Harvard University Press, 1981).

21 See for example Bernard Williams, 'A Critique of Utilitarianism', in J.J.C. Smart and Bernard Williams, *Utilitarianism: For and Against* (Cambridge, Cambridge University Press, 1973).

22 Nozick, op. cit., pp. 32–3.

23 Rawls, op. cit., pp. 27–33.

24 There are some excellent discussions in R.G. Frey (ed.) *Utility and Rights* (Oxford, Basil Blackwell, 1985).

25 Wesley N. Hohfeld, *Fundamental Legal Conceptions, as Applied in Judicial Reasoning* (New Haven, Conn., Yale University Press, 1919), is the starting-point of this modern preoccupation with the form of rights. More recent discussions include: H.L.A. Hart, 'Are There any Natural Rights?', *Philosophical Review*, 64 (1955); Joel Feinberg, 'Duties, Rights and Claims', *American Philosophical Quarterly*, 3 (1966); David Lyons, 'Rights, Claimants and Beneficiaries', *American Philosophical Quarterly*, 6 (1969); and Carl Wellman, *A Theory of Rights: Persons under Laws, Institutions and Morals* (New York, Rowman & Allenheld, 1985).

26 See H.L.A. Hart, *Essays on Bentham* (Oxford, Clarendon, 1982), p. 162.

27 See Bernard Williams, 'The Idea of Equality', in P. Laslett and W.G. Runciman (eds) *Philosophy, Politics and Society*, second series (Oxford, Basil Blackwell, 1969).

28 This is H.L.A. Hart's 'mininum content of natural law' in *The Concept of Law* (Oxford, Clarendon, 1961), pp. 289ff.

29 See the discussion between John MacDowell and Simon Blackburn in S. Holtzman and C. Leich (eds) *Wittgenstein: To Follow a Rule* (London, Routledge & Kegan Paul, 1981).

30 See Arendt, *Origins of Totalitarianism*, op. cit., ch. 9, and Michael Ignatieff, *The Needs of Strangers* (London, Chatto & Windus, 1984), ch. 1.

31 John Rawls, 'Kantian Constructivism in Moral Theory', *Journal of Philosophy*, 77 (1980); John Finnis, *Natural Law and Natural Rights* (Oxford, Clarendon, 1980); Alan Gewirth, *Human Rights: Essays on Justification and Applications* (Chicago, Ill., University of Chicago Press, 1982); Wellman, op. cit.; Ronald Dworkin, *Law's Empire* (London, Fontana, 1986).

32 For useful summaries of this trend, see Sandel (ed.) *Liberalism and its Critics*, op. cit., and Amy Gutmann, 'Communitarian Critics of Liberalism', *Philosophy and Public Affairs*, 14 (1985).

33 See for example G.W.F. Hegel, *The Phenomenology of Mind* (1807), edited by J. Baillie (London, Allen & Unwin, 1949), pt VI, sect. A(c), pp. 501ff., and Karl Marx, *The Poverty of Philosophy* (1846), in David McLellan (ed.) *Karl Marx: Selected Writings* (Oxford, Oxford University Press, 1977), p. 200.

34 For a critique along these lines, see Michael Walzer, *Spheres of Justice: A Defence of Pluralism and Equality* (Oxford, Martin Robertson, 1983).

35 See for example C.B. Macpherson, *Democratic Theory: Essays in Retrieval* (Oxford, Clarendon, 1973), ch. 1.

36 It seems that John Rawls has retreated under this sort of pressure from the universalism of his earlier approach to justice: see Rawls, 'Kantian Constructivism', op. cit., pp. 517–18.

37 Cf. Ronald Dworkin, 'What is Equality? – II. Equality of Resources', *Philosophy and Public Affairs*, 10 (1981), and Bruce Ackerman, *Social Justice in the Liberal State* (New Haven, Conn., Yale University Press, 1980).

38 David Hume, *A Treatise of Human Nature* (1739), edited by L.A. Selby-Bigge (Oxford, Clarendon, 1888), bk III, pt III, sect. 2, pp. 484ff.; Hart, *Concept of Law*, op. cit., pp. 289ff.

39 See Rawls, *Theory of Justice*, op. cit., pp. 8–9.

40 Cranston, op. cit., p. 50.

41 Nozick, op. cit., pp. 159–60.

42 ibid., p. 238.

43 Michael Oakeshott, *Rationalism in Politics and Other Essays* (London, Methuen, 1962), p. 127.

44 Edmund Burke 'Speech on Moving his Resolution for Conciliation with the Colonies' (1775), in *The Works of the Right Honourable Edmund Burke* (London, H.G. Bohun, 1854), vol. I, p. 501. Cf. Aristotle, *Nichomachean Ethics*, edited by D. Ross (London, Oxford University Press, 1954), bk I, ch. 3 (1094b), p. 3.

45 For example R.M. Hare, *Moral Thinking: Its Levels, Method and Point* (Oxford, Clarendon, 1981), especially chap. 3.

46 Bernard Williams, *Ethics and the Limits of Philosophy* (London, Fontana, 1985), p. 97.

47 'Nature, as we say, does nothing without some purpose; and for the purpose of making man a political animal she has endowed him alone among the animals with the power of reasoned speech' – Aristotle, *The Politics*, edited by T.A. Sinclair (Harmondsworth, Penguin, 1962), bk I, ch. 2, p. 28. See also Hannah Arendt, *The Human Condition* (Chicago, Ill., University of Chicago Press, 1958), pp. 175ff.

48 See Jeremy Waldron, 'A Right to do Wrong', *Ethics*, 92 (1981), pp. 36–7.

49 See for example Ronald Dworkin, *Taking Rights Seriously*, op. cit., pp. 134–6 and 226.

50 Cranston, op. cit., p. 50.

51 See Amartya Sen, 'Rights and Agency', *Philosophy and Public Affairs*, 11 (1981), for a discussion of what happens when rights conflict.

52   Universal Declaration of Human Rights (1948), Article 29(2).
53   Hume, op. cit., bk III, pt I, sect. 1, p. 457.
54   ibid., pt II, sect. 1, pp. 477ff.
55   Thomas Paine, *Rights of Man, Being an Answer to Mr. Burke's Attack on the French Revolution* (1791–2), edited by H. Collins (Harmondsworth, Penguin, 1969), pt II, p. 179.
56   Immanuel Kant, *Groundwork of the Metaphysics of Morals* (1785), edited by H.J. Paton, s.n. *The Moral Law* (London, Hutchinson, 1961), ch. 1, p. 69n. (p. 402 of the Prussian Academy Edition of Kant's works).
57   Hannah Arendt, *On Revolution* (Harmondsworth, Penguin, 1973), especially chs 4–5.
58   This is argued powerfully, though still within a liberal context, by Joseph Raz, *The Morality of Freedom* (Oxford, Clarendon, 1986).
59   Raz, op. cit., p. 166.
60   See Dworkin, op. cit., ch. 7.
61   G.W.F. Hegel, *Philosophy of Right* (1821), edited by T.A. Knox (Oxford, Oxford University Press, 1967), sect. 163, p. 112.
62   Sandel, *Liberalism and the Limits of Justice*, op. cit., p. 33.
63   Karl Marx, *Grundrisse*, in *Karl Marx: Selected Writings*, op. cit., p. 346.
64   What follows is largely taken from Waldron, 'Right to do Wrong', op. cit., and also 'Galston on Rights', *Ethics*, 93 (1983).
65   Taylor, op. cit.
66   Hart, 'Are There Any Natural Rights?', op. cit.
67   The approach taken in 'Are there any Natural Rights?' is repudiated in H.L.A. Hart, *Essays in Jurisprudence and Philosophy* (Oxford, Clarendon, 1983), p. 17.
68   Joel Feinberg, 'The Nature and Value of Rights', in his collection *Rights, Justice and the Bounds of Liberty: Essays in Social Philosophy* (Princeton, NJ, Princeton University Press, 1980), especially p. 155.
69   A.I. Melden, *Rights and Persons* (Oxford, Basil Blackwell, 1977), pp. 23–4.
70   See Thomas E. Hill, 'Servility and Self Respect', *Monist*, 57 (1973).
71   Jean-Paul Sartre, 'Preface' to Frantz Fanon, *The Wretched of the Earth* (Harmondsworth, Penguin, 1967).
72   John Locke, *Two Treatises of Government* (1689), edited by P. Laslett (Cambridge, Cambridge University Press, 1960), II, sect. 10, p. 291.
73   Nozick, op. cit., ch. 3.
74   This is in effect Rawls's argument in *Theory of Justice*, op. cit., pp. 259ff.
75   Cf. Ely, op. cit.
76   Rawls, op. cit., pp. 17ff.
77   See especially Sandel, *Liberalism and the Limits of Justice*, op. cit.
78   Thomas Hobbes, *Leviathan* (1651), edited by C.B. Macpherson (Harmondsworth, Penguin, 1968), ch. 14, p. 192.
79   Thomas Hobbes, *De Cive: The English Version* (1651), edited by Howard Warrender (Oxford, Clarendon, 1983), ch. 2, sect. 18, pp. 58–9.
80   Rawls, op. cit., pp. 175ff.

Bibliographical essay

The natural rights tradition

Richard Tuck, *Natural Rights Theories: Their Origin and Development* (Cambridge, Cambridge University Press, 1979), gives a detailed account of the development of the idea of rights from the fourteenth to the seventeenth centuries. The other major source for this period – Otto Gierke's two-volume work *Natural Law and the Theory of Society* (Cambridge, Cambridge University Press, 1934) – is much less accessible.

The best available edition of John Locke's *Two Treatises of Government* is that edited by Peter Laslett (Cambridge, Cambridge University Press, 1960). Laslett's edition is also available in paperback published by Mentor Books. Useful commentaries on Locke include Geraint Parry, *Locke* (London, Allen & Unwin, 1978) and John Dunn, *The Political Theory of John Locke* (Cambridge, Cambridge University Press, 1979). There is an excellent discussion of the immediate historical background in Richard Ashcraft, *Revolutionary Politics and Locke's Two Treatise of Government* (Princeton, NJ, Princeton University Press, 1986). The thesis that Locke's theory was intended only as a vindication of the claims of those individuals who belonged to the rising bourgeoisie is developed in C.B. Macpherson (ed.) *The Political Theory of Possessive Individualism: Hobbes to Locke* (Oxford, Oxford University Press, 1964). Locke's theory of rights is discussed alongside other rights theories in D.D. Raphael (ed.) *Political Theory and the Rights of Man* (London, Macmillan, 1967) and in Ian Shapiro, *The Evolution of Rights in Liberal Theory* (Cambridge, Cambridge University Press, 1986).

The Enlightenment

David Hume's essay 'Of the Original Contract' is to be found in *Hume's Ethical Writings*, edited by Alasdair Macintyre (London, Collier Macmillan, 1965) and also in Ernest Barker (ed.) *Social Contract: Locke, Hume and Rousseau* (Oxford, Oxford University Press, 1960).

The Age of Enlightenment, edited by Lester G. Crocker (London, Macmillan, 1969), contains a large number of useful extracts on morals and politics. Among commentaries on Enlightenment thought, the best is undoubtedly Peter Gay, *The Enlightenment: An Interpretation* (New York, Alfred Knopf, 1969). In the present context volume II of that work – *The Science of Freedom* – is likely to be of the greatest interest, particularly chapters 7–10. Gay's book also contains an excellent bibliographical essay. There is a somewhat sketchier, though more provocative, account in Anthony Arblaster, *The Rise and Decline of Western Liberalism* (Oxford, Basil Blackwell, 1984).

The French Revolution and the Declaration of Rights

I have taken my account of the drafting of the 1789 Declaration from L. Gottschalk and M. Maddox, *Lafayette in the French Revolution: Through the October Days* (Chicago, Ill., University of Chicago Press, 1969). There are also useful discussions in Joan MacDonald, *Rousseau and the French Revolution, 1762–91* (London, Athlone, 1965), and Eric Thompson, *Popular Sovereignty and the French Constituent Assembly, 1789–91* (Manchester, University of Manchester Press, 1952). There is a basic chronology of events in Norman Hampson, *The French Revolution: A Concise History* (London, Thames & Hudson, 1975); and a useful discussion of several of the issues raised here in George Rude, *Interpretations of the French Revolution* (London, Historical Association, 1972).

Jeremy Bentham

Anarchical Fallacies can be found in its complete form only in volume II of the Bowring edition of *The Works of Jeremy Bentham* (Edinburgh, William Tait, 1843). There are shorter extracts in Bhiku Parekh, *Bentham's Political Thought* (New York, Barnes & Noble, 1973), and A.I. Melden (ed.) *Human Rights* (Belmont, Calif., University of California Press, 1978). The full text of 'Supply Without Burthen' can be found in volume I of Werner Stark's edition of *Jeremy Bentham's Economic Writings* (London, Allen & Unwin, 1952). The comprehensive edition of Bentham's writings being put together under the direction of J.H. Burns and the Bentham Committee at University College London does not yet include these works.

The main source for Bentham's utilitarianism remains his *Introduction to the Principles of Morals and Legislation*, edited by J.H. Burns and H.L.A. Hart (London, Methuen, 1982). For an interesting critique read John Stuart Mill, 'Essay on Bentham', in the collection *Utilarianism, On Liberty, and Essay on Bentham*, edited by Mary Warnock (London, Fontana, 1962).

There is a growing secondary literature on Bentham. Ross Harrison's *Bentham* (London, Routledge & Kegan Paul, 1983), in 'The Arguments of the Philosophers' series, provides an excellent overview of Bentham's philosophy and a clear exposition of his moral, political and jurisprudential thought. H.L.A. Hart's collection of his *Essays on Bentham* (Oxford, Clarendon, 1983) is invaluable in relating Bentham's concerns to those of modern legal theory. Specifically on political philosophy, the most useful work is Douglas Long, *Jeremy Bentham's Idea of Liberty in Relation to his Utilitarianism* (Toronto, University of Toronto Press, 1977).

Edmund Burke

Burke's works have been published in many editions, and there is a new and authoritative edition of his *Writings and Speeches* emerging under the general editorship of Paul Langford (Oxford, Clarendon, 1981–). To date only a few volumes have appeared, and *Reflections on the Revolution in France* is not so far included. It is, however, readily available in the paperback edition edited by Conor Cruise O'Brien (Harmondsworth, Penguin, 1969); the 'Introduction' to that edition is an intriguing overstatement of the importance of Burke's Irish background in his political philosophy. For Burke's other writings and speeches it is, however, necessary to consult one of the older sets of his complete works; I have referred to the complete edition published in London by H. Bohun in 1854.

There is a powerful response to Burke's *Reflections* in Thomas Paine, *Rights of Man, Being an Answer to Mr. Burke's Attack on the French Revolution* (1791–2), edited by H. Collins (Harmondsworth, Penguin, 1969), and that debate is also presented in Marilyn Butler (ed.) *Burke, Paine, Godwin and the Revolution Controversy* (Cambridge, Cambridge University Press, 1984).

The secondary literature on Burke is considerable, and I shall mention here only those I have found particularly helpful or interesting. Alfred Cobban, *Edmund Burke and the Revolt Against the Eighteenth Century* (London, Allen & Unwin, 1960) is the classic discussion. Gerald W. Chapman, *Edmund Burke: The Practical Imagination* (Cambridge, Mass., Harvard University Press, 1967) is a thorough study, dealing with Burke's political concerns area by area ('Burke on India', 'Burke on America', etc.). More recently, Michael

Freeman, *Edmund Burke and the Critique of Political Radicalism* (Oxford, Basil Blackwell, 1980), and F.P. Lock, *Burke's Reflections on the Revolution in France* (London, Allen & Unwin, 1985), both provide helpful accounts. The latter includes useful chapters on Burke's life, and on contemporary and modern reactions to the *Reflections*.

Of the various revisionary interpretations, Peter J. Stanlis, *Edmund Burke and the Natural Law* (Ann Arbor, Mich., University of Michigan Press, 1958), argues for the natural law view; Isaac Kramnick, *The Rage of Edmund Burke: Portrait of an Ambivalent Conservative* (New York, Basic Books, 1977), helpfully raises the issue of Burke's sexual orientation; and C.B. Macpherson's little study, *Burke* (Oxford, Oxford University Press, 1980), in the Oxford 'Past Masters' series, presents the Marxist view of Burke as a bourgeois ideologue.

Karl Marx

'On the Jewish Question' is available in any edition of Marx's early writings. The best is David McLellan's *Karl Marx: Early Texts* (Oxford, Basil Blackwell, 1972). It is also available in McLellan's invaluable collection *Karl Marx: Selected Writings* (Oxford, Oxford University Press, 1977). That collection contains most of what a working political theorist, as opposed to a Marx specialist, might want to consult (apart perhaps from *Capital*). For specialists the three volumes of *Capital* are available in Penguin editions, and there is a complete edition of Marx's and Engels's writings in the authorized Moscow set.

David McLellan has also provided the best biography of Marx in his *Karl Marx: His Life and Thought* (London, Paladin, 1976), as well as a useful discussion of the Young Hegelians in *The Young Hegelians and Karl Marx* (London, Macmillan, 1980). There are excerpts from Young Hegelian writings in L.S. Stepelevich (ed.) *The Young Hegelians: An Anthology* (Cambridge, Cambridge University Press, 1983), and that includes an extract from the essay by Bauer to which Marx was responding in 'On the Jewish Question'.

The secondary literature on Marx's work is immense, though on his specifically *political* thought it is a little more manageable. J. Maguire, *Marx's Theory of Politics* (Cambridge, Cambridge University Press, 1978), and Shlomo Avineri, *The Social and Political Thought of Karl Marx* (Cambridge, Cambridge University Press, 1968), provide good starting-points. Avineri's essay 'Marx and Jewish Emancipation',

Journal of the History of Ideas (1964), is one of the few articles addressing 'On the Jewish Question' explicitly. Apart from these, H. Draper, *Karl Marx's Theory of Revolution*, volume I: *State and Bureaucracy* (New York, Monthly Review Press, 1977), may be helpful.

Recently considerable attention was been paid to Marx's use of concepts like *right* and *justice*, to see how much distance there is between his concerns and those of modern liberal theories of equality. *Marx, Justice and History*, edited by Marshall Cohen and others (Princeton, NJ, Princeton University Press, 1980) provides a good anthology. In addition, Allen Buchanan, *Marx and Justice: The Radical Critique of Liberalism* (London, Methuen, 1982), George C. Brenkert, *Marx's Ethics of Freedom* (London, Routledge & Kegan Paul, 1983), and Steven Lukes, *Marxism and Morality* (Oxford, Clarendon, 1985), are all good book-length contributions to that debate.

For more general overviews of Marx's work, see John Elster, *An Introduction to Karl Marx* (Cambridge, Cambridge University Press, 1986), and, if necessary, his monumental *Making Sense of Marx* (Cambridge, Cambridge University Press, 1985). Allen Wood, *Karl Marx* (London, Routledge & Kegan Paul, 1981) in the 'Arguments of the Philosophers' series, is also excellent.

E. Pashukanis, *Law and Marxism: A General Theory* (1929), edited by C. Arthur (London, Ink Links, 1978), is often taken as the starting-point for modern Marxist critiques of rights and law. See also Alice Ehr-Soon Tay, 'Marxism, Socialism and Human Rights', in E. Kamenka and A. Tay (eds) *Human Rights* (London, Edward Arnold, 1978), and Tom Campbell, *The Left and Rights* (London, Routledge & Kegan Paul, 1983).

Modern theories of rights

Ian Brownlie (ed.) *Basic Documents on Human Rights*, second edition (Oxford, Clarendon, 1981) provides a useful sourcebook. The 1948 Universal Declaration of Human Rights is subjected to detailed philosophical discussion in D.D. Raphael (ed.) *Political Theory and the Rights of Man* (London, Macmillan, 1967). See also L.J. MacFarlane, *The Theory and Practice of Human Rights* (London, Maurice Temple Smith, 1985), for a general, if not particularly deep, discussion.

There are several useful anthologies of articles on rights, including: A. Melden (ed.) *Human Rights* (Belmont, Calif., Wadsworth, 1970); E. Kamenka and A. Tay (eds) *Human Rights* (London, Edward Arnold, 1978); David Lyons (ed.) *Rights* (Belmont, Calif., University of

California Press, 1979); J.R. Pennock and J.W. Chapman (eds) *Human Rights: Nomos XXIII* (New York, New York University Press, 1981); and Jeremy Waldron (ed.) *Theories of Rights* (Oxford, Oxford University Press, 1984). R. Martin and J.W. Nickell have provided an excellent bibliography and discussion in their article 'Recent Work on the Concept of Rights', *American Philosophical Quarterly*, 17 (1980).

The revival of the modern liberal concern for rights and justice is usually associated with the publication of John Rawls, *A Theory of Justice* (Oxford, Oxford University Press, 1971). Other books in this area include Robert Nozick, *Anarchy, State and Utopia* (Oxford, Basil Blackwell, 1974), and Bruce Ackerman, *Social Justice in the Liberal State* (New Haven, Conn., Yale University Press, 1980); the former is a very right-wing defence of property rights and the minimal state, while the latter, like Rawls's book, presents a much more egalitarian theory. Ronald Dworkin's collection of his essays in *Taking Rights Seriously* (London, Duckworth, 1977) is an important landmark in the modern discussion of rights and constitutionalism; the legal theory on which his approach to rights is based is set out at length in *Law's Empire* (London, Fontana, 1986). In *Reason and Morality* (Chicago, Ill., University of Chicago Press, 1978) and *Human Rights: Essays in Justification and Applications* (Chicago, Ill., University of Chicago Press, 1982), Alan Gewirth has attempted to establish a meta-ethical basis for rights-theory in the Kantian tradition; opinions about the success of this attempt vary. Other recent books on rights include: Maurice Cranston, *What are Human Rights?* (London, Bodley Head, 1973); J. Donnelly, *The Concept of Human Rights* (London, Croom Helm, 1985); and Carl Wellman, *A Theory of Rights: Persons under Laws, Institutions, and Morals* (New York, Rowman & Allenheld, 1985).

There are helpful overviews of the modern liberal theories in Amy Gutmann, *Liberal Equality* (Cambridge, Cambridge University Press, 1980), and Ian Shapiro, *The Evolution of Rights in Liberal Theory* (Cambridge, Cambridge University Press, 1986).

Modern critiques of rights

There is very little in the way of detailed criticism of rights in the enormous modern literature on the subject.

In the late nineteenth century the idea of natural rights was attacked by D.G. Ritchie in *Natural Rights: A Criticism of Some Political and Ethical Conceptions* (London, Muirhead Library, 1952). The idea that the rights of the individual could be set up against the social interest came under close scrutiny from writers in the English idealist tradition, such as T.H. Green, *Lectures on the Principles of Political Obligation* (Oxford, Clarendon, 1882).

In the twentieth century Hannah Arendt's *The Origins of Totalitarianism* (New York, Meridian, 1958), particularly chapter 9, raised serious questions about the substance and efficacy of human rights concerns in the modern world, while her later work *On Revolution* (Harmondsworth, Penguin, 1973) took issue with the 'naturalism' implicit in the idea of human rights. The latter theme is also taken up in chapter 1 of Michael Ignatieff, *The Needs of Strangers* (London, Chatto & Windus, 1984).

The debate between theorists of rights and utilitarians is continued in anthologies like J.J.C. Smart and Bernard Williams, *Utilitarianism: For and Against* (Cambridge, Cambridge University Press, 1973), Amartya Sen and Bernard Williams (eds), *Utilitarianism and Beyond* (Cambridge, Cambridge University Press, 1980), and R.G. Frey (ed.) *Utility and Rights* (Oxford, Basil Blackwell, 1985). There is a vigorous defence of the ability of utilitarianism to generate the sort of protection for individual interests that rights theories are calling for in R.M. Hare, *Moral Thinking: Its Methods, Levels, and Point* (Oxford, Clarendon, 1981). In this regard the modern debate over the interpretation of John Stuart Mill's classic essay *On Liberty* (1859), edited by C.V. Shields (Indianapolis, Ind., Bobbs Merrill, 1956), is interesting: for example J.A. Gray, *Mill on Liberty: A Defence* (London, Routledge & Kegan Paul, 1983), presents a picture of Mill's essay in terms of two-level utilitarianism.

Other recent work in which the idea of rights is subject to critical scrutiny includes: Kai Nielsen, 'Scepticism and Human Rights', *Monist*, 52 (1968); Herbert Marcuse, 'Repressive Tolerance', in R.P. Wolff, B. Moore, and H. Marcuse, *A Critique of Pure Toleration* (London, Jonathan Cape, 1971); W. Nelson, 'On the Alleged Importance of Moral Rights', *Ratio*, 18 (1976); Robert Young, 'Dispensing With Moral Rights', *Political Theory*, 6 (1978); Charles Taylor, 'Atomism', in A. Kontos (ed.) *Powers, Possessions and Freedom: Essays in Honour of C.B. Macpherson* (Toronto, University of Toronto Press, 1979); John Charvet, 'A Critique of Human Rights', in J.R. Pennock and J.W. Chapman (eds) *Human Rights: Nomos XXIII* (New York, New York University Press, 1980): R.B. Louden, 'Rights Infatuation and the Impoverishment of Moral Theory', *Journal of Value Inquiry*, 17 (1983); and Joseph Raz, *The Morality of Freedom* (Oxford, Clarendon, 1986). There is an interesting feminist critique in J. Hardwig, 'Should Women Think in Terms of Rights?', *Ethics*, 94 (1984).

The new communitarianism

The 'new communitarian' critique of rights is well represented in Michael Sandel (ed.) *Liberalism and its Critics* (Oxford, Basil Blackwell, 1984). In addition one can refer to a number of important monographs that have appeared in recent years. Alasdair Macintyre's *After Virtue: A Study of Moral Theory* (London, Duckworth, 1981) is a comprehensive attack on what he takes to be the bankruptcy of modern moral philosophy; Macintyre calls for a return to a more Aristotelian style of thought about ethics. William Galston, *Justice and the Human Good* (Chicago, Ill., University of Chicago Press, 1980), and John Finnis, *Natural Law and Natural Rights* (Oxford, Clarendon, 1980), both argue that a concern for justice and rights is unintelligible without a full-blooded ethical account of human goodness and the value of community. Charles Taylor, 'Atomism', in A. Kontos (ed.) *Powers, Possessions and Freedom: Essays in Honour of C.B. Macpherson* (Toronto, University of Toronto Press, 1979), argues that liberalism is self-defeating in the absence of such an account. Michael Sandel, *Liberalism and the Limits of Justice* (Cambridge, Cambridge University Press, 1982), is presented as an attack on Rawls's work, but develops also a more general critique of the liberal conception of the self and of its relation to communitarian commitments. That attack is also developed in Sandel's essay, 'The Procedural Republic and the Unencumbered Self', *Political Theory*, 12 (1984). Michael Walzer, *Spheres of Justice* (Oxford, Martin Robertson, 1983), questions the universalism implicit in modern liberal theories, and suggests that justice is dependent on and relative to local understandings in each community. Other communitarian themes are developed in Roberto Unger's books *Knowledge and Politics* and *Law in Modern Society* (New York, Free Press, 1976), and in an article by Richard Rorty, 'Post-modernist Bourgeois Liberalism', *Journal of Philosophy*, 80 (1983).

The historical dimension of communitarian thinking is discussed in Charles Taylor, *Hegel and Modern Society* (Cambridge, Cambridge University Press, 1979): John Charvet, *A Critique of Freedom and Equality* (Cambridge, Cambridge University Press, 1981); W.R. Newell, 'Heidegger on Freedom and the Community', *American Political Science Review*, 78 (1984); George Kateb, 'Democratic Individuality and the Claims of Politics', *Political Theory*, 12 (1984); and B. Yack, 'Community and Conflict in Aristotle's Political Thought', *Review of Politics*, 47 (1985).

So far not much has appeared in the way of a response to

communitarian concerns. John Rawls's Dewey Lectures, 'Kantian Constructivism in Moral Theory', *Journal of Philosophy*, 77 (1980) and his 'Political Theory: Political not Metaphysical', *Philosophy and Public Affairs*, 14 (1985), represent perhaps strategic retreats under the communitarian onslaught. Stouter resistance is offered perhaps by Michael Ignatieff in the final chapter of *The Needs of Strangers* (London, Chatto & Windus, 1984), by Amy Gutmann in her essay, 'Communitaran Critics of Liberalism', *Philosophy and Public Affairs*, 14 (1985), and in a symposium by various authors on 'Civic Republicanism and its Critics', *Political Theory*, 14 (1986). My own essay 'When Justice Replaces Affection: the Need for Rights' will be published in *Harvard Journal of Law and Public Policy* (1988).

Name Index

Subject Index